The Knights Templar of the Middle East

THE KNIGHTS TEMPLAR OF THE MIDDLE EAST

THE HIDDEN HISTORY OF THE ISLAMIC ORIGINS OF FREEMASONRY

HRH PRINCE MICHAEL OF ALBANY
AND WALID AMINE SALHAB

WEISER BOOKS
San Francisco, CA / Newburyport, MA

First published in 2006 by
Red Wheel/Weiser, LLC
With offices at:
500 Third Street, Suite 230
San Francisco, CA 94107
www.redwheelweiser.com

Copyright © 2006 by HRH Prince Michael of Albany and Walid Amine Salhab. All rights reserved. No part of this publication may be reproduced or transmitted in any form or by any means, electronic or mechanical, including photocopying, recording, or by any information storage and retrieval system, without permission in writing from Red Wheel/Weiser, LLC. Reviewers may quote brief passages.

ISBN-10: 1-57863-346-X
ISBN-13: 978-1-57863-346-3

Library of Congress Cataloging-in-Publication Data available upon request

Book design by Dutton & Sherman
Cover design by Donna Linden
Typeset in Adobe Caslon
Cover photograph © National Library of the Netherlands

Printed in the United States of America
RRD
10 9 8 7 6 5 4 3 2 1

The paper used in this publication meets the minimum requirements of the American National Standard for Information Sciences—Permanence of Paper for Printed Library Materials Z39.48–1992 (R1997).

Contents

Introduction: Scotland, Templars and Ancient Freemasonry ix

Part One

CHAPTER 1	The Making of Christianity	3
CHAPTER 2	The Rebirth of Jerusalem	15
CHAPTER 3	The Rise of Islam	24
CHAPTER 4	To Bring the West into a Better Age	37
CHAPTER 5	Cordoba: The New Alexandria	45
CHAPTER 6	Popes, Emperors and the Tribulations of Survival	57
CHAPTER 7	White Robes and Cross Pate	65
CHAPTER 8	Rex Deus, Ismaeli and Nusayri	86

Part Two

Chapter 9	Betrayed for the Sake of a Debt	99
Chapter 10	Scotland: A Kingdom in Need and a Safe Haven	116
Chapter 11	Secret Templars and Hidden Orders	126
Chapter 12	Let There Be Light	132
Chapter 13	From Operative to Speculative	139
Chapter 14	James VI: I, the Solomon of Britain	146
Chapter 15	Operative Masonry in Scotland	156
Chapter 16	The Auld Alliance and Secret Services	168
Chapter 17	Excommunicate Them!	174
Chapter 18	Divide and Conquer: The End of an Auld Lang Sine	184

The Mohammedan descent of Hugues de Payens and Teresa, ruling Countess of Portugal 195

Acknowledgments 198

Bibliographies 199

The publisher is pleased and honored to present this marvelous and particularly timely work concerning the Knights Templar. The authors offer an informative and provocative history of perhaps the most controversial military order in the history of western civilization. It is inevitable that controversy will also surround any piece of literature authored by someone who is, or claims to be, a titled member of one of the royal houses of Europe. In this particular instance the publisher believes the work stands on its own as a valuable contribution to our understanding of this important subject, and that it is neither proper nor necessary to endorse, deny, or otherwise make judgments concerning the contentions and complexities of European nobility.

Introduction

Scotland, Templars and Ancient Freemasonry

This book is about much more than the Templars. Like it or not, when one wishes to find out about them, the researchers will end up becoming enthralled with Judaism, Christianity, Islam, and secret societies, and will find themselves on a journey that will take both the writers and the readers towards Freemasonry. Worldwide and popular within many sections of society, Freemasonry is also misunderstood and feared by some. It is, of course, a closed society with secrets (as opposed to being a secret society), and it is this that has helped Freemasonry gain rather a bad press lately. During the past two decades, Freemasonry has had to put up with financial scandals involving, from the early 1980s, the Vatican Bank, the Italian Mafia and corruption from many individuals belonging to various governments. In Britain, the latest political administration, New Labour, is now insisting that all police personnel, those involved within the legal profession, as well as members of parliament, should state whether or not they are members of Freemasonry. It can be said to have reached a deadlock situation, with Masons claiming that their civil right to belong to an organization is being infringed upon. In this thinking, they are quite right. Also, Freemasonry functions through a properly drawn up constitution, which is more than can be said of the British institution of Westminster or even the devolved UK Parliament sitting in Edinburgh. (Few people are aware that Britain is the only country in Europe not to have a written constitution.)

The biggest difficulty that Freemasonry faces today is the fact that its rituals are only for those in the know. The same, however, could be said for any boardroom meeting of any business. Whether one likes it or not, the inner workings of any organizations, their strategies, those to be invited to join the boards, even their politics, for all organizations are political, are all run by a chosen few. They carefully vote who should join the inner sanctum and who should remain within the periphery of the outer one. This is nothing new. What is new is that a government is taking steps to impeach one of the oldest institutions in Great Britain simply because Freemasons come from many walks of life and Freemasonry claims to have no political affiliation.

The other problem is one that any institutionalized organization in this world faces: the "rot" problem. This is what happened with Freemasonry, not so much in Scotland but rather in Europe and the various "Grand Orient" types of Freemasonry that pervades the world of business, banking and politics. The political Mafia and the Vatican Bank, particularly, overtook Italian Freemasonry. The Grand Orient of Italy was infiltrated in order to help the Roman Catholic Church disguise its investments and income from arms dealing and to help the Mafia launder money from drug trafficking. The problem became so embarrassing that murder, in order to keep many people silent on the matter, was committed all over Europe. It reached the shores of Britain when banker Roberto Calvi was found hanging dead under Blackfriars Bridge in London in 1982. Calvi had links with the Roman Lodge P2 and was also known as "God's banker." Certainly, the fact that he acted on behalf of the Vatican with the bank Ambrosiano did not pay him much. The publication of *The Messianic Legacy* by Michael Baigent, Richard Leigh and Henry Lincoln in 1986, made the public aware of the illegal activities of some European lodges. These activities have, by implication, tainted the whole concept of Freemasonry as being entirely corrupt and politically created by the powers that be.

It became so bad that in 1992 I was required to travel to Italy where I was asked to point out that there was a fundamental difference between the Grand Orient of Italy and the few Jacobite lodges coming under the protectorate of the Royal House of Stewart. Both the newspapers and the various television and radio stations had a field day when I mentioned the corruption and the Mafia links with the Grand Orient of Italy and the Vatican. I was based, for the duration of the exercise, in Calabria, then Mafia country, and my safety was in the hands of a team of people connected to the local police. However, while there are problems with many trends of Freemasonry, I must emphasize that these problems do not really apply to Scotland, and it is high time that this prejudice against Scottish Freemasonry be corrected.

The questions that remain in people's minds are "what is Freemasonry and where does it come from?"

Much has been written about the roots of Freemasonry, most of it confusing, most of it outrageous, most of it based on the concept of misinformation by people who have a problem with Freemasonry. But the worst aspect of the misinformation is that very few nonoperative Masons themselves know what Freemasonry is all about. Most lodge meetings, proceedings and rituals end up at the nearest bar where most members will congratulate each other on a job well done. Should you ask them what Freemasonry is all about, you will get conflicting answers from all present, from the good charitable work Freemasonry achieves (which it does) to the fact that it is as old as Methuselah himself (which it isn't).

What can be said about Freemasonry, without making an outrageous claim that could be rejected by Masons (save perhaps those belonging to the Grand Lodge of England), is that it evolved from a remnant of Knights Templar who settled in Scotland following the order's demise in 1307. As it evolved and transformed itself, it was disseminated by Scots throughout the world from 1688 onwards, the first extant written records of a masonic constitution being found in Scotland in 1598. The roots of Templarism itself, and thus those of Freemasonry, are actually deeply linked not so much to Christianity, but rather to Islam and particularly to Muhammadism. To think of Hugues de Payens, the founder of the Templar Order, as Christian is to take history, the propagandists and the Christian status quo very much for granted. There are, inevitably, two sides to a coin and the other side of the Christian coin is the inheritance that the whole of Europe gained from Islam. One must remember that religion is based on faith while history is based on facts. Yet, depending who is politically in charge, either one can be used in order to enhance the prestige of the other, though only after the events making up the history of our ancestors have taken place. In truth, the conquerors wrote their interpretation of history and the opposition was required to remain silent on the matter.

A look at the historical events taking place in Europe and the Middle East is needed to trace the roots of both the Templars and Masons in the ancient world of post-Roman history and medieval Christendom. Actually, this book will look much further back to the true historical biblical land, based in western Arabia rather than Palestine. The true secret of the inner circle of the Order of the Templars was such that, had they revealed it, would have rocked the cradle of Christian and Judaic beliefs. In their infinite wisdom, the inner circle decided to keep the historical facts and finds to themselves and their Islamic allies. Is the world ready to handle a few home truths? Are those organizations claiming a Templar connection to have survived to this day still aware of the secret that their knightly brothers took to their graves? Can historical facts rebalance one's faith back to its original concept rather than the dogmatic impositions of the Church? Whoever you are, know that this book is for those whose minds are open to hidden historical truths, not for the fundamentalists and their sad interpretations of both faith and history.

Introduction

Part One

Chapter 1

The Making of Christianity

To many people today, particularly those professing the Christian faith, Islam is seen as an enemy religion, one whose entire belief and traditions should be fought to the point of no return. This is manifestly wrong, because without its Islamic link, Europe, even the Western world, would be no more today than a stagnating pool void of intellect. Westerners are unaware that this psychological crusade—for make no mistake, this is what it is—is being fought from within the fringes of the extreme right wings of the Catholic and American evangelist churches, about one hundred million people alone in the United States of America. This crusade is lead by such institutions as the papal condoned Opus Dei; by the very descendants of the Inquisition, the Papal Order of Jesus Christ, whose members are known today as "The Soldiers of Christ"; and by the American-created state of Israel. They wage this holy war by promoting racism and portraying Muslims as lazy, second-rate citizens. Add to this the might of the banking world, more or less still within the hands of a Jewish hierarchy and with political connection the world over (including to the Vatican), and one will soon realize that Islam is bound to fight back for the very survival of its own religious tenets. But Islam is young and has yet to fully understand how the Christian church has been able to keep it at arms length. Propaganda is the key to power and if anyone knows how to use propaganda, the church does.

To that effect, history has been rewritten to emphasize the trend of Christianity, first against Judaism (on the grounds that it totally rejects Christianity) and then against Islam (despite the fact that it acknowledges Christianity). Christianity, according to Rome, is and must be the only religion that should be practiced by all people. Actually, what the Church of Rome means is that only its own trend of Christianity must prevail over all others, emphasis on the "all." Catholicism must become the monopoly of planet earth. To that end, even dictionaries have been written to promote that concept.

A typical example on the matter is *Roget's Thesaurus* of synonyms and antonyms published in 1972 by E. Kroiz and printed in Israel. Within this work, the words "revelation" and "pseudo revelation" are defined as "Word of God; Scripture; Bible; Book of books; Holy Writ; Inspired writings; Gospel." The thesaurus then mentions the various books (Jewish and Christian) that are concerned with the word "revelation." "Pseudo" means false and the word is described in the *Oxford English Dictionary* as "professed but not real." As "Pseudo-religions," *Roget's Thesaurus* names the Koran, Alcoran, Ly-King, Shaster, Vedas, Zendavesta, Vedidad, Purana, Edda, Gau-tama and the Book of Mormon. These are then followed by the names Buddha, Zoroaster, Zedhurst, Confucius, Mohammed, Baal, Moloch and Dagon under the heading of "false prophets and religious founders." Clearly, all guns are out against those that have rejected Christianity.

Two questions, however, remain to be answered: where does Christianity come from, and is it based on historical facts? When was Jesus Christ born? Some believe that he was born in 7 BC, others the year 12 BC. The date of his crucifixion is also a confused issue. It definitely was not AD 33 but rather AD 37. In any case, Jesus the man was either forty or forty-nine years of age when he ended up on the cross (although even this event is debated by some).

The term "Christian" is one that was first used in Antioch in the early AD 60s and is thus of Eastern origin. The word came from Antioch's pagan population and denoted a community that was neither simply Jewish nor simply Gentile, because it was composed indifferently of both. The simple truth is that the creation of Christianity, an uphill struggle that took over six hundred years, was no more than a fantasy gone wrong. Moreover, it was concocted by a bunch of rather sick but ambitious individuals who not only lied through their teeth, but also sent millions of people to their death with the sole purpose of dying, so they thought, in the name of "The Lord." The history of Christianity is bloody, savage and cruel. In the early days of the ministry of Paul, Peter and their subsequent successors, the common people were pawns in the hands of bishops bent on pleasing political leaders. The growing number of people following Christianity provided the bishops of Rome, and many other towns ruled by Roman procurators, with a ready supply of victims for the games of the Roman emperors. Christians were butchered to death by lions, leopards and gladiators, and crucified in public to become human torches. The bishops would then send for their remains and boil their bones free of the flesh so as to enrich their own gruesome collections of relics. A made-up history of how, when dying, these various Christian individuals "shouted with joy in the glory of the Lord" was written by those various bishops and the concept of martyrdom, followed by that of sainthood, was born.

It is a fact that most Roman Catholics, quite wrongly, believe that popes have existed since day one of the Christian church and that the first pope was Peter. It is ignoring the fact that, historically speaking, the title of pope was not used by the bishops of Rome before the rule of St. Syricius, bishop of Rome from AD 384 to 399. Until then, the See of Rome had no ecclesiastical authority over anyone but itself.

Actually, few are aware that there were many popes across the early Christian world. The *Catholic Dictionary* describes the word as "originally a childish word for father (Latin Papa) . . . given at first as a title of respect to ecclesiastics generally."

> Among the Greek Orthodox Church at this day it is used of all priests, and was used, as late at least as the Middle Ages, of inferior clerics. In the West, it seems to have become very early a special title of bishops. Thus the Roman clergy (Cyprian, Ep VIII, I) speak of the bishop of Carthage as "The blessed Pope" (*Benedictum Papem*). Even as late as the sixth century the title of pope was sometime given to metropolitans in the West. Gradually, however, the title was limited to the bishop of Rome, and we find a synod of Pavia in AD 998 rebuking an archbishop of Milan for calling himself pope. Gregory VII, in a Roman Council of the year 1073, formally prohibited the assumption of the title by any other than the Roman bishop. It is of course in this last and most restricted sense that we use the word here.

So here we have it. Unlike the belief that Rome had popes from day one, it was not till the days of Pope Gregory VII (1073 to 1085) that Rome finally got the exclusive right to using the form. Most Catholics also forget the fact that there has been an alternative papacy known as the anti-popes, amounting to no less than thirty and spanning over a period of some nine hundred years. All were legally elected by bishops and cardinals, all ruled separately from various parts of Italy and Europe.

From the time of Pope Symmachus, who ruled from AD 498 to 514, the so-called apostolic succession became seriously compromised. Laurentius was the first anti-pope set up against the hierarchy of Rome, and he ruled until AD 505. With this precedent set within the apostolic succession, the rule for objection and alternate succession became pretty much entrenched within the Roman Catholic Church. The anti-popes have, however, been hidden in the mist of the rewritten history of Rome through a clever propaganda campaign, emanating from the Inquisition, now known as the Doctrine of the Faith, a Church department that was previously headed by the present Pope Benedict

XVI. Roman Catholic Church promotes a history that is, to say the least, rather edited. In fact, from the point of view of the proper historian, there is little truth to the historicity of the Christian church as a whole.

As for the Gospels, all were written years after Jesus' death and were an amalgamation of history written in code (for those with ears to hear and eyes to see) to reach an exclusive Jewish Essenic membership. While the actual writings of the Essenes survived within the Dead Sea scrolls, most of the original Christian writings dating back to the sects led by Peter (supposedly bishop of Antioch but never that of Rome) and Paul were destroyed by Emperor Diocletianus. (Paul, seemingly, is a member of the Herodian dynasty of Judaea, being descended from a sister of Herod the Great.) One must remember that Diocletianus (AD 284–305) was one of the fiercest opponents of the Christians. By the time he died, most writings relating to the early Roman Church had been burned to cinders and very little remained to make a coherent history of the Christian faith in the Roman world. Furthermore, most of the known world was, at that time, Roman, and so the edicts of the emperor were followed to the letter. It was not just in Europe that the Diocletian persecutions took place, but also in Africa and the Middle East.

With the advent of Constantine the Great, the persecutions came to an end in AD 313 and Christianity truly came into its own. It did have a clean slate to work with and it is with the Council of Nicea of AD 325, attended by Constantine himself, that the tenets of the Catholic (that is to say universal) faith as we know them today were concisely shaped and promulgated to the masses. But in no way did that faith resemble anything that the early Christians had practiced.

To begin with, Christianity was no more than a cult, or to be precise, no more than cults. The known world of our ancestors, ruled by and from Rome, was one where mystery religions ruled the day but, above all, where the worship of the emperor was also expected. Enter Judaism, or rather Rome enters Judaea, the last remaining enclave, so we are led to believe, of the ancient kingdom of Solomon. There is a problem that Rome must face with this conquered land in the East. Its religious belief is unlike that of any others in the empire. Elsewhere, gods and goddesses are worshiped and sacrificed to. In Judaea, there was only one god, and not just one god but "the" god that ruled the lives of his "chosen" people. Moreover, the Judaean people saw the imposition of any other gods within their land as an insult, a slap in the face of the traditions and ancient history of the people of Judaea.

Jerusalem at that time was a city rife with high priests, aristocrats and other Jewish political factions, all vying for power. It also boasted numerous individuals claiming the crown of Solomon. The Herodians ruled through the tight grip of Herod the Great, who came to power through marrying

Mariamme, the heiress of the royal Hasmonean house. But even the Hasmonean minor heirs made themselves heard, and their bid to power culminated in a marriage, held at Cana, between a descendant of the royal house of David, Jeshua ben Joseph, and a Hasmonean princess, Myriam of Migdal. Today, they are better known as Jesus Christ and Mary Magdalene. People tend to forget that power can be attained only through strong alliances. Some you win and some you lose. At Jesus' Crucifixion, the Hasmonean/Davidic alliance seemed to have lost the day. But while it lost the battle, it did not lose the war. It was suppressed, even wounded, but as most Christians believe, not mortally. Jesus' physical survival from the Crucifixion, as explained by Sir Laurence Gardner in *Bloodline of the Holy Grail*, is no fiction but a fact that many at the time were aware of, not least Pontius Pilate, since his wife was an Essene.

The other aspects of historical Judaea at the time were the various religious political sects vying for power, the most prominent active one being the Zealots. While the Zealots were the Judaean warriors fighting the might of Rome through assassinations, as well as hit-and-run tactics, the Essenes were a deeply orthodox religious group that had decided to separate itself from the rest of the collaborating Sadducees and Pharisees sections of Judaic societies. While orthodox in thinking, the Essenes added a concept of asceticism and cosmological end of the aeon, meaning "age" (as opposed to the mistranslation "end of the world," when the word "aeon" was expunged by the church to be replaced with "cosmos"), to their tradition. Myriam of Migdal belonged to the Zealot faction; Jesus belonged to the Essene one. That they had children is not in doubt. The rule prevailing at that time required royals to produce heirs. Once born, these children were taken into the care of the community so that they would, in time, produce the next generation. In some instances, they had to be hidden. The descendants of Jesus and Myriam became so important to the Jewish diaspora and the Gnostic Christians in the Roman world that, over subsequent centuries, both the Roman emperors and the bishops of Rome persecuted them, trying but failing to bring them to extinction.

The "Children of Jesus" (the descendants of Jesus and Myriam leading a strong Essene group throughout the Roman empire) decided to take the Roman world to task and pursued a policy of religious invasion. But they were not Christians; they were Jews offering the mystic world of mystery religion a belief unlike that world had known before (i.e., monotheism). Moreover, what has to be remembered is that the Roman world housed more Jews than the kingdom of Judaea ruled by the house of Herod. The Jewish diaspora dated from 174 BC, when the last true high priest of Jerusalem, Onias III, was toppled out of power by his brothers. Onias III went into exile and settled in Egypt under the protection of the ruling Greek Ptolemies and was given land in the Egyptian delta, which became known as a separate small principality known as the "land of Onias." Its princes would be hereditary high priests fully recognized by the kings and queens of Egypt. In fact, during the days of Cleopatra VII, Prince Malachai, high priest of the land of Onias, and his descendants would be granted the formal title *Socius Atque Amicus Populi Romani* ("Friend and Ally of the Roman People") by Cleopatra's husband, Julius Caesar. He also granted all the Jews, throughout the Roman Empire, the right to send the yearly temple tax from countries other than Judaea itself. To the Jews of Judaea, Caesar gave back the port of Joppa, declared that they were exempt from military service, and abolished the tax farming. In 149 BC, Onias III's son, Onias IV, built an exact replica of the Jerusalem temple at Heliopolis for the use of the Jews in Egypt and Cyrene. Thereafter, the Mediterranean world of Africa, together with the South of Spain, France and Italy, was open to these exiled Jews. They became the backbone of the import/export trade. This Jewish diaspora, still keeping in touch with the hierarchy in both Heliopolis and Jerusalem, knew perfectly well who was who in terms of priestly and royal successions. Needless to say, the subsequent Jewish royals, though no longer ruling in effect, were quick to put this extra human asset to good use.

When it came to the Judaic conversion of the Gentiles, the family of Christ decided at the Council of Jerusalem, held in AD 50, to allow the Greek community led by Paul, a convert to the Essenic rites, not to insist that Gentile converts should observe the Mosaic law of circumcision or the Levitical ceremonial regulations of the Jews, except for the "abstention from what has been sacrificed to idols and from blood and from what is strangled and from unchastity." From then on, the group would evolve as the Roman Catholic Church claimed that the Jerusalem hierarchy had allowed for an apostolic succession outside the fringes of Judaism. In this belief, the church is wrong. Jerusalem agreed to a compromise that would make its rule more appealing to the pagan western world that new little about Judaic practices, but that did not mean that it had given Paul the right to start a new separate movement. With Paul going it alone and creating his concept of the sacrificial Jesus Christ, we have the birth of European Christianity as it evolved today. However, what the Church of Rome, which was supposedly built upon the rock of Peter, omits is that the followers of the two protagonists from whom Catholicism took its present form, Paul and Peter, became bitter enemies over Pauline and Petrine doctrines. It led to their respective followers being led to the slaughter like lambs to the butcher. There are no proofs, for example, that Peter ever visited Rome in the first place, and the saying about Peter being Jesus' rock is, once again, a deliberate mistranslation. What was meant was "upon this faith shall you build my church." What we should beg to ask is, of course, "What faith?"

Certainly not the faith of the "son of man" but rather the "faith" of a few ambitious individuals bent to render our lives difficult and narrow minded.

From then on, the early fathers of the church behaved like predators, stealing rituals from other faiths, sucking the blood of other religions. Think of it. Christ is represented with a halo and was originally referred to as "The Sun God," in the same manner that the pagan religions depicted their own deities, Sol Invictus and Mithras (both described as "the son of god and the light of the world.") Jesus' original birth date was changed from March 1 to December 25, now referred to as "Christmas Day," which is really the celebration day of the winter solstice. Lo and behold, this was the very birth date of the gods Osiris, Adonis, Dionysus and Mithras.

Mithraism had, among its tradition, a vision of hell and paradise, a last supper and both a physical sacrifice and ascension. Being a branch of the cult of Zoroaster, it firmly believed in the concept of resurrection, and this resurrection was denoted in the worship of the dying and rising of the sun, representing both the death and resurrection of life. This was symbolically represented by the sign X in the architecture of their temples and as a halo in their writing. The Easter resurrection, celebrated the Sunday following the first full moon after the spring equinox, was originally the very day that the god Dionysus came to life again. In fact, it reflected the turning of winter into spring. The depiction of the Christ child sitting on the lap of his mother, the veiled Mary, was taken from the more ancient depiction of the child Dionysus sitting upon the veiled mother earth's lap and had artistic links to the Egyptian goddess Isis holding the infant Horus. Bishops, the world over, bless their congregations with the sign of Sabazios. As for the crook they carry, it is that of the god Attis, the good shepherd. Take, for example, the feast of Advent, whereby Christians celebrate the days preceding Jesus birth in Bethlehem. Little do Christians know that the word "Advent" comes from the Latin "Adventus" and celebrated, not the entry of Jesus into the world but rather the entry of the emperor of Rome into Rome following one of his war victories outside Rome. Nothing in the Christian church, even the Eucharist (originally practiced by the Druids with mead and bread), is original. Everything in the Christian church is borrowed, stolen and transformed from earlier pagan religions for the purpose of imposing upon the European Roman/Greek world a faith based on fear, where women had no rights but to cook and to give birth to endless children, where submission to the words of bishops and to blind faith ruled the mob. Peter and Paul, and their immediate successors, followed a policy where freethinking became strangled and suppressed through the fear of hell.

The churches of Paul and Peter were indeed opened to all, regardless of class, culture or race. Whether you were poor or rich, literate or without education, you had the right to join the Church of Christ. There was, however, a price to pay. You had to submit to the system of organization that ruled the church. That organization was made up of three elements: doctrinal first, ritual second and clerical hierarchy third. Anyone challenging any one of these elements was excommunicatd, or kicked out of the church. According to Paul, but none of the other apostles writings, God appointed in the church first the apostles, then prophets, followed by teachers, then the miracle workers, healers, helpers, administrators and the speakers in tongues (translators). Origen, one of the church fathers, interpreted Paul's teaching to mean that without bishops, there was no church. Since without the church, there could be no salvation, the only voice to salvation was through the bishops.

The belief of individual contact with God or even the preaching of individual freedom that was based on the power of Christian truth was strongly denied. But the most perverse concept that the Church fathers came up with was that the Roman world and empire had been created by God to fulfill the destiny of Christ upon earth. One emperor, one empire, one god, one church, one bishop, that of Rome. Those that would not submit to this concept of church authority had to be disposed of, that is to say they had to be eradicated physically. Pagan temples had to be pulled down or taken over. Although it took over three hundred years to achieve it, the church managed to do just that, at the cost of loosing the feminine and benign aspects of the deity.

The same did not apply to the Gnostic church and that trend of Christianity imbued with hidden knowledge led by the descendants of the family of Jesus. The Gospel of John was the one upon which the Gnostics based their beliefs. Theirs was more of a spiritual church, and they believed that Christ was a redeeming and revealing spiritual being ascending and descending at will among them. This tradition was known as "angel-Christology." Like the Essenes, the Gnostics saw the Son of Man as the highest prince of angels, the archangel Michael, and believed that he occasionally descended to earth and became the man Jesus Christ. While rejecting the divinity of Jesus, Gnosticism kept the Judaic tradition of a monotheistic god. The Gnostics had both male and female bishops (one of the very precept that the Church of Rome denied at all time was a role for a woman within he Church and the idea of a female bishop was something that was fought against by Rome from the fifth century onwards) and the movement they led would settle both in the South of Spain, particularly in the area of Andalucia, and in the South of France. Their descendants were the Albigensis and the Cathars.

If the Cathars had women priests and bishops, it was no less the case (though Rome would dearly love to forget the fact) in the earlier history of the Roman Church. Artistically, for example, the Roman Church of Santa Prassede shows mosaics of a female bishop by the name of Theodora. The

Vatican library attests to the fact that the Church had a "Femina Episcopa," a woman bishop. Southern Italy and the region of Calabria in particular have graves stating that those buried below were "presbiteras," that is to say, women priests. It is interesting to note that Pope Gelasius I (492 AD to 496) confirms this to be so in various letters. The graves date back to the mid-fifth century. We have also to bear in mind the advent of Pope Joan, eradicated from the papal record. Although thought by the Roman Church hierarchy to be a man when she was elected, Joan, who ruled the church as bishop of Rome and pope between the rules of Pope Leo IV and Nicholas, was found to be a woman when she gave birth in a Roman street (now referred to as the *Vicus Papissa*, or street of the woman pope) to a boy during a papal procession leading from the Colosseum to the Latheran Palace. A fifteenth century portrait of Pope Joan survives to this day in one of the frescoes in the Piccolomini Library in the Duomo in Siena.

The Cathar concept of the world was that of a demonic nature, one in darkness upon which fell a divine spark of light. Paradise was to be restored through knowledge, as taught by Jesus, and passed on from one generation to another, orally. It makes sense. After all, we have, to date, no writings by Christ himself. Not until AD 90, twenty-six years after his true physical death around AD 64, were the Gospels put down on paper. Moreover, when they were written, they had no resemblance to the Gospels as we have them today. John's Gospel is a slight variant of Gnostic doctrines and is, probably, the most authentic. Both the virgin birth and the resurrection are missing in John for this is a Gospel of facts, not of fictions. As far as John is concerned, the world is not evil but divinely created. While mankind made the world evil, John states that it is redeemable through the belief in the Essenic traditions of Jesus. (Or this was very much how John has come to be interpreted by the Church today.) Other gospels used by the gnostic movement were those of "truth," the secret gospel of "Thomas," that of "Philip," the "Apocryphal Gospel of Mary" and so on. All of these were banned by the Roman Catholic Church.

The Gnostic movement spread far and wide. In Africa, the original Essene ministry had been led by Jude, the third son of Mary and Joseph, who had settled in Mauretania (present day Morocco). In fact, his daughter Anna married into the Mauretanian royal family, which, in turn, descended from Queen Cleopatra VII and her fourth husband, Marc Anthony. (History tends to forget that Cleopatra was quite fruitful. She gave birth to Julius Caesar's son, Ptolemy Ceasareon, and gave Marc Anthony two sons, Alexander Helios and Ptolemy Philometer, and one daughter, Cleopatra Selene.) Cleopatra Selene married King Juba II of Mauretania (thus bringing a strong lineage from the Barcha family and an ancestry that can be traced as far back as the sister of Hannibal the Great.) It is from this union that both Jannai (John)

Marcus bar Ptolemy (later to be known through a deliberate mistranslation as the apostle Bartholomew) and the later Idrisid kings of Morocco are descended. From North Africa, it soon spread to the European continent.

The family of Simon (another brother of Jesus) remained in Jerusalem till the last Jewish Rising of AD 132, when Simon's granddaughter, Myriam, fled from Palestine into western Arabia and married Mudar ibn Nizar, rightful high priest of the Temple of Makkah (now in Saudi Arabia). On the family tree, she is referred to merely as "al-Riyab" to disguise her identity from Roman spies. Her son, being the son of a Jew of royal lineage, was given the Jewish name of Ilyas (Elijah). This link brought to that part of the world an Essene community that would evolve in an Arabian trend of Christianity. Moreover, Muhammad, the Seal of the Prophets, was one of his descendants. Ilyas is the only Jewish name to be found in the Prophet Muhammad's family tree.

The family of Jose, the last son born to the biblical Mary and Joseph, settled in Syria where they founded a ministry based on Essene teachings. It is from these separated communities that the Gnostic church evolved. The family of Jacob (also known as James), second born son of Joseph and Mary, high priest of Jerusalem and, in effect, the first bishop of the Christian Church, ended up settling in Great Britain. Through his descendants evolved the hereditary Celtic Church in Ireland, Wales, Cornwall, Spanish Galicia, Portuguese Sintra, Brittany, Glastonbury, Northumbria and Scotland. As explained by Sir Laurence Gardner in his book *Bloodline of the Holy Grail*, James, on becoming of age, took the title and Essenic status of Joseph, the Rama Theo (meaning "divine highness"). In later history, it would be purposely mistranslated as "Joseph of Arimathea."

By the third century AD, two particular church fathers, Iraneus and Tertullian, had extrapolated upon the Pauline and Petrine doctrines in a more sophisticated fashion. Both individuals would be categorized today as "fanatics," and I have no doubts that psychiatrists would have a field day trying to unravel their mysterious warped minds. Iraneus was particularly keen to obliterate the belief of the Gnostic Christians. Through his efforts, the church declared the followers of Gnosticism to be heretics. From then on, the Latin cross and crucifix (from the Latin "cruciare," meaning "to torture") became the symbols of Christianity instead of the original fish and the peaceful equal-armed cross. The latter symbol represented, through its balanced vertical and horizontal elements, the perfect union between male and female. The concept of the apostolic succession of bishops can be traced back to Iraneus. Tertullian was a staunch theologian, albeit one with tunnel vision. He was a polemicist and a moralist, and he was instrumental in making ecclesiastical Latin the official language of the Roman Church. By prevailing over the Greek tongue, Tertullian can be said to have shaped the vocabulary and narrow-minded thought of western Christianity.

Martyrs fascinated Tertullian. A native of Carthage, now in Tunisia, he became a leading member of the Christian church in North Africa. In AD 225, that part of the world counted no less than seventy bishops, few answering to Rome, most leaning to the concepts of the Gnostic movement. Tertullian set to work putting them back on what he termed the right track, that of Rome and the fear of hell. He soon became a fanatic, and God helped those who came under his hammer. Three of his books included the word "against" in their titles. "Against Marcion," an Anatolian who believed that the physical world had been created by the evil god of the Jews; "Against Hermogenes," a Carthaginian painter who claimed that God created the world out of preexisting matter; and "Against Valentinus," an Egyptian philosopher and founder of Alexandrian schools of Gnosticism. (Notice that these three individuals are not natives of western Europe. The first is from Asia Minor, Turkey to be precise, the second is from Greece and the third is from Egypt. All had rejected from its early days the authority of Rome from its early days. All had come under the authority of the family, or desposiny, of Christ.)

It is now that the role of women within the Church was defined. St. Thomas Aquinas compared the female sex as "misbigotten men," arguing that women were inferior by nature and therefore incapable of leadership. St. John Chrysostom (347 AD to 407) says: "The whole of her bodily beauty is nothing less than phlegm, blood, bile, rheum and the fluid of digested food. If you considered what is stored up behind those lovely eyes, the angle of the nose, the mouth and cheeks, you will agree that the well-proportioned body is merely a whitened sepulchre."

St. Augustine (354 AD to 430) states in his confessions: "By the sex of her body, she womankind is submissive to the masculine sex. This is analogous to the way in which the impulse for action is subordonate to the rational mind's prudent concern that the act is right." He also taught that menstrual blood turned wine sour, made crops barren, rusted iron and infected dog bites with poison.

It is Tertullian who gave the church the first book on baptism. His writings on the Christian doctrines on man, the soul, prayer, devotion, marriage, remarriage, monogamy and chastity shaped the views of later fathers of the church, which evolved into Christianity as we know it today. He was also the first one, it must be noted, who mentioned a Celtic Christian Church in Britain.

While the Celtic Church will be dealt with in-depth in chapter 4, it is interesting to note that it was not till the Council of Constantinople of AD 551 that the Celtic Church was perceived as out of the norm. Indeed, its prime spiritual aspect of reincarnation was something that, till then, had been quite acceptable. Moreover, Celtic Christians quoted from both excerpts of ancient Christian literature and from saints. St. Augustine, for example, is quoted saying, "Was I not alive in another body before entering the womb of my mother?"

Clement of Alexandria declares that this is a truth that was transmitted and authorized by St. Paul. St. Gregory of Nicaea (AD 340–400) states that "the immortal soul must be healed and purified; and if she was not so during her life upon earth, the healing will be done through successive lives." (Note that he refers to the soul as a feminine entity!) St. Justin speaks "of souls that live several times in a human body," while Origen (AD 185–254) says, "Does it not conform within reason that each soul is introduced within a body in relation to its passed merits and actions? Each soul comes into this world reinforced by the victories or weakened by the defeats or previous lives." The sixth century would see this ancient natural belief of our ancestors eradicated by the Church in Europe. This elimination of reincarnation was a radical step for it made the Church Catholicus (meaning universal) the only salvation for our soul. The church of fear was truly born.

By AD 325, Christianity was to take over the Roman world, sweeping away the ancient notions of the old gods, and of the goddess, which, for millenniums, had prevailed within the life force of our ancestors. Christianity was to have the full backing of an emperor who, although not a Christian till on his deathbed, would die a Christian.

CHAPTER 2

THE REBIRTH OF JERUSALEM

By the fourth century AD, Christianity had finally attained the status of the state religion of the Roman Empire then ruled by Constantine the Great. However, this was not because Constantine was a Christian, but rather because his mother Helena held the faith. Constantine was a follower of the cult of Sol Invictus and it was not till he was lying on his deathbed that he was baptized into the Christian religion, probably against his will. The Empress Helena was originally a member of the native British royal house and was a descendant of high priest James of Jerusalem, known in Britain as Joseph of Arimathea, the founder of the Judaic Celtic Church. It was this link, together with the time she spent with Bishop Macarius of Jerusalem, which persuaded Helena to support the new, emergent western Christianity. In fact, she became its greatest supporter and would spend the remainder of her life providing the early fathers of the church with a forum within the imperial ear. She persuaded her son to tolerate the Christian faith, which he recognized following his signing the Edict of Milan in AD 313. At the Council of Nicaea (in present-day Turkey), held in AD 325, the emperor was persuaded that only by uniting the entire empire under a Christian religious uniformity could the might of Rome prevail in the West. During the council, Christ was voted "God incarnate" on earth, while the New Testament was collated, edited and released for the clergy. This is the crux of the matter. The Holy Book, whether the Old Testament or the new one, was not faxed to us from heaven by God but rather was the product of man and the historical record of a particular people. It was later edited several times through numerous mistranslations. Moreover, some eighty works were considered for inclusion but seventy-six were then deemed to be too controversial (even though some were based on the apostles Thomas, Philip, Bartholomew and Jude's writings).

It is at the council of Nicaea that the Nicene Creed was formulated and the four Gospels, although very much in an edited form, were postulated. What is interesting about this new council is that it was held in Byzantine territory and not in the city of Rome. In fact, the bishop of Rome refused to attend the council in person, as did most Latin bishops. This is quite significant as it gave the Byzantine Church, the Orthodox Church, a new impetus, a new growing power, and an imperial assent to dominance. Byzantine bishops were quick to realize this and put it to good use. As such, the Byzantine approach to editing and producing the Gospels became more prominent. The truth is that the New Testament was written in Greek first (the most common language of the day) and translated into Latin much later. It was concocted for a Greek audience rather than a Roman one.

What must be remembered as well is that when the original Gospels were composed, they were written directly by the apostles themselves or by their own scribes, who made accurate copies. These were written on papyrus paper that were then rolled or assembled in codices. Most of these originals, written in Greek and some in Aramaic, did not escape the Diocletian destruction, and only a few fragments survived the vagaries of the second and third centuries. Indeed, the totally new, edited, complete copy of the New Testament was not produced before the year AD 340, fifteen years after the Council of Nicaea. If we now compare all the various edited versions of the New Testament today, compiled since AD 340, what is staggering to find is that the reader is faced with no less than 250,000 variants in words and interpretations. Moreover, the discovery of the Qumram finds makes it obvious that our version of the Old Testament is by far the more accurate of all the books in the Christian Bible. It is certainly more accurate in essence than any of the books of the New Testament. Over eighty original books were rejected for the New Testament because, like the Gospel of Thomas (which spoke of Christ's brothers and sisters and a bridal chamber), the secret Gospel of Philip and many others, they embarrassed the new emergent church.

At the council, Christ was truly deified through the concept of a virgin birth. The reason for this is quite simple. Within the Greek psyche of those days, a deity could only be a deity if born from a virgin who had been impregnated by a god. The worship of a man, such as Julius Caesar for example, is nothing new. A Roman aristocratic descent demanded an ancestry related to that of a god. Julius Ceasar claimed descent from Hercules. Marc Antony, on the other hand, although sharing a common ancestry with Ceasar, adopted Dionysus as his very own god. The Hellenistic world was no less pervaded with demigods, sons and daughters born to Zeus and virgin mortals, giving rise to the stories of individuals such as Heracles (worshiped as Hercules in Rome), son of Zeus, and Alcmene, a granddaughter of Perseus. In order to create the concept of the virgin birth of Christ, the Greek hierarchy of the Christian church called upon the "evidence" that Mary had been impregnated by the Holy Spirit. This, however, was not merely far fetched, it assigned the wrong gender to the deity. In Judaic tradition, the Holy Spirit is referred to as "she who flew over the waves of the water." The Holy Spirit is to be understood as the female emanation of the Judaic deity. The question we must then ask ourselves is: can two women sexually create a child together? The answer is obvious. But the Greek population did not particularly care about this theological mishap because it was not told who or what was the Holy Spirit. As far as they were concerned, those scholars had confirmed that Christ was born from a mortal virgin and a god and that was good enough for them. Jesus Christ was merely added to the great pantheon of deities, which the people worshiped as a matter of fact.

One of the aspects often missed in the Roman Catholic history of the papacy is that the Council of Nicaea decreed that bishops already holding a bishopric could not be elected pope in Rome. The understanding was that one was a bishop of one bishopric for life and could not leave it for another. So who could be elected, and moreover, who could elect a bishop of Rome? The answer, I am sure, will surprise quite a few readers. Deacons, abbots and priests, even monks, were those entitled to be elected, and the electors, more often than not, were no others than the people of Rome themselves. Not only was the concept upheld at Nicaea in AD 325, but it was also subsequently put into practice by the people of Rome. Moreover, due to a short life expectancy in those days, bishops of Rome were usually quite young, and popes could be as young as twelve years of age, as in the case of Benedict IX. Pope John XI was twenty, while Pope John XII was eighteen; Pope Gregorius V was twenty-four, and Pope Innocens III was thirty-eight years of age when the papal tiara was settled upon their heads. Some popes just succeeded their fathers. Pope Innocens I was the son of Pope Anastasius I and Pope John X was the son of Pope Sergius III. The concept of a pope being elected by cardinals was very much a later event, cardinals not emerging within a Roman Catholic hierarchy before the eleventh century. This is where the concept of an episcopal line right back to St. Peter (never a pope himself) goes out of the window.

It was at the Council of Nicaea that December 25 was decreed the birth date of Christ. During the rule of Roman emperor Aurelian, the winter solstice fell, in the year AD 274, on December 25. The emperor proclaimed the date as "Natalis Solis Invicti," the festival of the birth of the invincible sun. Not to be outdone, Pope Julius I, then leading the Roman Catholic Church, decided, in AD 320, to adopt December 25 as the official birth date of Jesus Christ. Constantine the Great, to unify his empire under the Christian faith, decreed that the ancient pagan solstice celebration would be from then on an immovable feast that would be celebrated as the birth of Christ. There were good reasons for doing this.

To pagans, the winter solstice was a celebration of the goddess. According to tradition, the Great Mother gave birth to the new sun on the night of the solstice, thus heralding the new cycle of the seasons. In the north of Europe, the festival was called Yule and was celebrated by throwing a huge log, the Yule log, on a communal bonfire, around which people would dance and sing in order to awake the sun from its winter sleep. In Greece, it was celebrated as the birth of Dionysus, and in Egypt, as that of Osiris. During the days of the Roman Empire, the winter solstice became the celebration that honored both Saturnus (the Roman harvest god) and Mithras, the ancient god of light. The latter had come to Rome as a form of worship from Syria, together with the worship of Sol Invictus. Of such importance was December 25 to the world of the Romans that the church had to adopt it as one of its own festivals—and what better than making it Christ's official birth date!

It is also from AD 325 that Jerusalem became recognized as the Christian holy of holies. Strangely enough, it had little to do with the Christian faith but was based upon the concept of financial gain. Until Empress Helena began supporting the Christian church, Jerusalem was of little consequence to Western Christians. Few traveled there and, if the truth told, there was little to see in the city. Following its destruction by Titus, Emperor Vespasian's son, in AD 70, what was left was a city of rubble with a few anchorite monasteries scattered here and there. The temple had been destroyed, its treasures taken to Rome as Titus' trophies and were never heard of again. Also, since the days of Emperor Hadrian in AD 132, Jews were banned from entering the Judaean capital following their last revolt against Rome. In fact, the city of Jerusalem, by name, had been thereafter eradicated from all Roman records. Hadrian had what remained of the original city totally razed to the ground and rebuilt in a Roman style, giving it the new name of Aelia Capitolina.

Bishop Macarius of Jerusalem wanted to change all that by creating a bishopric unlike any other in the Christian world, where the name of Jerusalem would take prominence over all, Rome and Constantinopolis included, where pilgrims would travel and worship but, most of all, where they would spend money. Macarius invited Helena to travel back with him to his holy city. The octogenarian empress rose to the challenge and crossed the sea to Palestine. When in Jerusalem, Helena pointed out, at random, the various sites that the church would claim to relate to Jesus Christ and his ministry. Until the feet of Helena walked the dust of Jerusalem, all that could be found was nothing more than one remaining Herodian wall (that of Phasael), now worshiped by Orthodox Jews as the Wailing Wall, and a few pagan temples built by Roman emperors.

By the time she left the city, the grotto at Bethlehem, were Jesus was supposedly born; the Mount of Olives, where Jesus, so the Bible claims, had instructed his disciples; and Golgotha, the alleged site where Jesus found martyrdom and where Hadrian's temple to Venus stood, had been carefully chosen. The temple of Venus was pulled down, and the foundation of a new Christian basilica settled on top of it. The Church of the Holy Sepulchre was born. Helena would later choose other significant sites, such as the house of Caiaphas, the high priest of Jerusalem and Jesus' nemesis; the Praetorium of Pontius Pilate; even a beam of the true cross. All these added to a growing collection of buildings and artifacts that brought both the church and the Byzantine state a hefty revenue from visiting pilgrims. The concept of holy relics for sale also became endemic to this financial arrangement. But before then, Jerusalem meant little to the early Western Christians: they paid only lip service to the forgotten city and, occasionally, to its bishop.

In fact, the first record of a pilgrimage to Jerusalem by a traveler, known as only "the Bordeaux pilgrim," does not date back until after the raising of the basilica in the late fourth century AD. The record of this lone individual states that he traveled to Jerusalem because "he had less religion, less knowledge, and had not the finishing strokes of their virtues, unless he had adored Christ in those places whence the Gospel had first shone forth from the Cross." Whoever was in charge of the public relations department of Bishop Macarius's new plan knew what he was doing. From then on, there was no stopping those pilgrims from traveling to Jerusalem. Rome, of course, thought this new pilgrimage to the city of Jerusalem rather silly, till they saw the coins filling the coffers of the Byzantine Church. From then on, they wanted a piece of the action, and so Rome created a Latin patriarch of Jerusalem. Rivalry became sharp and, occasionally, rather brutal.

While western Europe was basically but surely being taken over by Catholicism, the same cannot be said of Spanish Gallicia, Portuguese Sintra, French Septimania, Brittany, mainland Britain and Ireland. In those kingdoms, it was the Celtic Church that prevailed. Roman Catholic apologists have always tried to link the Celtic Church to the Roman one. By doing so, they clearly go against all the precepts and available records that link the Celtic Church to the original Essene Judaic church of Jerusalem and the Syrian and Coptic Essene churches of the Middle East. Though Celtic Christians were a minority within European society, had it not been for this link, the history of Europe would have evolved much differently and probably rather for the worst.

But despite the common sense of the Celtic Church, the years of strife and rivalries between Rome and Constantinople continued. The Roman Church in the West and the Orthodox Church in the East became hotbeds of theological debates on the Christian faith and the nature of Christ. Was he merely a man, was his nature divine, or was he even both? These various dogmas became more sophisticated as the years passed by, and the bishops, both Roman and Orthodox, upholding them became more forceful, excommunicating one another left, right and center. Christianity was literally split between those espousing Nestorianism, Arianisn, Monophositism, Gnosticism, Celticism and so on.

Actually, by AD 395, the Roman Empire had been split between west and east, with the city of Constantinople as the eastern capital of the Roman Empire. When Roman emperor Theodosius I died in AD 395, the Roman Empire was divided between his two sons. Honorius (ruled from AD 395 to 423) inherited the western part of the empire (which consisted of Italy, Africa, Spain, Illyricum, Gallia and parts of Britain) while Arcadius (ruled from AD 395 to 408) received the eastern part of the empire, Byzantium (composed of Macedonia, Dacia, Egypt, Orientis, Pontus, Thracia and Asia) and followed the old precept of "divide and conquer" in order to keep its hold on the whole.

So Constantine got it all wrong. Christianity did not unite the empire at all; it merely made the empire uniformed for a short while. The Western Roman Empire expired in August AD 476 when its last emperor, Romulus Augustus, was toppled during the Visigoth invasion of Italy. The Western Roman Empire had lasted 503 years and six months. Rome, the imperial seat where the eagles of ancient and famous legions once flew, became a forgotten city in a forgotten country. When Rome collapsed in AD 476, Constantinople took over and thus was truly born the Byzantine Empire. The problem is, you can only do this for so long. Something is bound to break at the seam after a while or an individual is bound to rebel against it all and rally people to his or her banner against the unfairness of the system.

What is more, the Church of Rome decided to retaliate against the Eastern Roman Empire. Out of the ashes of the Roman Empire rose a "Pontifex Maximus" (a title which Julius Caesar, as high priest of Rome, had held from 73 BC till the day he died and which his own ancestors had held for some two hundred years before him). A Roman pope suddenly claimed supremacy over all other bishops and branches of the Christian church. The claim was not new, but this one was made in such a forceful theological way that many people in the west took it seriously. Historically, the culmination of this process is referred to by the Roman Catholic Church as "the Donation of Constantine." The eastern Christian Church of Byzantium thought the whole thing to be pretty dubious and, today, we know that it was nothing more than a lie, a Roman fabrication and that the document supposedly issued to bishop Silvester I of Rome (AD 314–335) by emperor Constantine the Great was no less than a downright forgery.

Constantine died in the Eastern Roman Empire, having taken over the one-thousand-year old city of Byzantium and made it into his capital, aptly renamed "Constantinopolis," (today's Istanbul). Astride his horse and using a spear, Constantine redefined the boundaries of the city, enlarging it and encasing it within a defensive wall. Like Rome, Athens, Lisbon and Edinburgh, it boasted of seven hills, and both the court and administrative language was Latin. The newly redefined city was divided into fourteen administrative wards, as Rome was, and it would not be long before Constantinople became the more important of the two capitals.

The truth is that Constantine was much fonder of the eastern part of the Roman Empire, Byzantium, by then far more sophisticated than Rome, which was then on the road of political and military decline. He had left Rome behind, seeing it as a second best to the city that bore his name. As far as he was concerned, Rome could go to pots and the true seat of Christianity was Constantinople. Rome, stripped of her self-proclaimed spiritual right was not likely to let the matter lie. The Donation of Constantine, a Roman forgery, was Rome's answer to Constantinople's spiritual rise. The fact that Constantinople was the new Rome was actually set in stone by the Byzantine church with words attributed to Constantine: "O Christ, Ruler and Master of the world, to Thee have I now consecrated this obedient city and this scepter and the power of Rome. Guard and deliver it from every harm." A rival city dedicated to Christ was not, was never, to be tolerated by Rome.

Rome, however, would not rule supreme for many, many years yet. Both the Byzantine emperors and various invaders saw to that. In AD 410, during the rule of the western emperor Honorius and Pope Innocens I, Alaric and his Visigoths invaded Italy and laid waste to Rome. Augustine was so shocked at this event that he wrote "The City of God," a treatise famous for its pessimism with regards to Rome's survival as a religious entity in western Europe. During the rule of Pope Leo I (AD 440 to 461) and Emperor Petronius Maximus (AD 455), Rome was threatened of yet another invasion by no less than Attila the Hun. While the Roman emperor tried to flee the city and was caught by the people who tore him to pieces for being such a coward, it was Pope Leo who faced Attila and asked him to spare the city. Attila was so impressed that he gave in to the pope's intercession. It was this small victory that gave Leo I the impetus to claim that Rome was the fount of all authority for the entire Christian world and that this Christian world was dependent to the See of Rome. Rome has clung to this concept ever since. Some forty years later, in AD 493, Theodoric, king of the Ostrogoths, invaded Italy (quietly pushed to do so by Emperor Anastasius I of the East) and proclaimed himself king of Italy. He ruled until AD 526, settling a dynasty that lasted till AD 553. Theodoric, deemed by Pope John I to be heretical in his beliefs, had the pope seized and imprisoned for ten years. Pope John died in his cell, never seeing the light of day. The situation became so precarious that the emperor's exarch and representative in Rome decided to move his quarters to Ravenna.

Rome, although considered a satellite city of the Byzantine Empire, was suffering and was soon losing the luster that the early Roman emperors had put upon the city. As if contending with invasions from pagan tribes were not enough, Rome and her popes had to contend with the wrath of eastern emperors as well. Pope Vigilus (AD 537 to 555) was, for example, kidnapped by Emperor Justinian I and brought to Constantinople, where he spent eight years in prison. Released in AD 555, he died on his journey back home. A century later, Emperor Constans II had Pope Martin I (AD 649 to 655) forcibly taken from his sick bed by the imperial guard and brought to Constantinople, where Martin was publicly flogged. Constans wanted to actually put him to death but the eastern patriarch interceded, and Martin was told to make his way back to Rome. Martin died before getting to the "City of God."

Ten years later, the Byzantine emperor visited Rome and had the entire Roman aristocracy and the papacy bowing and scrapping to his every wish. When he left Rome, he helped himself to what was left of any splendor, taking away priceless statues, gilded bronze tiles and other treasures. Rome was left with very little, aesthetically, to look at.

This physical split was heightened when Rome lost her last emperor. Severed from its other half, Rome had to look elsewhere for imperial leadership. Gaul came forward when Clovis I, the victor of the Battle of Tolbiac, on condition that the church endorsed his hereditary right to the Western Roman Empire. But Rome had to pay a price for this new supportive emperor. Loyalty to the Merovingien House of France, descended from the reviled desposiny of Christ, was expected from Gelasius I, bishop of Rome. The Roman Catholic Church has a rather nice story relating that Clovis I converted to Catholicism when, before doing battle against the Alemmanni (Germans), he called upon Christ to sway the victory in his favor. Of course, Clovis won the day and was baptized straight away by St. Remi, bishop of Reims, into the Christian religion. This, needless to say, is an echo of Emperor Constantine's spurious conversion to Christianity following the battle of Milvan Bridge (though he did not convert until he laid incapacitated upon his deathbed).

While Rome, supported by the Merovingiens, was gradually able to regain some sort of supremacy in the west, its power on the east had been totally rendered to sweet nothing. This meant that Western and Eastern Christianity would be at loggerheads for hundreds of years. (Technically speaking, they still are, since the Eastern Church has its own pope.) The battle would bring both Europe and the East into theological chaos and religious disruption, with communities finding themselves rather confused as to what they should believe from one morning to the next. Since Christians resided both in Palestine and Arabia, where the native population considered the Byzantine Church to be westernized, the same applied to them as well. By the early seventh century, the Middle East was ripe for a religious revolution and political reforms. One man rose to the challenge of bringing common sense into both the religious and political equation. The new faith would be that of Islam, and the name of its leader was Muhammad, the Seal of the Prophets. Islam's religious impact upon the West would be a turning point in our history.

The Islamic religion is, for one born within the Christian faith, difficult to fathom, but only because there is little mention—in fact there is no mention—of Islam in the Christian teaching, be it at Bible or Sunday-school levels, or even from an educational perspective. I am lucky. One of my closest friends, Walid Salhab, a Lebanese filmmaker and a lecturer on Media at Queen Margaret University College in Edinburgh, was taught both in Islamic classicism and the Christian Maronite religion. I doubt I would have been able to write this book had it not been for his help, dedication and interest. The project has been a journey, even a spiritual one, for both of us. It has been a journey of theological debate in the best tradition of two close friends wanting desperately to make sense of the crazy, so-called religious world around them. We searched, traveled, looked up records, both Islamic and Christian, photographed, surfed the Internet, read books, theorized, concluded on our findings and came to one simple realization: all we found between our two worlds, which are supposedly so religiously different, was an incredible commonality (with a capital C) that should bring mankind closer together rather than separate us all.

My mother surprised me during a telephone conversation when she said that, as far as she was concerned, Islam, when properly practiced, was the most gentle and the fairest of all religions. The biggest problem today is religious fundamentalism, be it Christian, Judaic or Islamic. Neither Christ, Solomon or Muhammad would condone it. In fact, they would tell the fundamentalists where to get off and go back to the roots of things. It is the interpretation of the word in the holy books by men that has lit the flames of many jihads and crusades. Those battles are the dividing factors between faiths. Yet, for all that, the common denominators between the basics of the Christian, Judaic and Islamic religions are of much greater value than people will ever be led to understand and believe. The unknown, as is often reflected by the enlightened ones, tends to terrify most people into rejecting it. It is time for this trend to be broken and for some home truths to be said on a subject that has so much in common with true Christianity and little to do with "Churchianity."

CHAPTER 3

THE RISE OF ISLAM

Few people in the western world are aware that Muhammad (known in the West as Mohammed), he that would be historically and reverently blessed and referred to as the Seal of the Prophets, was born into one of the most influential families in the Middle East. Moreover, his family had held for generations the title of "Lords of the Temple of Makkah." Makkah, and Mecca, as the city is known in the West, is much more important than people think. So what about the Holy of Holies of Islam and what do we know about it?

Makkah is mentioned in the Old Testament in Psalm 84, being referred to by its older name of Bacca: "How happy are those whose strength comes from you, who are eager to make the pilgrimage to Mount Zion. As they passed through the dry valley of Bacca, it becomes a place of springs; the autumn rains fill it with pools. They grow stronger as they go; they will see the God of gods on Zion." Thus Makkah has a biblical proportion that has been ignored by both the Judaic and Christian traditions for well over fourteen hundred years. An article entitled "Ka'bah as a Place of Worship in the History" by M. S. M. Saifullah, found on the Islamic Web site *www.islamic-awareness.org*, says, "the Arabian translation for Baka' a [Bacca] is 'lack of stream' and seems to throw some light on the nature of the valley before the appearance of the stream of Zam-Zam near Ka'bah which was a dry place with no vegetation and water whatsoever." Saifullah also says that its further interpretation as the "'valley of weeping' makes sense because of the distress which Ha'gar [sic] underwent when she was left with Ishmael in the barren desert with no means of living." This is, of course, Old Testament history.

Abraham had two wives, Sarah (whose original name was Sarai) and Hagar. Hagar came from the Egyptian court of Pharaoh Amenemhet I

(Twelfth Dynasty) who had usurped the throne from Mentuhopep IV (Eleventh Dynasty). It is probable that Hagar was a younger daughter of Mentuhotep, and that Amenemhet (originally Mentuhotep's vizier) gave her to Abraham as a wife. In those days, nobles had more than one wife, the wife major (who was charge of the household), and the wife minor (taking over her functions when required to do so). Sarah was rather envious of Hagar. She intimated that Abraham had to choose between the two and had Hagar expelled from the marital home, son and all. The story is reflected in the name "Hagar." It means "of flight" and was not her true birth name. Hagar and her infant, we are told in the Old Testament, walked the desert and, as one would expect, ran out of water. Looking at her infant son Ishmael, she cried to God, begging him not to let her son die. On hearing Hagar weep, God was touched and brought forth a stream (Zam-Zam) so that she and her son Ishmael would survive. This is when she was informed that Ishmael would be the ancestor of a great nation (Genesis 21).

There are many things that do not fit geographically in the story. Makkah, today, is in Saudi Arabia, desert country. One can only walk so far in the desert (as in a few miles) before one dies of thirst. This means that Abraham and his family lived within the vicinity of Makkah itself and not, as some biblical scholars tend to think, anywhere near Egypt. We are facing a historical controversy with which we will deal in a later chapter.

So, biblically speaking, Makkah stands in the "valley of Abraham." Arabian tradition and the Koran ascribe the building of the Temple (Ka'bah), then dedicated to single God, by both Abraham and his elder son, Ishmael. Notice that it has no connection with his younger son, Isaac. This, in effect, simply means that the faith of Islam does trace its roots in the Old Testament, and the family of Muhammed descended from Ishmael, son of the patriarch Abraham (who is known within the Islamic faith as the prophet Ibrahim) and his wife Hagar. In other words, Islam is related to the Christian Church and the Jewish faith since they both claim their roots through Isaac (half-brother to Ishmael), the son of Abraham and Sarah, herself the daughter of Princess Nfry-ta-Tjenen (better known as Tohwait, the Tehama) of Egypt and Terah of Ur Kisdim (seemingly the father of Abraham by wife Yawnu). The Sarah/Abraham connection is explained, at length, by Laurence Gardner in his book *Realm of the Ring Lords*. From Ishmael's twelve sons, namely Nebaioth, Kedar, Abdee, Mibsam, Mishma, Dumah, Massa, Hada, Tema, Jetur, Naphish and Kedamah, all mentioned in Genesis, were descended twelve tribes. However, they evolved separately from those later Jewish tribes in the kingdoms of northern Israel and Judah.

What can be said about both Ishmael and Isaac is that they were extremely well connected. Their ancestries were royally Egyptian on the maternal side, while their paternal ancestors are believed to be of Sumerian origin, Abraham being, according to a mistranslation in the Greek Septuagint, a prince of the city of Ur of the Chaldeans. This mistranslation will be dealt in a later chapter.

There were neither Arabs nor Jews as yet in the days of Abraham. According to the Koran, both Abraham and Ishmael built Makkah, which, from then on, became a center of worship. Then, from the days of Muhammad, some two thousand five hundred years after Abraham's death, Makkah became a center of pilgrimage as important to the Muslims as Rome became to Roman Catholic Christians. According to the Koran, Abraham was required by God to give up his elder son Ishmael as a sacrifice, just as he was later required to do with his younger son Isaac. Abraham's sacrifice of his eldest son took place in what is today's Saudi Arabia, roughly west of the nearby plain of Muzdalifa, halfway between Mounts Arafat and Mina. However, the Koran states that God, in his infinite bounty, told Abraham not to kill Ishmael but to sacrifice a sheep instead. The story is thus identical to that of his half-brother Isaac. Before Muhammad decided to categorize the Islamic faith under the aegis of a lunar calendar, what was practiced in Makkah was a solar religion, the remnant of the Aten worship of the eighteenth Egyptian dynasty. This is confirmed in the dynasty's archives and letters dating back to Pharaoh Akhenaten.

Historically speaking, Makkah is as old as some of Egypt's most ancient temples. On the Web site *www.islamic-awareness.org*, author M. S. M. Saifullah writes, "Diodorus Siculus was a Greek historian of 1st century BC who wrote Bibliotheca Historica, a book describing various parts of the discovered world." Saifullah then quotes Edward Gibbon's English translation of Siculus, found in Gibbon's *Decline and Fall of the Roman Empire*: "And a temple has been set-up there, which is very holy and exceedingly revered by all Arabians." According to Gibbon, Saifullah's article says, the Homerite kings (who ruled southern Yemen from their capital Zafar) seven hundred years before the time of Muhammad (200 BC), first offered the linen of silken veil that entirely covers the temple.

Saifullah also quotes from the 1905 book *The Penetration Of Arabia* by D. G. Hogarth, which says that Claudius Ptolemy of Alexandria, the Egyptian mathematician and astronomer, compiled an atlas that mentioned some 114 cities and villages, including Makkah, which was already then sacred.

> For example, *Dumaetha*, placed by Ptolemy just outside the northern boundary of Arabia Felix [comprised of southwestern and southern Arabia in what is today Asir and Yemen], must be the mediaeval Arabian *Daumet*, which is today the chief village of the great oasis of Jauf. [Jauf was ruled by the Minaean kings of Ma'in from 1000 BC until the second century BC.] *Hejr*, famous in the "times of ignorance" [mean-

ing prior to 312 BC] as the seat of a [Nabataean] kingdom, and now Medayin Salih, is Ptolemy's *Egra*. His *Thaim* [again ruled by Nabataean kings from the first century BC to the first century AD] is *Teima*, now known for its inscriptions to have had temples and some sort of civilization as far back as 500 BC. It is the *Tema* of [the biblical] Job. In *Lathrippa*, placed inland from Iambia (Yambo), we recognize the *Iathrippa* of Stephan of Byzantium, the *Yathrib* of the early Arab traditions, now honoured as *El Medina*, the City of Cities.

finally, Saifullah cites G. E. Von Grunebaum's 1970 book *Classical Islam: A History 600–1258* as saying how Makkah is referred to as "Macoraba" and is identified by Ptolemy as "a South Arabian foundation created around a sacred sanctuary."

From its earliest tradition, this Temple is known to have an unpretentious, cubelike architecture and for some four thousand years has housed a black meteorite. It remained in the custody of the descendants of Ishmael, as high priests of Makkah, until they were dispossessed of it by the clan of banu-Juhrum. The latter were later dispossessed by the banu-Khuza'ha who introduced idol worship. What is not generally known about Makkah is that in its pre-Islamic history the Temple was also dedicated to the triple goddess Manat, Al-Lat and Al-Uzza, the "Old Woman." The stone (Kabba) was also linked with the name of Cybele (Kybela), the Great Mother of the gods. Apparently, the stone (now in pieces), like the black stone worshiped by the Votaries of Artemis, bore an upturned triangle, the emblem of the yoni, which is the symbol of the maternal womb and fertility.

finally, the power of the priesthood was wrested from the usurpers by the Quraysh family, the rightful descendants of the original line of high priests descended from Ishmael, who kept it till the days of Muhammad. It is then that the patriarchal fundamentals overtook the feminine symbolism. However, the priests of the Kabba are still known as "Sons of the Old Woman," commonly referred to in ancient times as "the Widow." The historical antiquity of Makkah proves one thing, namely that it is older than the temple of Solomon in Jerusalem. Further, it was rebuilt several times, but its architectural basics never changed. It was built on such architectural principles showing representation of cube, square, circle and triangle. The entire structure is orientated so that its corners roughly correspond to the point of the compass, and its interior contains nothing but three pillars supporting the roof from which a number of gold and silver lamps are suspended. To the Muslims, it is the most sacred spot on earth.

As "Lords of the Temple of Makkah," the Quraysh made treaties with both the Byzantine and Persian empires, and with the kings of both Yemen and Ethiopia. They also were in charge of the trade routes within the Hejaz (present-day Saudi Arabia) and caravans making their way to and from India. Makkah was one of the many trading centers in the known eastern world. As well as the Quraysh power, other dynasties had entrenched themselves in the Arabian Peninsula. Two related royal families from Yemen, the Lakhmid (who ruled from the third century AD to AD 602) and Ghassanid (a Byzantine-created dynasty, whose headquarters was situated east of the Sea of Galilee) dynasties, had allowed Christians of the Nestorian and Monophosite persuasions to settle respectively within the confines of their kingdoms. The Ghassanid kings were, as a matter of fact, Christians of the Monophosite (Coptic) persuasion, and Muhammad was one of their most direct descendants through Hubba, princess of the Khosites and a Christian, who married Quasay Zaid, governor of Makkah.

Quasay, of course, was not a Muslim, being Muhammad's three times great grandfather, and thus preceding the Islamic religion by some one hundred years, but this marriage to Hubba introduced an eastern Coptic Christian trend in the area. There was a much more provocative link to early Christianity in Muhammad's ancestry. His earlier ancestor, Mudar, married Myriam, the great niece of Jesus Christ and the granddaughter of Christ's younger brother Simon. Their son was given the name of Ilyas (Eliah), and that is the only Jewish name in Muhammad's ancestry.

Myriam had escaped from Jerusalem following the Judaean revolt of AD 132, which was led by her brothers, James and Sokker bar-Kochba. From then on, the Christine family had to disperse to various parts of the Middle East and Myriam, together with a brother by the name of Jose and quite a few Essene followers, made it to the safety of western Arabia (in today's Saudi Arabia). In order to remain there, she married the local tribal chief and high priest of Makkah, thus giving her people the right to settle within her husband's rulership. Her brother Jose, together with his followers, decided to settle in Yathrib (now Medina) and some (though not all) of their descendants would play a crucial part in Muhammad's fight to promote the new faith of Islam. While not powerful, these two links were outside the grasp of Rome and would have been able, somehow, to influence the family in a different way of thinking. In Egypt, the Coptic Christians had a church of their own which dated back from the first century AD and which was based in Alexandria.

Jews were still extant in the Middle East though their numbers had been greatly depleted when Roman emperor Vespasian dispatched 1.3 million of them to their deaths in AD 68. The Jewish population of Judaea never really recovered from the slaughter and most of those who had survived left Palestine for the shores of Egypt, North Africa, southern Spain and southern France.

Actually, already during the days of Cleopatra VII of Egypt (she died in 30 BC), more Jews lived in Alexandria than Jerusalem itself. In AD 70, Vespasian's son, Titus, had the temple of Jerusalem dismantled stone by stone, scattering them so that it could never be rebuilt again. The Jews, then, like the Christians in Palestine and Arabia, were not a consequential power.

Muhammad was born in AD 574 and was orphaned from a very early age. If we had to relate his family background in terms of our own days, he would be equated with the various princes of royal families who have lost their thrones generations ago while retaining some political influence over the people their family used to rule (such as the Hapsburg dynasty of Austria today). Moreover, unknown to most people, Muhammad belonged to the Christine family of Jesus Christ. In their book *The Messianic Legacy*, Michael Baigeant, Richard Lee and Henry Lincoln infer that Muhammad's father may have been a member of a Nazorean sect (an offshoot of the Essene community) and that Muhammad may have been raised in that particular tradition. They also mention that one of his wives is reported to have been Jewish and, by implication, Nazorean. Actually, while this speculation may be far fetched to some, the fact is that it is the genealogical link to Simon, a younger brother of Christ, which brought the Nazorean/Essene tradition within western Arabia. As for Muhammad's wife Myriam being Nazorean, the truth of the matter is that she was an Egyptian Coptic Christian. The fact that she was a Copt is mentioned in the Koran.

Muhammad's education, which was oral, the norm in those days, fell to his grandfather. The history and tradition of his family helped Muhammad to understand one thing about the religious world around him. It needed to be simplified, purified and codified, and centralized. He realized that a very tight unity among the tribes of Arabia was required if both the concept of paganism, which Muhammad abhorred, and the loss of political power were to be fought on a practical level.

Muhammad was a very well-connected man. He was also very devout and had a concept of how the world of his own people should function. Visionaries, in those days, were a power in their own right, particularly if their prophecies proved to be correct. Muhammad was a man of charisma, and of deep religious belief, living in an era when the common people were suffering at the hands of the various empires ruling over them. The time was ripe for a change, on a social as well as political and religious levels. And so, Muhammad prayed for guidance, and God, through the offices of the angel Gabriel, sent to him words of wisdom through the power of visions. Notice the angel Gabriel, is the same one that announced the birth of Christ. Gabriel, was the name style adopted by the Essene ambassador whose duty was to proclaim a major royal event or birth within the Christine family. Again, the Essenic trend of angel-Christology comes into play.

Muhammad's first vision came to him in AD 610, when the angel Gabriel appeared to him and, as recorded in the Koran, required Muhammad to "recite in the name of the Lord who created all things, who created man from clots of blood. Recite, for thy Lord is the most generous, Who taught by the pen, Who taught man what he did not know." Notice the difference between the Koran and the Christian Bible and the Jewish Torah. Whereby in the latter two, man is formed from clay (implying that we evolved from a carbon structure), the Koran rightly states that man was genetically created from clots of blood. Purely from a medical and scientific point of view, this genetic statement, made to Muhammad in the seventh century AD, is indeed quite a revelation. God's original emphasis on education is also paramount.

Further visions came to Muhammad and urged him to persuade his people to abandon their idolatrous beliefs and follow the one, single, universal god of their ancestors Abraham and Ishmael. Since Muhammad could neither read nor write, he dictated his visions to an Egyptian Coptic (though some say that he may have been Armenian) Christian priest friend of his who wrote down Muhammad's dreams and prophecies. This literary partnership between the Prophet and the Coptic priest echoes one of the main points of Muhammad's visions: that the Christian church, from the Middle Eastern perspective, had gone astray. Muhammad emphasized that Christianity should be brought back to its true roots of monotheism.

From the outset, Christianity of the Coptic and eastern trend was not a problem for Muhammad but rather the way it was practiced by its Western followers. As previously stated, one of Muhammad's wives was a Coptic Christian by the name of Myriam who would be the mother of his son Ibrahim. She must have been of consequence and high birth because all of Muhammad's wives were not only rather well connected but also were related to one another. It was Myriam who asked Muhammad to be kind to those following the Christian religion in Egypt. In fact, the Coptic priest who transcribed Muhammad's visions was her brother. As far as Muhammad was concerned, the New Testament had been inspired by God and as such, despite having been transgressed against by its priestly hierarchy, had the stamp of God.

The Coptic priest must have sense the truth of it and decided to record Muhammad's prophetic words exactly as given to him, without making any changes and alterations that would give a different interpretation to these revelations. If anything, the revelations show how much the Christian communities in the East lacked an understanding of the local needs of the population it was supposed to take care of. Being Egyptian, the Copt would have had no qualm in espousing the concept of going back to a root common to the new covenant of Christ: that Christ never claimed to be the Son of God, but rather referred to himself as "the Son of Man," a title given to all princes in succession from King Yehoiachim of Judah and taken from the book of Daniel in the Old Testament.

Muhammad believed in common sense and a religious life void of dogmas. To him, the rule was what mattered, and that rule had to ingratiate itself into a way of life. The Coptic priest would have been particularly aware of the ancient "Law of Mat" whereby the population of Egypt had been required by the ancient lines of Pharaoh to live by the "rule of truth."

In Egypt, truth was also equated with justice. With the emergence of Christianity in Egypt, this way of life had been eroded and had, indeed, almost disappeared. To transpose it to Arabia in the way Muhammad wished to promote it made perfect sense. What Muhammad and Islam quite rightly believe is that "surely God (Allah) should be more than enough for each and everyone of us." The idea of believing that Jesus Christ was "God incarnate on earth" must be a concept that even Christ would himself reject since none of the original sources of the New Testament claim that Christ was born or died a god. Purely from a traditional Jewish point of view, "Messiah" simply meant "anointed," or "king." All Jewish kings and high priests were declared a "messiah" when ascending to the throne of Judah and the high priesthood of Jerusalem. The same term, for example, also applied to the kings of Pontus.

To translate the Koran is difficult because of the Arabic language. It is a bit like Scots Gaelic inasmuch that it can be descriptive in so many ways. Unless one is fully fluent in either Gaelic or Arabic, the nuances of the languages will be lost. The words of the Koran are shaded in meanings (the Essenes typically used that particular trick as well), but Muhammad's codified religious law finds an answer for any kind of eventualities and aspects of life. This way of life can be referred to as "Muhammadism." It is liberal, tolerant, and polite, rendering unto the temporal power what belongs to it and rendering unto the priestly power what belongs to it. It does reject the Christian concept of a "god incarnate on earth" and thus the divinity of Jesus Christ, but upholds him in the Koran as a "prophet" and actually refers to him as the "shadow of God." The Koran also denotes Jesus' physical royalty by mentioning that he was born under a palm tree (a reference to the Solomonic Psalms). Until Muhammad came to power, all people in Arabia, whether from Makkah or Medina, prayed towards Jerusalem. Muhammad put an end to this by decreeing that all followers of the Faith should pray physically towards Makkah.

This rule seen by many as arrogant, but, in fact, it makes perfect sense. After all, all Roman Catholics are supposed to pray for the pope and make a visit, at least once in their lifetime, to Rome. To the staunch Roman Catholic, the word of the pope prevails over that of the law of the country he or she may be born. And many a time have the words of a pope been known to clash with the law of a land. Democratic legislation has no sway over papal utterances. (The papacy's stand against birth control or, indeed, the democratically legislated right to abortion in many countries proves the point.)

Muhammadism is, in concept, very socialistic, asking those better off to take care of the less fortunate. Muhammad, for example, decreed that both Jews and Christians had the right to worship according to their own conscience. Admittedly, they had to pay a tax for the right to do so (though women, children and elderly people were exempt from it). What the Christian church fails to clarify on the matter is that the money collected from non-Islamic followers, like that which each Muslim had to give to the Beyt al-Mal (meaning the ministry of finance), would then be used to support those less fortunate of the community in which they lived, regardless of their religious denomination. Until then, Middle Eastern Christians had provided little financial support to the community within which they lived. They were practically exempt from tax. By introducing this tax, Muhammad introduced a system of financial equality against one of privilege. This is, of course, socialism practiced at its best. Little is said of the fact that Muhammad stood against the practices of slavery. Islam is a religion that accepts Christianity and Judaism as equals.

While the whole Christian philosophy dismisses the faith of Islam as one that totally rejects Christianity, the truth of the matter is that it is the Christian church and the tenets of Judaism, no matter which mainstream protagonist of them, which rejects all other faiths. In fact, for the greater part of two thousand years of its history, the Christian church has actively fought against them all, be it the Jewish faith, the Islamic faith, the Tibetan faith and any other faiths on the face of this planet.

Unlike Christianity, the Islamic religion truly drew from its own native culture and tradition. Becoming active within its society in the name of God, it used both military and nonmilitary idealism to counteract a failing, fragmented Christian church in the Middle East. Islam is a faith expecting its followers to truly believe that cleanliness is next to godliness, requiring them to wash before their prayers (five times a day), which thus helps eradicate diseases. It requires the faithful not to drink if they are going to pray but it does not forbid anyone to drink. What Muhammad simply said was "if you intend to pray, do not drink," in the same manner as drivers today are being told "if you intend to drive, don't drink." In Islamic terms, a prayer offered to God under the influence is not acceptable to God.

What most people outside the faith of Islam also fail to realize is that with the advent of Muhammad, the Middle East regained an arena of political and historical order it had lost under the emergence of the Roman Empire. One has to remember that the emergence of any religion is nothing more than a reaction to the political environment people are coping with. So with Islam in the Middle East, Anglicanism in England, Hinduism in India or Southern Baptists in the United States of America.

However, like Christianity and Judaism, Islam would become, after the death of Muhammad, the Seal of the Prophets, opened to misinterpretation and extreme fundamentalism. This is not a criticism on Islam, merely a reflection of what happens to an ideal following the death of its leader. Women, for example, contrary to popular belief, were never required to veil themselves during the days of Muhammad. The decision was merely one of choice. Incidentally, women, under the laws of Muhammadism, did acquire rights for themselves, which they did not have before, including the right to inherit and run a business.

While the religion of Islam has now been, albeit grudgingly, accepted by the West as mainstream, it is a mistake to believe that the population of Makkah followed Muhammad's new religious ideal overnight. Truth be told, the people of Makkah viewed his religious concepts with such distaste that Muhammad had to flee the sacred place in AD 622 and went into forced exile in Medina (then al-Yatthrib). There, settling in a humble house, he was asked to take up his priestly position and adjudicated on various matters put to him by the people of Medina, among whom lived the very descendants of the earlier Nazorean/Essenes that had settled in the city some four centuries before. This event in his life proved to him one thing: the tribes of the Hijaz must become united, even if by force if need be. The one way to do this was by disrupting the trade routes, and thus the income, that were under the authority of the Quraysh tribes, his tribes. By the year AD 630, following eight years of military clashes, Muhammad was back in Makkah, in charge of the temple. It was only then that the new faith was taken up by the entire population of the Hijaz and the Quraysh tribes. Two years later, Muhammad died, leaving a legacy that would grow into one of the greatest religious and scientific empires and that would show Rome to be no less than a limping second best.

When the leader of a great faith coming from an old dynasty dies, there must be a succession working on behalf of the faith. Muhammad was married four times. None of his sons survived him. Only one of his daughters, Fatima, produced children. Two of his fathers-in-law succeeded to him. The first was Abu Bakr as-Siddiq, who led until he died in AD 64. (His name means "the upright," but the title Siddiq may have roots in the Judaic priestly title of Zadok.) The second was Umar. Umar decided, in order to expand the faith, to declare a holy war, a jihad, and invade Syria, Palestine, Mesopotamia, Egypt and Persia. By doing so, the caliphate of the East became a political equation of such a magnitude that Byzantium had to recognize and acknowledge it. The loss of Jerusalem in AD 638, was not even particularly difficult for Byzantium to bear because it was then no more than a very small city peopled by very few Jews and a small population of Christians. (People tend to forget that Jerusalem had been lost to the Persians in AD 614, when most of its population had been put to the sword by the emperor Khosrau II, head of the Sassanid Empire. In fact, no fewer than 60,000 Christians had been butchered and another 35,000 sold into slavery. Technically speaking, Jerusalem had become Persian territory. While the Eastern emperor Heraclius reconquered the city in AD 629, his forces based in Mu'tah near the southern tip of the Dead Sea were fighting the first waves of Islam against the Byzantine Empire.)

Umar I was certainly kinder than Khosrau. In reverence for the sites where the feet of the Prophet Jesus Christ had walked, Umar made a covenant with both the Jewish and Christian population of Jerusalem. In the act of surrender, the Christians were assured of "the safety of their persons, possessions, churches, crosses, their healthy and sick persons, and all of their community . . . They will not suffer for their religion, nor will any one of them be molested or injured." Following this act, he had a wooden mosque built.

Caliph Abd al-Malik would later build a more spectacular building that truly would dazzle the sense and introduce Muslim architecture to a world that had been aesthetically starving for years. Construction of the Dome of the Rock in Jerusalem began in AD 687 to be finished and dedicated in AD 691. No one had seen anything quite like it. What is not known to most Christians is that the greater part of the Arabic calligraphy on the walls mainly refer to Koranic passages relating to Jesus, so as to commemorate the location of the city that witnessed the climax of Jesus' teaching. The Dome of the Rock not only emphasizes Islam's link to Christianity but is also concerned with reintroducing Jesus ethnic birthright as a Jew. It is the first building with the concept of ecumenism, in which the three main spiritual faiths are celebrated as one.

The Dome of the Rock also reintroduced the architectural harmony of sacred geometry in the Middle East. It had not been done for centuries. Even Constantine I had not been able to achieve a revival of sacred geometry in his new Byzantine capital. Constantinople looked stunning because the use of colored porphyry, not because of the geometry used within its architecture. Furthermore, Constantine had merely expanded the boundaries of the city. While the city became bigger, what filled the space was the equivalent of any modern city's suburbs. Nothing substantially new was built to be remembered today. Even the statues that Constantinople boasted of had been pilfered from conquered pagan cities. At the time Christian geometry was, to say the least, rather stale. With Islam and the Dome of the Rock in Jerusalem, all this would change. Elegance of proportion was the keynote. While simple, the formula of circle enclosing two staggered squares, the latter of which, when extended, determined the dimension of an octagon was one that, once upon a time, had been used in the sacred geometry of the great pyramids of Egypt. All the parts not only blend together in size, but they also relate to one another aesthetically, proportionally, mathematically, geometrically, structurally and decoratively. The architectural concept of the Dome of the Rock would be later borrowed by the Christian church in its endeavor to establish the gothic style of architecture in Europe. For this is what the Dome of the Rock was, the precursor of the gothic arch.

It was clear to the emperors of Constantinople that Umar's capture of Jerusalem in AD 638 was only the first wave of invasions. Following the death of Umar I in AD 644, Uthman I ibn Affan, son-in-law of Muhammad, succeeded Umar as third caliph. It is he who issued the authorized version of the Koran as we have it today. As a leader, he was unpopular and was murdered by disaffected Egyptian troops while reading the new edition of the Koran. The fourth caliph was Ali, a cousin and another of Muhammad's son-in-law. Until Ali's assassination in AD 661, the successors to the Prophet had been elected. They were considered to be the wisest of their peers, but with Ali's death, this would change. When the Umayyads took over the reins of power from Ali's sons, al-Hasan and al-Husayn, pressurizing them to abdicate their rights, the system was changed from a democratic choice to a succession of primogeniture. These Islamic dynastic disputes are what probably saved the Byzantine Empire from being Islamized straight away.

With the Umayyads coming unto the political field, we come into a further age of expansion. Moreover, the seat of Islam was no longer held in Makkah in the Saudi Arabian Hijaz but was transferred to Damascus, which had been a Byzantine Christian stronghold up to AD 635, when the army of Umar I conquered it. Damascus' surrender actually set the pattern for all future conquests.

The formal terms of surrender reads: "In the name of Allah, the merciful, the compassionate, this is what Khalid ibn al-Walid would grant to the inhabitants of Damascus ... He promises to give them security for their lives, property and churches. Their city wall shall not be demolished; neither shall any Muslim be quartered in their houses. Thereunto we give to them the pact of Allah and the protection of his Prophet, the Khalife and the believers. So long as they pay the tax, nothing but good shall befall them."

There, in Damascus, among Christians, the Umayyads established the caliphate as a quasi-temporal hereditary monarchy. They also occasionally married Christian wives. They even, from time to time, signed treaties with Byzantine emperors. The Umayyad's expansion was two-fold: territorial and scientific. Territorially, they had extended into India and Northern Africa when the Exarchate of Carthage was overwhelmed in AD 698. By AD 711, the Islamation of Spain had begun. This was to be Europe's best break and would lift her out of her intellectual stagnation. It would bring us an impetus of sciences and religious liberalization. It would transform Europe with a concept of chivalry that has never been seen since.

Chapter 4

To Bring the West into a Better Age

Many things have been written about the coming of Islam to Spain. The words "Spain was invaded by Islam in AD 711" is what one usually reads in the history books; however, this is what I call a Catholic simplification. Nothing was further from the truth. Islam did not invade Spain. It was invited to come to Spain.

Spain, the kingdom presently ruled by King Juan Carlos I, did not come into being till AD 1474 (some 160 years after Scotland had fully regained its independence following the battle of Bannockburn). Originally part of the Roman Empire, Spain had been invaded by the Vandals before falling to the Visigoths in the fifth century AD. Toledo had been the Visigoth capital in Spain from the early fifth century, and the city capitulated to the Moors (AD 711) for various reasons, not least the fact that Catholicism had been imposed upon Jews who had been threatened with slavery or death if they did not conform to the Christian "Catholic" faith. Most people tend to forget that there were more Jews outside Judaea, even before the days of Christ, than in Judaea itself. Julius Caesar, who died in 44 BC, had declared the Jews "Friends of the Roman Empire" (it was reiterated by Marc Antony as Ruler of the East) and, by doing so, gave them the right to travel and trade all over the empire. With the fall of the last Western Roman emperor, Romulus Augustus, in AD 476, the whole of Europe became fragmented. In France, the Merovingien dynasty, partly Jewish by descent and monarchical practices, took over control of the Roman administration and expanded as far as Italy and Germany.

The South of France, that which was termed "Septimania," was ruled from the late fourth century AD by Visigoth invaders who assumed the title of "king of Toulouse." From Septimania, the Visigoths crossed the Pyrenees and invaded Northern Spain in 412. By AD 466, most of Spain was under the rule of King Eurico of Toulouse. A century later, the kings of Toulouse removed their capital to Spanish Toledo. By then, the Visigoth kings had followed the Aryan branch of the Christian church. It was this allegiance that made both the Visigoth rulers and the people over which they ruled heretics by the standards of both Rome and Byzantine Constantinople and in the view of mainstream "Roman" Christianity, by then firmly espousing the tenets of Catholicism. By AD 586, King Recaredo I had abjured Aryanism and brought Spain within the fold of the Catholic Church of Rome.

The problem with this turn towards Catholicism was the fact that it restrained the rights of the Jewish community in Spain to trade and to worship in their own way. By the late seventh century AD, this persecution had become untenable to the Spanish Jews. By then most of them were aware that the Islamic faith was more favorable to the Jews in the Middle East as a people of the Book (the Torah, the Bible and the Koran) than the Church of Rome. Some Spanish Jews had decided to leave for the safer and more liberal shores of the south of France. The break for those non-Christians in Spain came on the death of King Witiza in AD 710. At his death, Witiza left a son called Agilla, who thought that he should be king after his father through a succession based on primogeniture, in the manner of all other kings in Christendom. However, Visigoth royal succession was not hereditary but elective; the people decided otherwise and elected a military leader by the name of Rodrigo to be king. The Witizan party decided upon a civil war to wrest power from Rodrigo and invited the Islamic Moors of North Africa to side with them in putting Agilla on the throne.

This North African involvement into Spanish affairs should not surprise anyone. After all, North Africa, then called Mauretania, and Spain both had been provinces of the Roman Empire, and, as such, they had traded with one another for centuries. For a political party in Spain to call upon the neighboring Moors was, in fact, nothing new. North Africa had been conquered by Islam when the exarchate of Carthage, now in Tunisia, succumbed to the Umayadds in AD 698. This meant that the Byzantine Empire had lost a rather big chunk of its western territory. While newly conquered on behalf of Islam, the Arabian influx of people was not excessive, so the flow of trade with Spain and other parts of Mediterranean cities had on gone on as usual. Except for converting to Islam, little changed in the life of the native Berbers.

When the call came from Spain, the Moors were quick to oblige and sent crack troops under the leadership of Tariq ibn Ziad, then governor of Tangier. (He first took the "rock" that lay in the straits between Spain and North Africa and gave it his name, Gibr al-Tariq, hence Gibraltar.) His arrival was the opportunity that the Spanish Jews had been waiting for. As said before, Islam recognized both Judaism and Christianity as equal with itself. When the

Moors came to Spain, the Jewish population understood that being ruled by Islamic leaders was a better and safer bet than being ruled by a Catholic hierarchy. Rodrigo was ousted while Agilla was set aside and the Spanish Jews opened wide the gates of Toledo, cheering the liberating Moors. By AD 714, virtually all of the Iberian peninsula had been taken over by the Moors, and an emirate was established in Cordoba in AD 756.

Actually, a tremendous amount of native Spaniards were quick to realize that the new Islamic hierarchy was much fairer than the old Visigoth one. Tax wise, the burden was less onerous and serfs who converted to Islam immediately gained their freedom and enrolled in some conquering Islamic aristocratic houses as paid dependents. The next three centuries of social and economic improvement in Islamic Spain would make sure that many Spaniards converted to Islam. Jews were freed from Christian persecution and found themselves placed on an equal footing with the Hispano-Romans and Goths who still professed, freely, the Christian faith. This religious equality had never been achieved before in Europe. Al-Andalus, as this independent emirate was called from AD 711 to 756, came under the authority of the Umayyad dynasty based in Damascus. This new expansion into Spain stretched the Umayyad Empire across four thousand miles. Wherever the sword of Allah was carried, trade followed, and Muslim merchants soon became the middlemen in the world of imports and exports. In fact, a Muslim merchant could sell Persian saffron to China, Chinese porcelain to Greece, Greek brocade to India, Indian iron to Aleppo, iron from Aleppo to Yemen, stripped Yemeni material back to Persia. This is how vast the Islamic Empire was. By AD 732, Islam had even made a foray into France when the army of Emir Abd-ar-Rahman al-Ghafiqi crossed the Pyrenees to be defeated near the city of Tours by Charles Martel.

It would also be a mistake to believe that all of Visigoth Spain followed Catholicism. The Celtic Church had also become entrenched in Gallicia and had two sees functioning in north west Spain, in Bretona and Santiago de Compostella, and one in Portugal, in Sintra. We find these sees mentioned in Spanish church records as surviving independently until AD 800 (thus well after AD 662, when the Roman Catholic Church claimed that the Celtic Church had dismantled). These sees calculated Easter based on the British Celtic calendar, and thus on the Jewish Passover, as opposed the calendar of Catholic Rome. The interesting thing about the Celtic Church in Spain was that it was left in peace by the Islamic authority. Actually, it was not merely left in peace, it was positively seen as the more acceptable side of Christianity by the religious Muslim hierarchy. The question that comes to mind is why?

Catholic apologists have always denigrated the eastern origin of the Celtic Church. It seems that at no time could the Church of Rome accept the fact that the Celtic Church had a fundamentally better pedigree than Rome. The roots of the Celtic Church were twofold. The first sprung from the Syrian Church, which had a proper Hebraic hierarchy and answered to the Church of Jerusalem and the leadership of the successors of the high priest James, brother of Christ. The second root was Alexandrian which, although based in Egypt, was influenced by the ancient Hellenistic trend of worship. This Syrian-Alexandrian background applied to the Gallican Church of Gaul (France) as well. Both the Celtic and Gallican churches used similar ritual texts, and ideas and introduced the Syrian practice of using hymns and psamoldy within their church services. The Celtic Church drew from its native religion as well. Furthermore, like any other high priesthood anywhere in the world, it was hereditary within the family, and gave women equal rights to men. In Britain, Druidism had much in common with the Essenic concepts of dual messiahship of king and high priest and the afterlife. It was also extremely nationalistic and anti-Roman. Like the nationalist Jews, the Celtic tribes were always quick to try to reassert their independence from the Roman Empire.

The Roman Catholic Church, never mindful of the truth, has always been extremely slow to admit, for example, that the second bishop of Rome, Prince Linus, was the son of King Caractacus, a native British king who ruled a part of England stretching as far as the Wash and the Cotswolds between AD 40 and AD 80. Caractacus had been carried to Rome by the emperor Claudius in AD 43. Caractacus's family members were brought to Rome as trophies of war for the usual display during the emperor's triumph. In AD 58, the children of Caractacus converted to the Christian sect led by Jesus Justus (not that of St. Paul or St. Peter as claimed by the Catholic Church). In fact, some archives claim that Caractacus's family was already Christian, belonging to the Church of St. James. This is crucial to the Celtic Church equation. We know that Saint Paul did not make it to Rome before AD 62. In fact, some scholars believe that he did not make it till after AD 65, and others believe that he never made it to Rome at all. Linus, a Celtic Christian, became bishop of Rome sometime after AD 64, probably AD 67, and died about AD 79. His sister Gladys, who adopted the Roman name of Claudia, married the Roman aristocrat Rufus Pudens. They are the Claudia and Rufus of the St. Paul's epistle to the Romans. Their children were Timotheus, Novatus, Pudentiana and Praxedes, all of whom are revered saints of the Roman Catholic Church. During the days of King Cyllinus, Bishop Linus's brother, infant baptism took place in Colchester, and Linus's brother-in-law, Salog, founded the town of Salisbury. But when Linus succeeded as bishop of Rome, neither Peter or Paul were part of the equation, rather the bishop and high priest of Jerusalem, St. James, was the man to whom Linus answered to. Linus could hardly ignore the religious influence of Joseph the Rama Theo (the Essene "divine highness") to whom his family was related. Nor should we be surprised at the British family marrying into a Roman one. Linus's aunt, another

Gladys, had already set the trend by marrying Aulus Plautius, a Roman commander. Taking this genealogical link into consideration, it is more than probable that the Judaean Essenic church was already entrenched in Britain. This makes Glastonbury's claim to be the root of the Celtic Church in Britain all the more probable, and something that Rome, later coming fully under the Christian Pauline sect and a Petrine succession (even though Peter was never bishop of Rome nor buried there), decidedly has great difficulties accepting.

In order to give credence to its alleged god-given right and precedence over all others of the Catholic Church, Rome claims the Celtic Church was introduced to Europe between AD 176 and 208. The main item used by the Catholic Church against an earlier date for the Celtic Church was the fact that Irenaeus, bishop of Lyons, failed to mention it in his writings. Irenaeus's main task, however, was to fashion a literary negative movement against not just Gnosticism and its concept of dualism, but also against any other nonconformist trend of Christianity. Though born to Greek parents in Asia Minor before AD 140, Iraneus was extremely influenced by Paulinism. As a child, he heard and saw Polycarp, the last known living connection with the apostles, in Smyrna, before Polycarp was martyred in AD 155. When he succeeded to the bishopric of Lyons, the previous incumbent had been none other than the Christian martyr, Pothinus. The Roman concept of martyrdom became an obvious way to propagate the faith. Iraneus instigated the concept of a canon of scriptures and the doctrine of an "apostolic succession" from bishops recognized only by Rome, none of whom were, of course, Gnostics or Celtic.

The only and safe guides to biblical and scriptural interpretations, according to Irenaeus, were those Roman Catholic apostolic bishops. Any trend of Christianity claiming an oral tradition from Jesus Christ had to be eliminated. By doing this, the fact that most things in the Middle East were transmitted orally was to be totally ignored and repudiated. I find it very strange that no one has ever been surprised that no writings by Jesus Christ himself, nor any original papers by any of the apostles, save perhaps those of the secret Gospel of Thomas, have ever been found. The New Testament, and it has been edited many times before being presented to us as we know it today, was not written until many years after the death of the individual in whose name it was claimed to have been written. The oral tradition is something that the early fathers of the Catholic Church, including Irenaeus, do not wish to entertain. In fact, they want it eradicated from the people's mind.

Tertullian (born before AD 160) does, of course, mention the Celtic Church. So how did the Celtic Church evolve in the various parts of Europe and did it ever sway any kind of power?

Except for the use of a Latin mass particular to itself, the Celtic Church can in no way be connected to the Pauline and Petrine movements from which derives the Roman Catholic Church. Fundamentally, Druidism recognized the divine message of Jesus Christ and acknowledged him as a prophet, very much in the manner that Muhammad did some six hundred years later. It is James (brother of Jesus Christ), high priest and first bishop of Jerusalem, who first brought the Essene faith to Britain in AD 37. When he reached the shores of these Islands, he was known as "Joseph Rama Theo," which would later be mistranslated as "Joseph of Arimathea." Together with the original Essene bishopric of Jerusalem, the Celtic Church can claim to be one of the oldest Christian churches in the world, as can the Syrian, African and Coptic churches.

By AD 62, the Celtic Church had been imbued with a touch of the liberalism of the declining Greek influence of the post Ptolemic era within the east. Moreover, it was recognized by the various Jewish movements of the diaspora, particularly that of Alexandria in Egypt. It was the Alexandrian, and thus Coptic, form of the Mass, together with the Egyptian anchorite monastic system, that the Celtic Church would use in its missionary zeal to propagate the faith. This missionary zeal stretched across the whole of Europe, from Greenland to the very gates of Rome. Early Catholic bishops were so despised by the Italians that many were deposed by the native populations and replaced with traveling (Peregrini) Celtic bishops passing through their towns. Like the Jerusalem succession, the Celtic apostolic succession was kept within the family, passing from father to son, uncle to nephew or cousin to cousin. Ancient gods and goddesses became the early saints of the Celtic Church so as to create an easy way to conversion. Within the early Celtic Church, episcopal and priestly celibacy was encouraged but not required, and infant baptism did not exist, unless the life of the child was deemed to be in danger. Holy communion was celebrated twice a year, at the Jewish festival of Passover, which became the Celtic Easter festival, and at Michaelmass. Moreover, the Celtic Church did not believe in the concept of the original sin, but rather believed that people became sinners as they grew older. The tonsure of Celtic monks was different from that of the Roman Catholic monks. Heads were shaved from ear to ear and hair was allowed to grow long at the back as in the Essene tradition.

Unlike the Roman Catholic Church then, Celtic bishops were anointed exactly in the same way as the high priests of Jerusalem, that is to say hands and head as prescribed in the ritual of ordination of Leviticus 21:10. This anointing was not borrowed from the Celtic Church by the Roman one before the ninth century, despite its promotion in the influential Roman forgeries known as the "pseudo-Isodorean decretals," which gives the impression that this practice was an ancient one within the Roman Church. It would not be before the late sixth century that Roman Catholicism would be introduced in the south of England by St. Augustine in AD 597, when he was sent to the court of King Aethelbert I of Kent, by the Benedictine pope Gregorius I.

Aethelbert allowed Augustine to settle in Canterbury, the latter claiming to be its first archbishop. He died either in AD 604 or 605. Until Augustine's coming, it was the Celtic Church that held sway in Britain, a Celtic Church that preferred willing conversion and that thus saw no wrong with pagan altars sharing common space with a Celtic Christian ones. This is why, within the records in Rome, it is stated that Augustine's mission failed the papacy.

However, by AD 663, Roman Catholic Canterbury, which had grown to rule the area of England south of Cheshire and Yorkshire, decided to counteract the power of the Celtic Church by calling a council to be held at Whitby in AD 664. The idea, of course, was to destroy the Celtic Church. Most history books, when mentioning Whitby, state that the Celtic Church came to an end and amalgamated with the Roman one. There is nothing further from the truth. What actually happened is that the hierarchy of the Celtic Church in Northumbria, bishops, priests, monks, congregation and all, simply removed themselves and crossed over into Scotland. There, they resettled among their own fellow Celtic Christians and thrived, without interference from Rome.

Most people are aware of the Irish born St. Columba, who settled in Iona, in Scotland, in AD 574. What most people are unaware of is that this hereditary Celtic Abbacy was firmly kept within the family till the death of Abbot John Mackinnon in AD 1555, almost one thousand years after the suppression of the Northumbrian Celtic Church at the council of Whitby. While the Celtic Church relegated the Roman trend of Christianity to second best, anything of Middle Eastern Christian tradition was firmly espoused. Other traditions included fasting on Wednesdays and Fridays, as well as during Lent; in terms of education, Greek grammar and philosophy, together with Latin speeches by Cicero were the norm within the Celtic Church. The Celtic tonsure, so despised by the church of Rome, was that of Simon Magus (former high priest of Jerusalem and thus proving the Celtic Church's roots with the Essenes) and the Abbots of Celtic monasteries, based on the eastern anchorite rites, were called "holy fathers." The chief festival of the Celtic Church was not Christmas but Easter (spring equinox) and they did not recite the service of Compline (last canonical hour).

With the import of Islam to Spain via North Africa, the African trend of Christianity, which had been totally accepted by the Islamic hierarchy, was then introduced and promoted in Spain. The Spanish Mozarabic Church was born and developed strong links with both the Sees of Santiago de Compostella and Bretona in Gallicia, as well as the see of Sintra in Portugal and thus with Celtic Ireland and Scotland. One aspect of the Mozarabic Church soon made its way into Celtic Church art: the use of the serpent as a common form of ornamentation in the elaborate illuminations of interlaced works, which can be found in both the Celtic Church's manuscript and iconography. This use of the serpent, together with the use of animal and geometric representations, is something the Celtic Church inherited from Africa via Egypt and Asia. Parts of the Gallician Mozarabic rituals also made their way to those of the British Celtic Church. The adjacent kingdom of the Asturias to the caliphate of Cordoba remained firmly Catholic, as did the eastern Spanish kingdom of Pamplona that engulfed the Basque countries. Within these two Realms survived the Hispano-Roman Visigothic traditions. It is mainly from the Asturias that the concept of the "Reconquidesta," the reconquest of Muslim Spain for the Catholic Church, was born and put into practice from the year 1050.

It is during this expansion into the West that a change of dynasty took place within the hierarchy leading Islam. In AD 749, the caliphate was transferred from Damascus to Kuffah. The problem that arose within the Islamic Empire was one of dynastic power. The Quraysh tribe was extensive and had produced various lines, all related to Muhammad, some descended from him. Needless to say, each vied for powers and, in AD 74, the Umayyad and Abbaside dynasties came to a showdown. The latter gained the upper hand, and the former had to give in to the inevitable. But where the Umayyads had been liberal and tolerant, the Abbasides would take a more fundamentalist stand, ultimately splitting the empire into two sides, some supporting what remained of the Umayyad caliphate, others supporting the new Abbaside administration. It was Abu-Djafar al-Mansur, the second Abbaside caliph (AD 754–775), who transferred the administration to his newly built capital city of Baghdad, in what is now Iraq. (Iraq was formed into a modern kingdom under the Hashemite dynasty in 1921, which was granted independence in 1932. It was declared a republic following a revolution in 1958.)

This situation was no good to the Abbasides, who wanted to rule a unified empire, and so the Abbasides decided that the Umayyad family should be slaughtered to extinction. And it almost worked. Having been invited to a huge family dinner by Abu al-Abbas al-Saffah, the new Abbasid caliph, all of the male Umayyad princes were put to the sword on entering the banqueting hall. Out of an entire royal family numbering into the hundreds, only one young member who had not attended the banquet was able to escape and make it to the safety of Spain. Abd-ar-Rahman I, the last of the Umayyad princes of Damascus, was proclaimed Emir of Cordoba in AD 756 and his dynasty would last for another three hundred years. One should say they were three hundred glorious years, not just for Spain but also for the rest of Europe. Spain's new capital, Cordoba, would be the keystone to importing knowledge from the East into Europe. Cordoba was a bridge between East and West and would shake Europe out of the dark years of Roman Catholic suppression.

CHAPTER 5

CORDOBA
THE NEW ALEXANDRIA

Few words have ever been written about Cordoba, which is very surprising considering the influence it had within the West for over three hundred years. In fact, Islamic Cordoba was the equivalent of a Western Alexandria. As well as being the largest city in Europe at that time, Cordoba could boast of eighty thousand market stalls, nine hundred bath houses (an unknown luxury on the other side of the Pyrenees) and a thousand mosques. To this must be added the many Christian churches and Jewish synagogues that functioned normally under the new Islamic hierarchy. As a city, Cordoba was famed for the most sophisticated metal works, for weavers producing the most beautiful textile works and leather works that had no equal anywhere in the world. Along the Guadalquivir River, five thousands water mills ground corn and irrigated the land that fed Cordoba's population. But it was as a centre of learning and as a city of libraries, with one particular library housing no less than four hundred thousand books, that Cordoba was best known. As such, it could then be equated with the library of Alexandria in Egypt. Cordoba was a literary center in the known world, an abode for those wanting to delve into the various spiritual faiths, past and contemporary, of their world.

There is a much more interesting aspect about this Islamic university in Europe, which many academics have missed. It is from Cordoba that the science and technology of architectural traditions, together with mysticism relating to tabernacle and temple buildings, spread throughout Europe. However, this mystic science and technology was not a Jewish tradition as commonly believed, but rather an Islamic one imbued with an Egyptian concept to which was added a zest of European Judaic philosophy. The Jewish nation of old is only remembered for three architectural feats in the history of their ancestors:

three temples (technically four), all destroyed and of which hardly any archeological records telling us what they looked like have survived. Furthermore, the dominant quarrying and stonecutting expertise in the Middle East can be attributed only to Egypt.

To Egypt alone can be attributed complex geometrical temple and tabernacle designs, numerical calculations and colonnades. One should remember that while the architectural concept of the arch comes from ancient Sumeria and that of the vault from Babylon, it is a fact, albeit one that present day Jewish historians would dearly like to forget, that both Jewish mysticism and Solomonic architectural lore drew from Egypt in concept. Islam never rejected the ancient knowledge of the countries they took over. In fact, it simply amalgamated the best from each into its own philosophy and propagated that philosophy to the far confines of its growing empire.

Suddenly, via the Islamic liberalism of Cordoba, the West was opened to popular works of medicine, astrology, geography and agriculture. Poetry reached a level as yet unparalleled, journalism came into being, academies of *belles lettres* were founded, books of grammar and pure mathematical sciences were printed. Astronomical data, such as the fact that the orbits of planets are not circular but ovoid (thus anticipating Johannes Kepler by centuries) were published, and astrolabes were introduced into the West. The first printed nautical maps originated from Muslim Granada. Muslim Spain, and Cordoba in particular, eclipsed all else in Europe, including Rome (but save perhaps Islamic-influenced Sicily).

While the Christian church had rejected, over the centuries, the Hellenistic views and treatises of great master philosophers (such as Plato, Euclid, Ovid, Horace and Aristotle), the scriptoria of Baghdad and Arrakesh in Morocco were busy translating them into Arabic in the tenth and eleventh centuries AD. These works were later translated, in Cordoba, into Latin and still later in the vernacular languages of western Europe, and would form the basis of the Renaissance period. The same applied to the works of Ptolemic geography, works of Sanskrit astrology, and to medical works from Hippocrates and Galen, all of which were first heartily embraced by both the Umayyad and the Abbaside dynasties. Arabic translations of these literary works were made from books originally written in both Syrian and Greek. What these Islamic scholars also did was check all the data over years and either corrected them when needed and improved on them all of the time. But Islamic Spain did much more than reintroduce the concept of wisdom. It introduced to the rest of Europe an age of science and philosophy uninhibited by the faith. This was the era of true freedom of artistic expression, and, for three centuries, Cordoba was a place where linguists and intellectuals could meet and talk without constraints, where metaphysics, pure arithmetic, optics (later borrowed by Leonardo da Vinci), meteorology, medicine, music, astronomy, astrology, alchemy, grammar, poetry and architecture, even fashion, was encouraged and practiced.

The use of the system of numerals called, in the West, "Arabic" and the adoption of the Indian concept of zero enabled the Muslims to make sophisticated calculations that were impossible for those Europeans using cumbersome Roman numerals. The complicated geographical and astronomical calculations measuring the extent of the earth and the passage of the planets (which they had used for some two hundred years) were finally codified in the eleventh century in the "Toledan" tables, a compilation made in Toledo by Muslim astronomers. A late thirteenth-century French recension of the tables was to prove useful to both astronomers and navigators alike when the "New World" was discovered. The astrolabe, the first of which, as a computing machine that could work out and exhibit the motions of the sun, moon and the known planets, can be traced as far back as 82 BC, was improved by the Muslim astronomer al-Zarqali in the eleventh century. As a navigational instrument in Christian hands, it made possible the voyages of exploration of the fifteenth and sixteenth centuries.

The healing arts were highly respected in medieval Islam, in contrast to the West where they had fallen into desuetude. The works of such Greek physicians as Galen and Hippocrates were translated into Arabic (though on practicing according to Galen, many Muslim physicians found him to be occasionally wrong). Medieval Muslim doctors thoroughly washed their hands before operating, were able to perform birth by caesarian and sterilized their surgical instruments both before and after an operation. In fact, most Christian rulers employed Muslim doctors and astronomers, even though this was frowned upon by Rome.

The three-course meal of soup, meat and dessert was, by the by, a Muslim introduction to Spain and adopted by Christian Europe, which was getting rather fed up with its rather monotonous diet. Cordoba, believe it or not, introduced the cultivation of rice, as well as that of sugar cane, to Europe. Until the introduction of sugar cane, Europe sweetened its food with honey. Not until Spain discovered America and its new West Indian colonies would the cultivation of sugar and rice in Europe die out. Printing and the manufacture of paper is something that Europe can thank the Muslims for as well though, admittedly, Islam acquiring the ways and means of it was purely an accident of war. Back in the early eighth century AD, an Arab force was besieged in Samarkand (in Uzbekistan), a city that they had conquered in 705, by a Chinese army. While in Samarkand, the Muslims learned the process of papermaking and afterward spread the manufacture of it from one end of their empire to the other. Cordoba, Valencia and Toledo, under Muslim rule, would become centers of paper manufacturing. With the availability of paper, Islam, together with other European countries, was able to propagate its literature. Their poetic themes was mainly centered upon chivalry and on love in all its varieties, that is to say heterosexual, homosexual, sensual, platonic, sophisticated, naive, fulfilled or frustrated.

Islamic literary works would later influence the lore of the Holy Grail. Some of the Grail stories can trace their roots to Arabian traditions and, indeed, to the very esoteric practices of what became known as the Ismaelite orders of the Assassins and Nusayri. The magical castle in which Lancelot meets the Grail king but fails to answer the question that would heal the king was very much part of an initiation ritual that was acted by Islamic acolytes under the eye of the Old Man of the Mountain, the master of the Order of the Assassins. The names "Parzifal" and "Fierefiz," first brought into play by Wolfram von Eschenbach (c. AD 1170–1220), are hardly Christian names at all, but have their roots in Arabia. The whole Grail concept was merely westernized when it was introduced in Spain. That it fitted so well within a pre-Roman concept of Christianity is not surprising. The desposiny of Christ had, after all, settled in Europe. The family, or desposiny, of Christ had, after all, settled and ruled parts of Europe. Ever aware of its eastern roots, the desposiny was able to influence the history of Europe with a zest of the eastern blend of tradition. The only thing needed to be done to westernize the Grail history was to graft the genealogies of the pertinent desposiny families in Europe upon it, and an entire esoteric history belonging to the East was introduced within the West.

Moreover, this new eastern grafting to western lore emphasized that Christians and Muslims could live together in harmony, like true brothers. In Grail history, Gahmuret married twice: first to a Muslim princess by whom he had a son called fierefiz, the "black and white" knight; secondly to a Christian princess by whom he had a son called Parzifal. What is more, Gahmuret is a dependent of the caliph of Baghdad, and it is in the Middle East, while fighting for his Muslim master, that Gahmuret dies. The legacy he left to his two sons was both a macro- and microcosmic alchemy proving that the two traditions, Christian and Islamic, have so much in common that they are not merely equal, but also could be amalgamated together in one whole liberating doctrine through the concept of Chivalry. Let us remember that the conceptual root of chivalry came from Arabia. The root for the word Elixir came, in fact, from the Arabian word "Al Iksir," as did the word "alchemy" ("Al kemy").

Think of it. Courtly love, the chivalric concept that can be found in the writings of such literary supremos as Chretien de Troyes, Wolfram von Eschenbach, Dante and Geoffrey Chaucer, came to them from Islam via Muslim Spain. In these works women were perceived as different beings from men and were described as remote and mysterious creatures. The mystery of woman would engender a cult of selfless devotion to the feminine. This cult can be seen in a painting from the ceiling of the Hall of the Kings at the Alhambra palace in Granada: the ceiling shows a knight-lover is rescuing the lady of his love from a wild-man, very much in the manner as Sir Lancelot was to do in Sir Thomas Malory's work *Le Mort d'Arthur*. The literary transmission by way of Flegetanis (Arab physician Felek Thani) to Kyot (a Provencal troubadour), then from the latter to Wolfram (German writer), Chretien de Troyes and Robert de Boron (both French) is easily defined. According to Robert de Boron, a master of traditional esoterism, "the great secrets were written in a sacred oral enlightened work guarded by the great Muslim clerks." No matter what the church may tell you about it, it is a fact that the concept of chivalry, which honored beauty and defense of the poor, orphans and of women, had been introduced in Europe via Islamic Spain. Christianity per se, certainly till then, had little time for women or the less fortunate. Only those in power mattered then. This concept of chivalry terrified the Roman Catholic Church.

The most important contribution Islamic Spain made to western Europe was architecture. From the fall of Rome and until the arrival of Islam, European architecture was plain, brutal and unsophisticated. It was "solid" and without aesthetics. Even the sacred geometry relating to Temple building had become a token of remembrance. With Islam, the architecture that was introduced was something that had been long forgotten but which had previously been seen in Celtic artworks. Islamic buildings showed stone, plaster and carved wood works of incomparable beauty, where nature came into full bloom, with intricate geometrical designs. This philosophy of beauty was everywhere, including gardens that were designed to please the eye, as well as to tame nature. Water, in this instance, played a great part in creating these formal gardens. It could be heard trickling by, traveling through ponds housing tropical fish, all this in the most arid of places. Gardens were the concept of paradise come true and it took over a thousand loaves a day to feed the fish of the ponds of the caliph's palace in Cordoba. The palace itself was built with roofs of gold tiles and translucent alabaster.

The mosque at Cordoba is of particular interest. It contains many designs that would later relate to those used by the Cistercian Order of Bernard de Clairveaux. One design in which in particular, the eighth century ceiling of the Cordoba mosque's "mihrab" antechamber, would be built, in the fourteenth century, in a ceiling of the Scottish border abbey of Melrose. The design represents the Dome of the Rock in Jerusalem, the first stone Islamic temple built outside Arabia. The mosque of Cordoba, now a Christian cathedral, compared to the plain Ka'bah in Makkah, shows in its magnificence the most grandiose as well as delicate architectural know how of Islam at its best. Ethereal colonnades would shade the believers in prayers. It would also show them the way to a promenade that would tune their psyche to reach God by themselves.

Cordoban Islamic architecture was light, airy and tall. Windows were the keys. It was so avant guard that it influenced that used by both the Cistercians and the Templars.

Cordoba and its caliphs were able to call to arms a standing army of no less than one hundred thousand men. It took one third of the country's income to keep the army maintained. The elite troops of the palace guard were Leonese and Frankish mercenaries, together with East European Slavs. The rest of the army consisted of Berber (North African, thus not Arab) and these Moorish troop units were organized and housed in such a way that tribal loyalties would be minimal, if not altogether nonexistent.

The various municipal administration posts were filled through the concept of merit and commitment. Loyalty was the key. In fact, ministerial cabinets as most governments have today were introduced by Cordoba. These ministers (viziers) specialized in matters such as finance, trade, justice, diplomacy and war. The concept of law, that is to say, civil rights, was also introduced in Europe via Cordoba. Municipal judges (cadis) heard personal, property, commercial and tax cases of all sorts (people could be taxed as low as twenty per cent or at most, in times of need, up to fifty percent but never more). These cadis protected, in law, the ordinary subjects, whether Muslims, Christians or Jewish, from the worst exaction of landlords, merchants and even high officials. They were also in charge of keeping a check on the coinage, weights, measures and the renting of market-stalls and warehouse space. Altogether, Spain under Islam was better off, more efficiently run and tolerant than it would become when conquered on behalf of the Church of Rome in the fourteenth and fifteenth centuries.

A Jewish Pope

One particular man who would be of great importance to the Christian church in the West, studied in Cordoba. His spiritual name was Gerbert d'Aurillac (born in AD 945), and in AD 999 he succeeded as Pope Sylvester II. It was Borrell II of Barcelona, then the vassal of the Caliph of Cordoba, who took d'Aurillac to the most important seat of learning in Europe. And in Cordoba, d'Aurillac was dazzled, studying with Arab mathematicians and linguists, with liberal Christians, Jewish scholars, Babylonian cabalists and Persian astronomers. It is d'Aurillac who introduced the word "croisade" (crusade) to the Christian vocabulary; however, his crusade was not one involving the military, but rather one involving an exchange of thought, idea, ideals, spiritual, cultural, even industrial. D'Aurillac was fluent in the Greek, Aramaic and Arabic languages (as well as Latin) and he entertained people of those nationalities in Rome. What Sylvester II wanted to prove was that the Christian faith, like that of Islam, could be one that was all embracing and liberating, and it need not be suppressive as it had been before his accession as pope. His knowledge of the Old Testament (including the books left out by the early Christian church fathers) was unsurpassed, as was his understanding of gemetria, mathematics, astronomy and alchemy, all of which he learned at Cordoba.

When d'Aurillac became the head of the cathedral school at Rheims, years before he acceded as pope, he decided to put the Cordoban system of education to good use and revived the liberal arts curriculum, which included the Trivium (comprising grammar, rhetoric and logic) and Quadrium (combining arithmetic, geometry, astronomy and music), which had fallen out of practice in the West. These would become the basic curricula in the Middle Ages. Some papal apologists would like us to believe that both disciplines have their roots with St. Augustine in the fifth century and the Visigothic saint Isidore of Seville of two centuries later. The truth, however, is that they were from Cordoba, with its new unsuppressed tradition of learning and education, and it was from Cordoba that d'Aurillac got the inspiration to reintroduce the Trivium and the Quadrium to western Europe.

No papal historian has ever wondered why Gerbert d'Aurillac ended up in Cordoba, the seat of Islam in Europe. Here we must disentangle the reality from the myth. What Rome tells the people about the origin of Gerbert d'Aurillac is definitely not the truth. Rome claims that this pope was, originally, the son of a poor shepherd. A monk came upon Gerbert counting the number of stars in the sky at night whilst looking after his sheep and asked him a few questions. Enthralled by the wise answers from the boy, he brought him to the monastery of Aurillac and decided to take up his education. The Roman Catholic Church hence claims that Gerbert adopted the name of the monastery. While a lovely story, it does bear the ring of a made-up one. In fact, the Roman Catholic Church forged this background for d'Aurillac, though not until after his death in 1003.

The papacy faced a few years of strife in the tenth century, when it was led by a woman, disguised as a man, historically dubbed Pope Joan. This pope gave birth in a Roman street during a procession back to the Vatican. After this scandal, Rome saw the holy seat of the papacy becoming the property of another very determined woman called Theodora. Though married to Theophilact (a Greek patrician), Theodora was also the lover of Pope John X (AD 914–928). She married her daughter Marozia to Pope Sergius III (AD 904–911), and their son succeeded the papal throne as John XI (AD 931–935). Marozia's grandson by her second marriage to Alberic, Marquis of Camerino, succeeded as Pope John XII (AD 955–964). Theodora's endeavor to found a papal dynasty that would make the Holy See of Rome hereditary within her family almost worked. In fact, following the death of Sylvester II, two great-grandsons of Marozia would become pope. Their papal names were Benedict VIII (1012–1024) and John XIX (1024–1032). Her great-great-grandson would succeed as Benedict IX from 1032 to 1044, then again in 1045 and finally from 1047 to 1048. (He died in 1049, having sold the office to both Gregorius VI and Damasus II.)

After having a woman secretly become pope and another woman engineer the papal office to become heritable within her own family, the Roman Catholic Church could not afford another scandal. It could not afford to admit that Pope Silvester II was, in fact, Jewish.

Gerbert d'Aurillac was a lawful Merovingien dynast descended from Theodoric IV, king of Neustria and Burgundy from AD 720 and deposed in 737 by Charles Martel. Loosing his French territories, Theodoric then succeeded to the Jewish kingdom of Septimania as Makir Theodoric and died with that title in 741. The title of "Makir" was settled upon Theodoric by no less than Caliph Hisham I of the Umayyad dynasty of Damascus, in other words by the head of the Islamic Empire. Moreover, even the exilarch at Babylon had agreed to Theodoric's succession on the say-so of the caliph. Theodoric's son, Guillaume de Toulouse, succeeded his father as the western Davidic sovereign and founded the Judaic academy of Gellone (St. Guilhelm le desert) in AD 791, dying with the French title of master of Aquitaine and second Count of Toulouse in AD 828.

Guillaume de Toulouse's son, Bernard, was the imperial chamberlain at the court of Louis I (Louis the Pious), son of Charlemagne. As well as holding the title of prince of Septimania, Bernard had married Louis's sister Dhoda. Caroloringien records show that Dhoda gave birth to two sons, both of whom died without issue. The Caroloringien tried to claim Septimania for themselves till it was pointed out to them by no less than an Islamic embassy from Cordoba that this could not be done because, firstly, Bernard's line was not dead as claimed, and secondly, Septimania came under the suzerainty of Cordoba. Islamic records were produced showing that Dhoda had a third son, Fulk de Rouergue, who took the title of his father in law, Fredegundus "de Rouergue."

And here starts one of the most important Jewish links in Europe. Fredegundus's father-in-law was Haninai, Jewish exilarch of Babylon, then in residence in Narbonnes (France). Aninai was a direct descendant of Aivu, founder of the Sura Academy and co-founder of the Babylonian Talmud. Aivu lived in the third century AD, and it is mostly due to his works that the ideals of the Babylonian cabbala were introduced within European Judaism.

In fact, the line of the exilarchy of Babylon actually linked with that of the kings of Persia, one of whom, Vaharan V (AD 420 to 438), recognized the rights of Zoroasterians and Christians to worship equally within the Persian Empire. It can be said that the religious traditions that were brought within the de Rouergue family were indeed unique.

Moreover, the Babylonian collateral branch of the de Rouergue family played a vital role in having the Bible translated into Arabic by Sa'adia ibn Joseph al-Fayyumi (Egyptian by birth) with Arabic commentaries. With the support of the exilarch David (a descendant of Haninai), Sa'adia became the pioneer of a Judeo-Arabic culture that came to full flower in Spanish Cordoba and French Septimania a century later.

With Sa'adia works backed by exilarch David, we see a clear stimulus for the revival of Jewish poetry. Sa'adia was an avid writer. The *Encyclopedia Britannica* states that "his translation of the Bible into Arabic and his Arabic commentaries of Scripture made the rabbinic understanding of the Bible accessible to masses of Jews. His poetic compositions for liturgical use provided the stimulus for the revival of Hebrew poetry." Above all, his rationalist commentary on the puzzling *Book of Creation* and his brilliant philosophic treatise on Jewish faith, *Beliefs and Opinions*, synthesized Torah (the divine law in the five Books of Moses and the rabbinic understanding of this revelation) and "Greek wisdom" in accordance with the dominant Muslim philosophical school of Kalam and thus made Judaism philosophically respectable and the study of philosophy religiously acceptable pursuit in the Christian west. With the exilarch David's cousin, Sherira, and son Hai, the Babylonian Talmud became the agent of basic Jewish uniformity as it grew in today's form. What is more, without the exilarch's link to Europe via the House of Toulouse, Judaism might not have survived within western Europe as an entity in its own right. But be under no illusion, Judaism as we have it today takes its trend from Babylonian roots and traditions.

Fulk's fourth descendant, Raymond III Pons of Toulouse, married three times. The first marriage, however, had been denied by the church because this first wife was the daughter of the Jewish exilarch of Babylon (then visiting the Jews of Narbonnes). In AD 945, she died in childbirth, having safely delivered a son. Gerbert was born. Then Raymond remarried Gersende of Gascony, who gave birth to William in AD 947. Gersende saw the young Jewish boy, and one must remember that a Jew is a Jew by the fact of being his mother's son, as a threat to her own progeny. Further, Gersende was a staunch Catholic. She decided to have Gerbert educated as a Christian in the not too far distant monastery of Aurillac. The monks, however, were liberal enough to recognize the importance of Gerbert's maternal inheritance. Years later, Borrell II of Barcelona (Gerbert's maternal uncle) took it upon himself to take the personable young man, Gerbert, now nicknamed d'Aurillac, to Cordoba.

This makes perfect sense. Anyone who was someone in the South of France was educated in Cordoba, then the seat of learning in Europe where three religions of the world, Islam, Judaism and Christianity, converged, worked, learned and co-operated together. Borrell II happened to be the vassal of the Caliph of Cordoba. Borrell II was an intimate of the Islamic Court in Spain, having himself spent fruitful years of education there. Morover, Borrell and Gerbert were cousins and both were descendants of the Merovingian dynasts recognized by the caliph of Cordoba as Jewish princes of Septimania. In fact, this line included not just Borrell II and Gerbert d'Aurillac, who later succeeded to the throne of St. Peter, but all succeeding counts of Toulouse, Limoges and de la Haute Marche. D'Aurillac's Jewish antecedents became of prime importance to him, influencing Vatican policies to the highest level.

When d'Aurillac took his pontifical office in Rome on April 2, 999, as Sylvester II, he took the unprecedented step to create the kingdom of Hungary and declare Stephen Arpad its king. Few people have ever asked why Sylvester II thought that Hungary should be declared an independent kingdom in its own right, but here, once again, it was the Judaic link that was important. Stephen's mother and grandmother were the keys. His grandmother was a daughter of the prince of Bikar Khazars. Her father, Maroth, was also the khagan of the Jewish Khazars between the rivers Theiss and Szamos. Originally from Turkistan, the Khazars had converted to Judaism in AD 740 and by the second half of the eighth century, the Khazar empire had reached the peak of its power. It extended along the northern shore of the Black Sea from the lower Volga and the Caspian Sea in the east, to the Dnieper River in the west. The Khazars controlled and exacted tribute from the Alani and other northern Caucasian peoples (dwelling between the mountains and the Kuban River), from the Magyars (Hungarians) inhabiting the area around the Donets River, from the Goths, and from the Greek colonies in the Crimea. The Volga Bulgars and numerous Slavic tribes also recognized the Khazars as their overlords.

Stephen's father, Taksony, had fought the emperor Otto the Great in AD 955 and had lost the fight against him. Already then, Taksony held the title of "Great Prince of Hungary" due to his Khazar inheritance. Following his father's death, Stephen took over in AD 970 under the regency of his uncle, Michael, the kuman of Samogy, a title held in right of his mother who belonged to the royal house of Samogitia, known as "The Royal House of the Sun." The Samogitians, like the Khazars, traced their ancestry to Old Testament Judaic tribes, and it is this connection that influenced Sylvester to form the kingdom of Hungary. Only after Sylvester II had created this new state, with a royal family akin to his own Judaic roots, did he declare his willingness to cooperate with Emperor Otto III in a semi-religious/political enterprise. Sylvester's goal was to introduce his ideal of a renewed Roman Empire based on pure and strict observance of Christian ethics.

As pope, Sylvester's policies were to reduce the power of the bishops down to a mere temporal one with no lordship over the judicial power of kings or the right to interfere in the elections of abbots. He further denounced simony (the buying and selling of ecclesiastical offices), and nepotism and promoted, though did not impose, celibacy within the clergy. He began the concept of feudalization by enfeoffing (investing with a fief or fee) several minor nobles in return for military service. He then ruled that the church could both borrow or lend money on an interest-free basis (or the least nominal interest if need be) and introduced the first western banking system in Venice and Genoa, all based on practices already used in the Middle East. By doing so, he tried to bring the West to an industrious level in relation to the East.

Sylvester II became such a frightening concept for the Roman Curia to deal with that they decided to get rid of him by poisoning him. Sylvester II died on May 12, 1003. The philosophical seed between East and West had been sown, though it would take well over one hundred years to reap the interests that Sylvester II had spread as far as the East.

Sylvester II was also a proponent of the return of Merovingien Davidic dynasts upon the throne of France, even that of Jerusalem, if it could be achieved. In fact, Gerbert d'Aurillac/Sylvester II is much more important to the equation of eastern desposiny meeting the western desposiny than people think. D'Aurillac, through his parents, could trace a direct ancestry to both the recorded Zerrubabels mentioned in the Bible. Unknown to most people, there are two quite distinct Zerrubabels in the Bible. One, from which Gerbert is clearly descended in the Old Testament; the other is to be found in the New Testament and from this latter one is descended from Jesus Christ. The Old Testament's Zerrubabel made him, Gerbert d'Aurillac, a Davidic dynast with a right of succession to the kingdom of Judaea. But what is more to the point is that, unlike the ancestry of Jesus Christ, the ancestry of this family can be traced back to David as stated in 1 Chronicles 3:17–23. Jesus' ancestry from Zerrubabel is only mentioned in the New Testament where both Luke and Matthew trace his descent from a previously unrecorded son by the name of "Abiud." However, this cannot be corroborated from the Old Testament, and thus Jesus' ancestry back to the Old Testament Zerrubabel can only be taken as conjecture and hearsay. While it cannot be disproved, it cannot be proved either. However, the one thing that we must bear in mind is the fact that the emirs, later caliphs, of Cordoba acknowledged the physical and genealogical survival of the descendants (desposiny) of both Jesus Christ and his immediate family as legal scion of King David. And Sylvester II was of that family, of the desposiny of Jesus, as well as being a direct recognized descendant of the princely line of the exilarchs of Babylon.

The other thing that most Christian writers fail to show is how closely related the Umayyad caliphs of Cordoba were to the Christian royal house of Pamplona. Abd al-Rahman III, for example, was a great-nephew of Queen Toda of Navarre on his mother's side. The present head of the Spanish de Lara family is a descendant of caliph al-Hakam II through one of his daughters. This means that the whole of Spain's aristocracy, together with that of France, England and Scotland, have origins taking them back to the foundations of the Islamic faith, even back to the Prophet Muhammad himself. If these various Islamic/Christian marriages had not taken place, the lack of this extra genetic implant would have prevented the present rulers and nonreigning de jure kings in Europe from being alive today. None of us would exist. None of the institutions upon which we rely and which we take for granted today, such as the post of prime minister, a banking system (the original concept being interest free), the insurance company, a free health service, the concept of a pension, even the minimum wage, would have been invented. With all due respect to the Labour Party (the old one, of course), these concepts were introduced in Spain by Islamic rule and were already old by then.

The last true Umayyad caliph of Spain, Hisham III, died in 1031. His death would fragment Muslim Spain into several smaller kingdoms known as Taifs. By 1050, Muslim Spain had been reduced to less than half of its original size, with the kingdoms of Leon, Castile and Aragon expanding and growing even less religiously tolerant. The counties of Portugal and Barcelona, however, grew to be both more prominent and liberal, within the new Spanish cultural and political equation. It was this new "Catholic" impetus of conquered territories that gave rise to the idea of the first crusade and the belief that if the Muslims could be defeated in Spain, they could be defeated in the Middle East.

Actually, a Roman Catholic conspiracy to topple the Byzantine Orthodox Church is what the first crusade was all about. Rome had had enough of rival popes in Constantinople. It wanted that which it considered a heretic church to be destroyed for once and for all. All that was needed was an excuse, any excuse, even if a made up one, to invade that lost part of the Western Roman Empire. All that was needed was for a pope to condone the idea. Pope Gregory VII found the ideal excuse, but died before he could implement it and so it would be left to Pope Urban II to put it into practice. The first crusade could have destroyed the Orthodox Church in Byzantium. The pope's plan was to sandwich the Greek Orthodox Church between a Roman Catholic West and conquered East in order to squeeze the life out of it. And the excuse for the crusade was the expansion of Islam, the loss of Jerusalem and the untrue claim that Muslims were killing Christians by the thousands in the holy land. That the crusade did not succeed was merely due to the Normans greed for land and titles, and the separate agenda of various families descended from the Merovingien royal family of France and Moorish princes who had settled in the French comte of Champagne and in the principality of Septimania.

CHAPTER 6

Popes, Emperors and the Tribulations of Survival

The first Crusade began in the autumn of 1096 when a number of west European potentates made their way to Constantinople. They were Hugues de Vermandois, Godefroid de Bouillon (Duke of Lower Lorraine) and his brother Baudouin, Bohemund and Tancred of Sicily, Raymond de Toulouse, Robert de Flandres, Robert de Normandie, Etienne de Blois (Count of Boulogne) and Adhemar, papal legate and bishop of Puy. They arrived in turn between November 1096 and May 1097 in the neighborhood of Constantinople. Most books, including the *Encyclopedia Britannica*, tend to take the view that the crusade was a Frankish affair but, in fact, it was no more than a plot concocted by a group of people closely related to one another. The plot was nothing less than an attempt to re-establish the rightful heir of Judaea upon his throne in Palestine and to recreate the empire over which, once upon a time, it was believed that King Solomon had ruled. To think of these related individuals going to Palestine on a spiritual mission is to know little of the history that these various families had in common. Christianity was the last thing on their mind. As for the papacy, few of them gave it credence, political, spiritual or otherwise. In fact, the last thing they wanted was for the papacy to interfere with their plans. It is also a fact that very few people today are aware as to why this crusade took place at all. I shall now try my best to explain what had transpired for some time to put the event in its proper perspective.

According to the *Catholic Dictionary* (edition of 1884), the crusades were the medieval Christian version of the ideal of holy war (equivalent to the Islamic jihad). It is further defined as a particular manifestation of the impulse to fight for the Christian faith against various great religions, which the church has characterized as an infidel, at various times and in various parts of the world. Actually, there were no less than nine crusades altogether, and some of them were fought on the very soil of Europe, in places such as Lithuania, Samogitia, the Balkans, even the South of France. In fact, many sections of society, which did not conform to the papal concept of "Roman Catholicism," were deemed fair game for genocide.

Alexius I Comnenus, emperor of the Byzantine Empire between 1081 and 1118, must have been rather perplexed in seeing, yet again, a second group of European people landing within the boundaries of his empire. The first wave, consisting of a large band of humble people under the leadership of Walter the Penniless and Peter the Hermit, had arrived in the late spring of 1096, having made their rather disorderly march from south Germany through Hungary. This band of thousands of people arrived in Constantinople hungry, destitute and very much unwanted. They also had been on the rampage, having massacred European Jewish communities by the thousands along the way to Constantinople. Alexius, seeing this multitude of unwanted people pillage, burn and rape his lands and people, decided to get rid of this rabble by shipping them all across the Bosporus to Asia Minor, where he knew most of them would perish at the hands of the Turks.

The main problem that Alexius I and his predecessors had been facing for several years was the fact that Turkish warriors had constantly raided the Byzantine borders of Asia Minor. Little by little, territory was being encroached upon by the rising power of Turkey and the Ghazis, which were growing extremely powerful under the Danishmend family, so much so that a Seljuk prince had to be sent to Asia Minor to keep them in check.

The problem, one must emphasize, was not the Islamic religion per se, but rather Turkey and its interpretation of Islam. Actually, what Islam did for the Turks was to unite them in a single military entity working on behalf of the Abbasside caliphate. Until then, the caliphs were using Persians to run their administration, and, following Turkey's conversion to Islam, they used Turkish soldiers for their territorial expansion. The Turks, of course, saw their chance to expand their own territory, and that could only mean taking lands that were technically Byzantine. Further, the Turks could be destructive. When they invaded, there were times that they left nothing behind but ruins and desolation. This was against the precedents of Islamic expansion.

This was the difference between the Islam of the Arabs, which would apply a tolerant approach to the Christian faith, and would amalgamate the knowledge of their newly conquered territory with theirs, and the Turks, who would not. If, say, the Umayyads had conquered Constantinople during the four hundred years of their rule, you may be sure that Constantinople would still bear its name today. But the Turks would overpower it in 1453, and its name was changed to Istanbul. While the faith of Islam was not the problem, the Islamic Turks embracing it in such a fundamentalist way would be.

Byzantine rule had been disturbed by the Turks. The old adage of "divide and conquer" had come to an abrupt end when the Byzantine emperors were no longer able to play the Seljuks and the Danishmends against one another. Byzantium could no longer bear alone the burden of defending the eastern frontiers of Christendom against the growing pressure from Turkish Islam. Turkey was reaching out to impose its rule over Syria and the various holy places of Palestine, a Palestine which, from AD 635 till AD 749, had been in the hands of the caliphs of Damascus and then those of Baghdad, then an ally of Alexius I. By 1070, the Seljuk Turks had wrested Jerusalem from the power of the caliph of Baghdad. A year later, the emperor Romanus IV had been defeated and both Syria and Mesopotamia were lost to the Seljuk Turks. In 1085, Antioch, the last Byzantine possession in Syria, fell. Desperate, Alexius I requested help from the West. What he wanted was merely to recuperate his lost territory in Asia Minor with the help of a Western army, which, in no way, involved the concept of a Christian crusade. Christian rights were still whole and respected in these lost territories now under Islamic rule. There was little Byzantine objection to the Islamic faith, only to the loss of cities. What Alexius wanted to do was simply replenish his military "Themes" (the Byzantine military regiments based on the old Roman legions) in order to fight the Turks. But as to lead a crusade to Palestine in order to free Jerusalem from Islam, Alexius had no notions of it.

In western Christendom, things were actually getting better for the Roman Catholic faith. The tide had finally turned in favor of the Catholic Christians. The Italians drove the Muslims from Sardinia and the Normans conquered Sicily. Sicily, from AD 827 till then, had been also ruled by Muslims, and, as such, the lifestyle on the island had been sophisticated for many years, so much so that the new Norman ruling family decided not to change a thing about it. Muslim doctors, writers and astronomers were retained at court and were able to practice their art. Meanwhile, the Pisans organized a successful expedition against al Mahdiya in North Africa. Only in Spain would the Moorish influence remain for another few centuries. This having been achieved in western Europe, the call from the Byzantine emperor fell upon ears ready and willing to colonize the East in the name of the Roman Catholic religion, the last thing on the mind of Alexius I, believer and upholder of the Orthodox Christian Church.

Pope Gregory VII, who had corresponded with eastern emperor Michael Ducas, first contemplated organizing assistance but he died in May 1085, leaving Urban II to give effect to the project. Alexius I's appeal to the Council of Piacenza in 1095, hurried Pope Urban II to preach for a crusade at the Council of Clermont soon after. The great papal conspiracy was born and Peter the Hermit, with the pope's blessing, inflamed the European populace's imagination with made up stories of disaster, massacre and doom for eastern Christians living under the yoke of the infidels. But it is with the Normans that the crusade proper was to be organized, mostly with the ideal of profit, land expansion and colonization. The Normans emphasized to the maritime cities of Italy, such as Genoa, Pisa and Venice, that an opportunity to develop direct trades with the East could be opened through Syrian ports.

When the flower of western European aristocracy arrived in Constantinople, Alexius I demanded their oath of fealty and got it from all of them save two, Raymond de Toulouse and Tancred of Sicily. Actually, what Raymond de Toulouse proposed was a different oath that would set his own house apart from all the others. This makes sense. As the descendant of the Jewish exilarchs of Babylon, Raymond has automatic rights that the others had not, even though they were related to him. Further, the Count of Toulouse was the eldest and most prominent of all the crusading princes and his army was by far the largest. Moreover, Raymond de Toulouse had strong imperial Byzantine blood himself. His adviser in this matter was none other than a man named Hugues de Payens, who would later become the first master of the Order of the Temple of Solomon. Having achieved this political understanding with Alexius I, Raymond of Toulouse remained one of the Byzantine emperor's most loyal supporters long after the crusade was over.

With the help of his newly gained army, Alexius marched on Nicaea and, on June 19, 1097, defeated the Sultan of Rum at Dorylaeum, where the crusaders secured for themselves an unmolested crossing into Asia Minor. Again, history is rather lax on the capitulation of Dorylaeum. Nobody captured it. Alexius made a deal with its Sultan who, in the middle of the night, allowed the Greek army of Alexius into the city while his retreated into the mountains. What the Sultan Kilji Arslan and Alexius agreed was that the city should not be sacked nor its population, comprising Christians, be put to the sword of the Western fanatics. No cities that capitulated, under the treaty that the Western leaders had signed with Alexius, could be sacked. Byzantine diplomacy and understanding of the Turkish Islamic thinking prevaricated and won the day.

When the crusaders reached Syria, Alexius thanked them, reminding them of their oath (which meant that any territories gained by them would come back under his authority and that of the Eastern Orthodox Church) and simply went back home, washing his hands of the whole enterprise. This took the leaders of the Western armies rather by surprise, as they believed that Alexius would come all the way to Jerusalem with them as their military leader. Faced with this new military equation, the campaign was duly taken over by the leadership of "the council of princes" led by Raymond de Toulouse.

They arrived in Syria during a dispute over the sultanate of Syria that had been developing since 1095. This dispute gave the first crusade the very thing it needed to succeed. In 1095, Tutush, brother of Grand Seljuk Sultan Malikshah, was killed in battle in a dispute over the succession to the sultanate. Already, there was bitter enmity between the Orthodox Islamic princes of Damascus and the fundamentalist Fatimid caliphs of Egypt. Tutush had ruled over Mosul, Aleppo, Damascus and Jerusalem. Following his death, his dominions fell to pieces with rivalries between his two sons, Ridvan of Aleppo and Dukak of Damascus, and prevented the dominions from joining together in order to fight the invading Christian army. What the Council of princes was counting on most was the considerable support and help from the Christian population in cities such as Edessa and Antioch. This they had and both cities did indeed capitulate due to the Christians desire to open the gates to them. Antioch was reached on October 21, 1097, and fell on June 3, 1098. Jerusalem was reached on June 7, 1099, and fell on July 15 following a very arduous siege and a fearful massacre of practically the entire population, Christians, Jews and Muslims alike. We are talking genocide on a massive scale here. Had it not been for Hugues de Payens, hurrying from Antioch after receiving words from the Count of Toulouse, the massacre would have gone for much longer and the entire population would have been eradicated. "Kill them all because God," the Catholic prelate Adhemar claimed, "would recognize his own." Many people had left the city before the crusaders had arrived and many inside the city survived the killings by hiding in the cellars of churches, mosques and synagogues. To the disappointment of the Roman papal legate, the Orthodox Christians of Jerusalem, Arab by ethnicity, reappeared in the city stronger than ever.

In effect, the papal concept of having an entire population eradicated in order to make way for a western Catholic influx of people failed miserably. History claims that by consent of the council of princes, Godefroid de Bouillon set up a government and, having declined the crown was proclaimed "Defender" (Advocatus) of the Holy Sepulchre. This, however, is not strictly true. The crown had been offered first to Raymond de Toulouse, who had sent a courier back to the court of Alexius I in Constantinople in order to get his assent (as per the oath that Raymond had given to the emperor). While his embassy was away, the council of princes objected to it and offered the crown to Godefroid of Bouillon. However, he too, was in a bit of a quandary about the offer of a crown, and so, unlike Raymond, he declined to represent the sovereignty of the Crusader state of Jerusalem but did accept an offer to be its administrator. Offering of the crown to anybody else would have been useless. Nobody else had as strong a claim to the desposiny as Godefroid and Raymond had. While declaring Godefroid "advocatus" of the Holy City and the Holy Sepulchre may have made sense to some, it simply meant that a new and totally alien hierarchy ruled over Jerusalem.

Raymond de Toulouse, as compensation, was offered the sovereign county of Tripoli in Lebanon. Raymond was keen on Tripoli for its situation, nearer to the Mediterranean coast than Jerusalem, would provide Raymond with a base better placed than Godefroid of Bouillon and his successors ended up with. The sovereign Crusader County of Tripoli was held within his family till 1187, when it was transferred to that of the princes of Antioch for the lack of a male heir. In effect, while the true heir to the ancient kingdom of Judaea, and to Jerusalem in particular, missed the opportunity to restore his rights to the throne of his ancestors, he ruled over a much more interesting part of the Middle East.

The history of Christianity rests upon the Holy Sepulchre, the site in Jerusalem where, it is presumed by Christian standards, Jesus was not only crucified and buried but also rose from the dead. The Church of the Holy Sepulchre was built to enclose the site of both cross and tomb. It is all rather nonsensical, of course, but faith will move many things. It can certainly titillate people's imagination. However, what most Christians must understand is that the sites of most of the places relating to New Testament events were first found, though in this instance one should say chosen, by the Empress Helena, the mother of Constantine I, and the site of the "Holy Sepulchre" dates back only to the days of Constantine the Great and the Church of the Holy Sepulchre being dedicated in AD 336. By AD 614, the Persians had burned the church, but Modestus, abbot of the monastery of Theodosius, had it restored by AD 626. When Jerusalem fell to Caliph Umar I in AD 638, the patriarch Sophronius actually invited him to unroll his prayer mat within the holy precinct. But Umar, realizing that if he should do so, the site would be claimed by Islam, thus creating a big divide between Christians and Muslims, diplomatically refused the offer and decided to have a mosque built nearby instead. This was a mark of respect for the Christian faith. In fact, Umar decided to sign a treaty of peace with the Byzantine Christian hierarchy in Jerusalem giving the followers of the church of Christ legal rights: "This peace . . . guarantees them security for their lives, property, churches, and the crucifixes belonging to those that display and honour them . . . There shall be no compulsion in matters of Faith." This was the principle of religious tolerance upon which the Islamic faith was based. What is not particularly known about the Church of the Holy Sepulchre is that, between the years AD 791 and 799, a treaty took place between Emperor Charlemagne and Caliph Haroun al Rashid, then based in Bagdad, whereby the caliph agreed to recognize that the site of the Holy Sepulchre as a Christian principality. Four hundred years later, the Church of the Holy Sepulchre was destroyed by Caliph al-Hakim and, once again, restored by the Byzantine emperor Constantine Monomachus. In the twelfth century, the crusader kings of Jerusalem carried out a general rebuilding of the Church of the Holy Sepulchre. Since then, it has been frequently repaired, and the present church dates mainly from 1810.

So not until the fourth century AD was the site acknowledged as being the place where Jesus died, was buried and rose from the dead. But the fact is that no one knows where the actual events that are the cornerstone upon which the foundations of the Christian faith are built, took place. The truth of the matter was that during the first three centuries prior to Constantine the Great unifying his empire under the Pauline church, the Christian church was unable to preserve an authentic tradition regarding the events. In fact, it could not have done so simply because it was the Church of Jerusalem that prevailed and that church was wholly Judaic. By AD 66, most of the members of the Jerusalem church, the Essenes and the Nazorites, had fled to Pella. Four years later, Titus, son of Roman emperor Vespasian, destroyed both the temple of Jerusalem and the city. By the fourth century AD, the Byzantine Orthodox Church lay claim to the city. Seven hundred years later, Godefroid de Bouillon was made guardian of it and the Roman Catholic Church had its beady eye on it.

Only when Godefroid's brother Baudouin, then king of Edessa, succeeded to him did the Crusader Kingdom of Jerusalem come into effect and only with Baudouin's succession were the pretensions of Daimbert, Latin patriarch, to turn Jerusalem into a Roman ecclesiastical principality, stopped effectively. Only when Baudouin I succeeded as king of Jerusalem was the overall conquest of Palestine begun in earnest, involving the fleets of Genoa, Venice and Pisa to protect the coastal towns. His kingdom of "Oultre-Jourdain" would stretch sporadically as far as south east of the Dead Sea, with Edessa, Tripoli and Antioch being fiefs of Jerusalem. When he died in 1118, his cousin Baudouin II (then king of Edessa) took over the succession of Jerusalem.

Many people, however, not least the Knights Templar, objected to his succession. They wanted the Count of Tripoli. While Baudouin II might not have been everyone's choice, he probably was the better man for the job. The problem with the crusading states in the Middle East is that they were just that: city-states holding on to a semi-independence within a territory which was mainly still within the hands of Islam. These crusader kings (Jerusalem, Edessa, Antioch and Tripoli) and smaller potentates (the Christian lords of Nablus, Ramleh, Beirut, Caesarea, Jebail, Sidon, Tiberias, Galilee and Sabyun) were able to keep what they had conquered purely through peace treaties with the local Islamic hierarchy. But to think that a crusader Christian empire stretched over the whole of the Middle East is rather far fetched.

By 1118, when galloping from Edessa to take hold of his new state kingdom, Baudouin II was faced with an entity that was even more powerful than he was himself. Not only that, it had the blessing of the Canons of the Temple (the

Christian church hierarchy in Jerusalem) and the Islamic hierarchy in Cairo. When he reached Jerusalem, Baudouin was welcomed by the rather distrustful and silent knights of the Order of the Temple of Solomon. Clad in white and astride their Arabian horses, they bid him to enter the city and proceeded to take him to his new quarters. Baudouin soon realized that he had to share these quarters with the knights and that it would be they who were in charge of it, not him. To add insult to injury, the ambassadorial network of Alexius I of Byzantium was very much in league with the leader of the knight Templars. The leader's name was Hugues de Payens, a rather impressive figure whose connection evidently stretched within both the Christian and Islamic hierarchies. Allowed to rest for a while, Baudouin was suddenly called upon by the patriarch of Jerusalem, Etienne de la Ferte, and presented with a charter to sign. The patriarch, together with the abbot of the Canons of the Temple, had already appended their seals onto this charter, which gave the Templars unique rights within the crusading kingdoms. Now, Baudouin was required to do the same without asking questions. His predecessor had already done so several years before in 1105 and, so Baudouin was informed, this was merely a formality.

Baudouin soon discovered that this formality pervaded his entire citystate. Worse to him, the knights behaved like natives, allowed the Muslims to pray to Allah in their mosques and even protected them from the enmity of newcomers. They were obviously allied with Emperor Alexius of Constantinople, had the ear of Bernard de Clairveaux, a growing power in France, and were kept abreast of Islamic politics by no less than Islamic embassies sent from Cairo in Egypt, Makkah in Arabia, Baghdad in Iraq and Cordoba in Spain. Baudouin's reaction was to leave the palace altogether to take residence in what was referred to as King David's Tower (built during the reign of the king Herod the Great and then referred to as the tower of "Phasael"). To top it all, Baudouin soon found out that Etienne de la Ferte was Hugues de Payens' cousin and that the knights had links with the Ismaelite Order of the Assassins and the Old Man of the Mountain.

The time has come to look at the real roots of the Order of the Knights Templar and put it in its proper perspective. In order to do this, we need to find out who Hugues de Payens really was and which families he was connected to. To paraphrase the lady in *All about Eve*, "Fasten your seatbelts, it's going to be a bumpy ride!"

CHAPTER 7

White Robes and Cross Pate

A lot of ink has been spilt by many historians with regards to the Order of the Knights Templar (or the Order of the Temple of Solomon). Most of them tend to support the status quo tradition that the order was founded for the benevolent purposes of keeping pilgrims traveling within the confines of the Holy Land safe from marauders, Christians and Muslims alike. Most historians have the order as permanent militia acting under the protection of both Baudouin II of Jerusalem and the Latin patriarch of Jerusalem. This could not be further from the truth.

To start with, we have to come to terms with the fact that there were thirty members when the order was founded, and out of these thirty, only nine were remembered in history. The second item that most historians have been unaware of is that all nine names recorded in the annals were related to the Count of Champagne through the de Montbard family. This connects them directly to Abbot Bernard de Clairveaux, son of the Tescelin le Saur, Viscount of Dijon and Lord of the Castle of Fontaine-les-Dijon, in the ancient royal duchy of Burgundy.

Further, the de Payens family, which also went later by the name of "de Paganis," was still in existence in France during the eighteenth century and held the title of "comte." Their archives survived the revolution and, interestingly, the family records shows them to have been involved with nonoperative Freemasonry from its earlier inception in France. But the most interesting aspect of the de Payens family is its genealogies, which spread across oceans, tracing it to imperial Byzantine and Merovingien houses and to the highest accolade of them all in the East, the Prophet Muhammad himself.

The family coat of arms is described today as *"Bande d or et d'azur, au chef de Bretagne, brise d'un lambel de gueulle, a la bordure componnee de Naples, France et Jerusalem,"* the latter being an addition granted by Baudouin II of Jerusalem. Actually, it does miss one heraldic representation, that of three Muslim heads, which can be found on the original family tree. What a later heraldic device states is that Hugues de Payens and company were not too distantly related to Raimond de Toulouse of Tripoli and Godefroid and Baudouin of Jerusalem, and it shows that the order was a family affair into which no interlopers were invited to join until after 1128.

The order had existed since about 1094 with Hugues de Payens as head of it from day one. Actually, this family was quite an extensive one and there were, in fact, two Hugues de Payens contemporary to one another. However, the Templar Hugues de Payens in Jerusalem (as opposed to his cousin in France) was the most prominent member of the family. Most historians simply see him as a crusader who followed Godefroid de Bouillon to Jerusalem where he set up the Order of the Temple of Solomon (the Order of the Templars). The truth is he followed Raymond de Toulouse, later Count of Tripoli (Lebanon), and settled in Jerusalem to look after Raymond's interests.

Furthermore, without Hugues de Payens, his contacts, the money made available to him, (and we are talking in millions already then), the kingdom of Portugal would never have emerged as an independent state with its own royal house. Indeed, it was Hugues de Payens who, in 1094, helped Henri of Burgundy, Count of Portugal by marriage, and his wife Teresa of Portugal (daughter of Alfonso VI of Castile and Leon and Zaida, princess of Dania and daughter of Muhammad III al-Mu'tamid, emir of Seville), to consolidate the country for themselves and their heir. Hugues de Payens' price was an agreement that the Muslim population would be left in peace to worship according to their own conscience. What is more surprising is that this demarcation line, which had been created in Spain by Hugues de Payens, would make sure that Castile, Navarre and Aragon's expansion into Islamic Spain would come to a standstill. It may have fortified what the Spanish Catholic factions had gained since the fall of the Umayadds, but this demarcation line certainly ended up being a buffer zone that gave the Moors the respite that was needed so that both their states and culture could survive for another three hundred years. In effect, what Hugues de Payens did was to create a sovereign earldom for a cousin of his, which, by 1139, was then transformed into a proper kingdom. In 1139, Alfonso I was referred to as king of Portugal, but it would not be before 1179 that the papacy acknowledged the existence of this kingdom. By the time Alfonso III (1248–1279) came to reign over Portugal, the country had finally acquired its modern boundaries, as we know them today.

The Spaniards cannot have been aware of this expansionist interference and, in fact, lands both in Catholic Spain and Portugal were donated to Hugues de Payens and his knights long before the order gained recognition from either the crusader king of Jerusalem or its patriarch. Many will find this difficult to believe. It is, however, interesting to note that land donations from Henri of Burgundy and Teresa, the parents of Alfonso I Enriquez of Portugal, date back to 1108, ten years prior the order being officially set up in Jerusalem. This is a historical fact that no historians, save Frenchman Jacques Rolland, have mentioned before.

But the most interesting item within the de Payens family tree is that Hugues's grandfather had Moorish links and was known as "Thibault de Payens, le Maure de Gardille." In fact, his name was Theobaldo and he came from Spain. Theobaldo's father was Abd ar-Rahman an-Nasir, better known in Spanish history as Prince Sanchuelo (little Sancho), the son of Muhammad al'Mansur, emir of Cordoba, and Abba, daughter of king Sancho II Abarca Garces of Pamplona. The heraldic design of Sanchuelo was the Islamic symbol denoting the number twelve in the Islamic zodiac. It is from this symbol that the croix pate traces its roots. The ancestry of Muhammad al'Mansur can be traced back to Muhammad, the Seal of the Prophets, through the Idrisid royal house, which ruled the earlier kingdom of Fez in North Africa.

Considering this high pedigree via the Moors (Maures), it then makes sense that Hugues was able, even allowed, to consolidate a territory that would emerge as the kingdom of Portugal. He is related to Teresa of Portugal, Emperor Alexius of Byzantium and many others within a very close degree. This is one of the reasons why the king of Portugal left his entire kingdom to the Templars in his will. Theobaldo of Gardille was also sent to the court of the caesar of the East, John Ducas (uncle to Emperor Michael Ducas VII, 1067 to 1078), to represent the last scion of the Umayyad caliph of Cordoba.

During this ambassadorial visit, Theobaldo fell in love with John's sister Angelica. They married according to the Orthodox rites. This link would later be of the greatest importance to Hugues de Payens. In fact, Theobaldo married twice, his second wife being the heiress Leotarde de Bagarris (a Roman Catholic), by whom he had another two sons called Jean and Hugues Herbert de Paganis de Bagarris. It is from this Jean that the comtes de Pagan are descended. Theobaldo's eldest son by his first wife, Thilbault, settled in Champagne, married Helie de Montbard, the aunt of Bernard de Clairveaux. It was within that family that Hugues de Payen was born in 1070. Between 1085 and 1090, he was given the fief of Montigny, near Lagesse, in the county of Champagne. Though born a Christian, Hugues's roots were so diverse that he was able to put them to good use on behalf of his various relatives, some Christians of both the Roman and Eastern persuasions, as well as those following the Islamic religion.

It is here that the genealogies become rather muddled up. In their book *The Holy Blood and the Holy Grail*, Michael Baigent, Richard Leigh and Henry Lincoln claim that Hugues de Payens was married to one Catherine de Saint Clair. This information was given to them by Pierre Plantard (who was, at the time, the grand master of the Priory of the Order of Sion, created in France in 1958) in his "dossiers secret." The authors were given genealogies, which claimed a de Payens/Sinclair connection. This claim was taken up by many other writers afterwards.

According to Pierre Plantard's dossiers secret, Hugues de Payens was a widower and the father of two sons when he went to Jerusalem. His wife, who died in 1093, was Catherine de Saint Clair, daughter not of a Scottish Sinclair but rather that of a French one, Robert fitzHamon ("son of Hamon") de Saint Clair, Lord of Thorigny, a crusader who traveled with Hugues to the Middle East. Robert had a paternal uncle, Walderne de Saint Clair, and it is from this Walderne that the Scottish Sinclairs are descended through his son William. Walderne had another two sons and from those were descended the Saint Clairs in Devon, Cornwall and Sussex. Their Sinclair name was inherited via the heiress of Saint Clair of Bassenville in the French district of Auge. She married Mauger le Jeune, archbishop of Rouen and younger son of Richard II of Normandy, and produced three sons, Hubert (follower of William the Conqueror), Walderne and Hamon.

While Catherine Saint Clair did indeed exist, she was not the wife of Hugues de Payens. Nor was he the father of two sons, but only one. The Christian name of Hugues's wife (whom he married between 1108 and 1114) was Elizabeth, but, sadly, her own family name has been lost to history. (Serious research is now taking place to establish who she truly was.) Their son, Thibault, became abbot of the monastery of St. Colombe in 1139, and the cartulary of the monastery states that he was the son of Hugues de Payens, first master of the Templars in Jerusalem. Except for authors Tim Wallace-Murphy and Thierry Leroy, whose findings are based upon proper documents and not on the spurious genealogies produced by Pierre Plantard in the 1980s, no other writers have rectified the faked family trees of the dossiers secret.

The de Payens family's Islamic background was Shiite and drawn from Sufism, a mystic belief in which Muslims seek to find divine love and knowledge through direct personal experience of God (the very thing which the Roman Catholic Church had declared a no-go area). The entire concept is based on mystical paths that are designed to ascertain the nature of man and of God. As an organized religious movement, it arose as a reaction against the worldliness of the early Umayyad caliphs who ruled from Damascus from AD 661 to 749 and then from Spain from AD 756. Traditional law was not enough for a particular strata of Muslim society because the Islamic Empire was so vast and encompassed so many diverse cultures, religious and otherwise. Sufism came into being as a common denominator among those many Muslim nations looking to ascertain a way (path) and a goal (reality) as an accepted alternative within the new world of Islam.

Sufism rejected theology and its rational deduction for a spiritual state of mind seeking a journey towards God. Sufis believe that a soul can be, either for a moment or for longer periods, purified and renewed with a new energy and higher religious expectation. It teaches that individuals, through this journey to purification and renewal, will become contented, reassured, and calm and will experience the overwhelming presence of God within their heart, a heart free of fear. Sufi followers tend to regard their life, prior to joining the Sufi order, as rather wasted. On joining the first stage of Sufi wisdom, the newly initiated member is given a robe of blue wool, the color of mourning and rejection of the material pleasure. After three years of study, and going through various stages involving robes of various colors, they are finally given a white woolen robe of purity.

For an order that believed in the saying that "he who knows God becomes silent," Sufism's composed meditations, commentaries and poetry were written in such a way that they conveyed the experiences of what followers called the "ineffable mysteries of God." Another one of their sayings is "he who knows God talks much." Sufi works were considered to be of the classical form and dealt with the concept of God and creation as two aspects of one reality. What was predominant in the religious belief of the Sufi order was, and still is, the right for followers to reach God. It was the "personal experience" that mattered. Typical of Sufi poetry is the hymn in praise of God, expressed in chanting chains of repetitions.

Sufism evolved in many different ways, including the dervish order, whose followers reached a state of ecstasy through dancing and whirling. The concept of praising God through music would be borrowed by the Cistercian Church, as would the individual approach to reaching the Lord. Following the fall of the Umayyad Spanish caliphate, a western trend of Sufism was taken to the South of France and introduced to the court of the counts of Toulouse, who were originally dependents of the Muslim court of Cordoba. Later, that eastern trend was taken to the court of the Count of Champagne and amalgamated within the teaching of its cabbalistic school, itself an offshoot from a Jewish cabbalistic school in southern France.

Another link that the de Payens family held dearly was its link with the Islamic Ahmadiyyah movement. This movement firmly held the views that Jesus had not been dead when taken off the cross and that he revived and was healed whilst within the confines of the tomb, to be then spirited away to end his life in Kashmir at a much greater age. This is a belief that Gnostics held in common with Islam. Both supported the desposiny of the Christ against the Christian church.

The county of Champagne was very Gnostic in its understanding of Christianity and had allowed Jews to open a cabbalistic school in 1070. This came at a time when the Moors in Spain were loosing grounds to the Spanish Catholic kingdom of Leon. In order to survive, Spanish Jews had to resettle somewhere else. The same, of course, applied to several Muslim families. Many Jews made their way to Septimania, then ruled by the counts of Toulouse, related to the counts of Champagne and the exilarch of Narbonnes and Babylon, and Muslims became an ethnic minority within a majority unorthodox Jewish population, which would later be labeled as Cathars and Albigensis. The Count of Champagne, together with his court at Troyes, was thus more liberated in its religious views than Roman Catholic northern France. Beside, the count himself had links with al-Andalous (Andalucia), the Umayyad Spanish caliphate, and the counts of Toulouse.

In the Champagne genealogies, we find that Ermengarde, daughter of Robert I, count of Auvergnes, and wife of Eudes II, Count of Champagne, is a direct descendant of Raymond I of Toulouse through the early viscount of Auvergnes. Indeed, the family got its appointment as ruler of Auvergnes by none other than Guillaume Taillefer, half-brother of Gerbert d'Aurillac, later Pope Sylvester II. When the Umayyads fell out of power in 1033, the main families supporting them would end up in Septimania, and some later relocated in Champagne, bringing with them the best philosophy that Cordoba had produced: tolerance of all faiths.

As previously stated, there had been many marital links between the Moorish royal family and the native Spanish aristocracy. Further, the Spanish royals married Umayyad princesses. Also, it looks as if the early Kingdom of Pamplona was the key to Islamic treaties with Christian Europe, trade treaties between kings and caliphs being sealed by a Christian/Islamic marriage. It also looks as if the reverse was of the norm, that is to say that Pamplonese kings married Umayyads princesses as well. When Sancho III died in 1035, his kingdom was divided into three parts for his sons. Ferdinando I took over Castile, Navarre was inherited by Garcia and Ramiro got Aragon. Ferdinando I married Sancha of Leon (thus gaining an extra Kingdom) and his son Alfonso VI of Leon (and later of Castile) married as his fourth wife the Islamic princess Zaida of Dania and Seville. Her tomb can be seen in the Chapel Royal of San Isidio of Leon with a Latin inscription stating that she was indeed Alfonso's wife rather than a concubine. In 1095, he settled the sovereign county of Portugal to their only daughter and child, Teresa, wife of Henri of Burgundy.

Because of these various marital links between the kings of Pamplona and the caliphs of Cordoba, most, if not all, the various royal families in Europe can trace an ancestry back to the family of the prophet Muhammad, even to the prophet himself. Taking all this into account, it thus makes sense for Hugues de Payens to use his ancestry and religious links between Christianity and Islam to help consolidate Portugal for Henri of Burgundy and his wife Teresa, since they are both related to him.

When the Templars arrived in Jerusalem in 1099, they were not housed in the stable of the royal palace as most historians claim. Godefroid de Bouillon housed them within the palace itself. Moreover, it was not to Godefroid of Bouillon that the Templars reported, but rather to the Count of Tripoli. Then, when Godefroid's cousin Baudouin II succeeded, he left the palace entirely to the Templars and moved to what the crusaders referred to as the Tower of David. This tower was, in fact, the tower of Phasael, a brother of Herod the Great, after whom the newly built edifice had been called. Nor did the Templars police the Holy Land on behalf of pilgrims, at least not till after 1128. No, for the first fifteen to twenty years of its existence in Jerusalem, the Order of the Templars, led by Hugues de Payens and his eight cousins and helped by the other twenty-one knights (with the blessing of Godefroid de Bouillon, his brother Baudouin I, and grudgingly that of their cousin and successor Baudouin II of Jerusalem), together with a workforce provided by these kings, excavated and found the secret cellars hidden beneath the ancient mosque built by Caliph Omar in AD 635 on Mount Moriah. A few years later, they would excavate below the Dome of the Rock, then built upon the very site where Herod had built his temple of Jerusalem. The Templars never asked for anything but to be in charge of the mosques ie the only place they were sure parts of the original temple of Herod had been built.

Their excavation beneath the stables of the palace, adjacent to the ancient temple of Jerusalem, is nothing more than pure invention. However, the stables' arches, vaults and roofs indicate that the stables were Templar-made buildings, which they may indeed have used for the purpose of housing their horses. The temple, originally built by Herod the Great in the late first century BC, was the third of its kind, and had been destroyed by the Roman legions in the first century AD. Following its destruction, the Judaic high priesthood had fled and itself scattered in the South of France, in what would later emerge as the Judaic kingdom of Septimania, and in Britain where it soon evolved into the Celtic Church in Scotland, Ireland, Portugal, Galicia, the Basque countries and Brittany.

Few people are aware that there have been at least three distinct successive Judaic priesthoods. The first emerged from 1364 BC, when the Hebrews left Egypt under the leadership of Pharaoh Akhenaten (Eighteenth Dynasty), the man known biblically as Moses. By 724 BC, the northern kingdom of Israel was overtaken by the Assyrians, and most of its population was deported to Assyria. By 586 BC, the southern Jewish kingdom of Judah was crushed by the Babylonian army, when the kingdom of Solomon's descendants was invaded and conquered. Thus fell the first temple, which Solomon had dedicated in 957 BC.

The second temple was built in 516 BC, when the Persians, who had meantime conquered Babylon, allowed the Hebrews to go home and rebuild their temple during the lifetime of Prince Zerrubabel. During the period of their second temple, their high priest Onias IV was exiled by the Syrians and ended up in Heliopolis, back in Egypt, were he set up new headquarters. Years later, during the reign of Ptolemy VI Philometer and Cleopatra II of Egypt, Onias' son and namesake, Onias V, was granted permission to build an exact replica of the Jerusalem temple at Heliopolis for the use by the Jews in Egypt and Cyrene. This replica stood in Egypt for 222 years, under the exiled hereditary priesthood, when it was destroyed by Titus (son of the Roman emperor Vespasian) in AD 70. In Jerusalem, the royal house of Maccabeus (also known as Hasmonean) took over as new priestly/kingly hierarchy (quite a heretical concept in Judaic terms) and would rule the land spiritually from 141 to 37 BC. This second temple in Jerusalem was desecrated during the Roman occupation of Palestine in 18 BC but was subsequently modernized and rededicated in 10 BC by Herod the Great, whose family had usurped the throne from the house of Maccabeus. But that third temple would be razed to the ground by the Romans in the year AD 131. Its priests were told to disperse, giving rise to what would become present-day Jewish rabinism.

What that last ancient high priesthood had not been able to take with them, they hid away in safe places, the very safe places that the knights of the Order of the Templars, linked to the Canons of the Temple, managed to locate one by one. These caches were bulging with gold and silver bullion sent by the various Jewish communities to the high priest in Jerusalem till the later days of the first century AD. Other major finds were the historical records relating to the Essene and Nazarene communities in Judaea from and long before the days of Christ and records of a second Jerusalem, which had been built over many years, a Jerusalem in the wilderness of Qumram.

Actually, the real secret that the Templars had found was much more fundamental than these things. Through their excavation, they realized that there were no foundations to be found for the first temple. There was a foundation for the second, Herodian temple, yes, and even something going back to the temple of Zerrubabel. But of the first temple, built during the reigns of David and Solomon, there was nothing. The question they were then asking themselves was where on earth can it be?

Interestingly, the newly conquered city of Jerusalem, when taken over by Godefroid de Bouillon, looked more Byzantine/Islamic than Jewish in architecture. In fact, the various quarters of the palace which became the residence of the crusader king and the Latin patriarch of Jerusalem, and then of Hugues de Payens and his cousins, were made of structures partly erected by the Roman emperor Justinian and mostly built by the caliph Umar I, who conquered Jerusalem in AD 638. The latter required the patriarch Sophronius to show him the holy site where Christ had worshiped and duly had a wooden mosque built upon it. The second and third mosque, the Dome of the Rock and al-Aqsa (the latter with a silver dome), were built in AD 691 by caliph Abd al-Malik ibn Marwan. The Dome of the Rock is, in fact, the oldest extant Islamic stone monument outside Saudi Arabia and is sacred to both Jews and Muslims. Within the Jewish tradition, it is here, upon this rock, that Abraham is said to have prepared for the sacrifice of his younger son, Isaac. The Islamic world believes that Muhammad made his spiritual assent to heaven from this very place. Thus, it is holy to both the Jews and the Muslims, as well as the Christians. Moreover, a great majority of the Arabic calligraphy that can be seen on its inside walls refers to both Muhammad and Jesus Christ, the latter being referred to as "the Shadow of God." The Dome of the Rock is as much dedicated to Islam as it is dedicated to Christianity, but this is Christianity in its purest and reverential form, where the deeds of men are remembered but where only God is worshiped.

The Dome of the Rock, however, was not built so much as a mosque but rather built as a shrine for all pilgrims, Jewish, Muslims and Christians alike. Unlike the Ka'bah in Makkah, it is of considerable architectural and aesthetic importance. It was also the first stone Islamic monument ever to be built outside Arabia. It abounds with mosaic, faience and marble. Admittedly, some of the latter concept was added over centuries. The building itself, octogonal in shape, has a slight Byzantine look about it and is sixty feet in diameter. It rises above a circle of sixteen piers and columns and is topped by a golden dome. The entire structure is full of windows, and its architectural plan would be borrowed by Templar masons and imitated in Europe. The architecture of the Dome of the Rock is the secret upon which the second masonic degree of sacred geometry is actually based. It was also the design upon which the Templar cross pate was based. It is an architecture sacred to God.

Adjacent to the south side of the mosque was a structure, which was known as well as the Temple of the Lord. In truth, this Temple of the Lord was possibly built, not on the site of the first temple, but on the foundation of the royal quarters erected by Herod the Great when the third and final temple of Jerusalem was built.

In the Dome of the Rock, Allah (God) was prayed to and both Muhammad and Jesus Christ were revered as prophets. The same, of course, applies today.

The al Aqsa mosque, with its silver dome, could be entered from four gates situated at the four cardinal points. That of the North was called "Bab el D'jannat" or gate of the garden. That of the south was known as "Bab el Kebla" or gate of prayer. The East entrance was referred to as "Bab ib'n el Daoud," which means gate of the son of David. The west entrance was known as "Bab el Garbi." It is in this mosque that Muslims gather for Friday prayers.

During the rule of the Muslims in Jerusalem (except during the rule of the Fatimid al-Hakim, AD 996 to 1021), Christians were allowed to get on with their business and worship. As previously stated, they had to pay a tax, although not any higher than the resident believer of Islam. Under the Templars, pilgrims, Christians and others, including Muslims, were allowed to visit and pray at the holy sites. It was left to Hugues de Payens and his order to see that this particular concept of tolerance was kept in place within the precincts of the Dome of the Rock, even by force if need be. As such, when the standard bearing the crescent symbol of Islam was replaced by one showing a golden cross, space was nevertheless set aside within the Temple of the Lord, now under the leadership of the Knights Templar, for Muslims to worship in their own way and towards Makkah.

This is a crucial equation. According to the Church of Rome, Muslims were heathens and were to be given no quarters, no rights, either to worship or function otherwise. One story recorded in the annals of the crusader kingdom of Jerusalem tells of a young Frankish knight entering the Dome of the Rock and being met by a Muslim praying towards Makkah. Loosing his temper, he intimated the follower of Islam that he was praying the wrong way. The Frankish knight then found himself taken to task by two Templars knights. They ordered him out of the holy precinct and told him not to come back till he had learned both manners and tolerance. The Templars then, on behalf of the expulsed knight, apologized to the Muslim individual for the Frank's obvious misguided attitude. This from an order that, so historians inform us, supposedly was totally Catholic in demeanour. However, the Templars ignored all directives from Rome and did the exact opposite, including giving Muslims the right to pray towards Makkah. The question that we must ask ourselves is: why?

Unknown to most western historians, the Arabic records talk about Hugues de Payens and his knights as far back as 1097. Imagine the scene of Hugues and the vizier of Egypt meeting and agreeing to a treaty in which the Middle East is, literally, partitioned between the two of them. The idea that a Muslim will allow a Christian to take over and rule part of any Islamic territory is unheard of, unless the so-called Christian is no Christian at all. The vizier of Egypt, al-Adjal, goes as far as writing of this plan and new development to Emperor Alexis Commenos of Constantinople, who does not object! Unfortunately, the Crusader Frankish hierarchy became aware of the plan, and

Hugues de Payens was required to back off, or so they thought. This treaty does beg the question about the order's early links with Islam.

The fact is that the Order of the Templars, certainly in the Middle East, was only Christian as an alternative to being Islamic. It was, fundamentally, Islamic in both essence and practice. Moreover, the Islamic hierarchy of neither Makkah nor Cairo made any military or verbal move to prevent the Templars taking over the charge of the Dome of the Rock, the second most holy site of Islam, and the al-Aqsa mosque in Jerusalem. The reason for their lack of enthusiasm to fight the Templars was simply because the contemporary Islamic records refer to the order as "the Knights Templar of Islam." Christians they may have claimed to be, but this was merely a ploy to keep both the Orthodox and Catholic churches out of the mosque, out of the Dome of the Rock, so that their true brothers could go on worshiping God while praying towards Makkah. The fact is that the Templars possessed a "Fatwa," the written word of an Islamic religious leader, an imam (probably that of Seville), confirming that it would be safe to let the order take over the charge of the Dome of the Rock. It would only look as if the Christians were in charge of it, and, as we know, image is everything.

But while the Templars were in charge of the dome, they had to reacquaint themselves with the world of Islam, with the traditions, the secrecy, the root of all that mattered, (spiritually that is). Purely from a historical point of view, their settlement in Jerusalem opened doors to understanding the Middle East from a perspective that had never been achieved by westerners before.

What the Templars found was that there was more to Makkah, or rather Arabia, than met the eyes. They became aware of this through their immediate involvement with the Muslims of the area. Their first treaty was with the "Old Man of the Mountain," the Ismaelite leader of the Order of the Assassins, seen by most orthodox Sunni Muslims as heretical. However, the Templar order's "Muslim" philosophy, which sprung from a Sufi trend of Islamism, was then Shiite in concept. The Ismaeli order was also Shiite in belief, and thus these two orders, that of the Templars and that of the Assassins are connected to one another albeit loosely so. It makes sense for Hugues de Payens, a descendant of Muhammad, head of a chivalric body disguised as a Christian entity, to ally himself and his fellow knights to one of the most powerful Islamic orders, itself headed by a descendant of the prophet Muhammad. In fact, in view of their common descent, they can only get together in a common cause. From the eleventh century on, Islamic records refer to de Payens's order as the "Templars of Islam." It is through this link with the Order of the Assassins that the Templars became guardians of an Eastern tradition that would put them at the forefront of Christian/Islamic politics. While other writers refer to the Order of the Assassins as killers, and I have no doubt that they removed leaders forcibly, both by kidnap and assassinations, the root of the word lies in the Arab word "Assas," meaning "guardian of knowledge." So to define them merely as killers is a bit far fetched. Rather, it was their arcane know-how that separated them from the other Islamic traditions.

Another aspect of the Templars, which all Christian historians have failed to mention on purpose, is the fact that the Templars acquired a fleet loaned to them, free of charge, by no less than the caliph of Egypt. Based in the Red Sea, it enabled our Templars to travel to Makkah disguised as faithful Muslims. This is quite important because unless you are a practicing Muslim, Makkah is closed to you. This rule, however, has not always been enforced. In its pre-Islamic days, Makkah was opened to all pilgrims, even Christians. When Muhammad took over the city and the Ka'bah, the rule applied (one of his wives was, remember, a Christian), even for a short while after his death. So long as the Christians properly asked for permission to visit and swore an oath to respect the holy ground where Muhammad had lived and died, they could visit the city and view, from a certain point of vantage, the Ka'bah. Today, however, no other pilgrims save those following Islam can visit the site.

At that time, all Muslim males were circumcised, but within the Pauline Christian church, circumcision was not, is not, required. Then, as well as now, Muslims in Makkah were required to clean themselves before prayer. Because pilgrims usually shared washing space with other pilgrims, non-Muslims would soon be found out. To be found out as a nonbeliever threading the sacred path of Muhammad means the loss of your life. What is interesting is that the early Templars agreed not only to convert to a faith different to that of Christianity but also did go through a circumcision rite.

In some quarters, the belief persists that the Templars, officially in charge of the Dome of the Rock in Jerusalem, had a free entrance within the city of Makkah. Strangely enough, the history of Makkah also claims that they had free access to the "Sons of the Old Woman" (also referred to as the "Sons of the Widow"), the priests in charge of the Makkah temple. Stranger still is the story of the sacred stone, kept within the temple in Makkah.

According to tradition, this stone was taken by Adam at the time of his expulsion from paradise. He then bequeathed it to his son Seth, and so it was passed down through the generations of the patriarchs till it came into the hands of Noah, who dedicated it as an altar to his family upon Mount Ararat in Turkey after the deluge. Here, his descendant Abraham found it, and it was this stone that Abraham's grandson Jacob set up for a pillar to commemorate his vision of the ladder. Moses (Pharaoh Akhenaten) carried it out of Egypt at the Hebrew exodus (1364 BC), and Solomon discovered it in the excavations for the first temple in Jerusalem. This stone bore the form of a perfect cube and engraved upon it was the ineffable name of God (Kybela). This name became the lost word of the Hebrew people during the dark days of the Babylonian captivity. To the people's forgetfulness of this stone and its sacred word was attributed the eventual demolition of the temple, the dispersion of the tribes and the complete destruction of Jerusalem. This is the keystone or cornerstone of legend, the Lapsit Exillis of the alchemists. This tradition equates the Ka'bah with the temple of Solomon that, supposedly, was originally built thousands of miles away in Palestine. So what is it doing in Makkah?

Many historians, save Graham Hancock and Tim Wallace-Murphy, would deny that the Templars traveled down the Red Sea, but serious excavations have now been done showing buildings in Ethiopia with architectural designs that are typically Templars and date back to the twelfth century. What must have struck the Templars as well is the Jewish links between some Ethiopian tribes and how historically the Ethiopian high priests related their offices back to the days of Solomon. In fact, Templars found a Jewish population that was of far greater importance in Ethiopia, even Yemen, than it was in Judaea.

What became also obvious to the Templars is that the original Jerusalem of Solomon, the pre-Babylonian-invasion Jerusalem, was not that which the crusaders were occupying in Palestine and from which these various crusader kings were ruling from. How they became acquainted with this knowledge is quite simple. Their archeological digs revealed much to them, including the fact that Old Testament name places could not be found in Palestine. When they looked at the history related within the Old Testament, they realized that something within the religious facts was amiss with the archeological finds.

Historically speaking, Babylon overtook Jerusalem in 586 BC and the entire population of the kingdom of Judah was taken away. For over fifty (some say seventy) years, the Jewish people lived in Babylon and became acquainted with the various religious trends of that part of the world, so much so that they decided to borrow from them, Judaized them and claimed their antiquity for their own. Some of the writings pertaining to the Jewish faith date back to the pre-Babylonian exile, but most of it belong to the post-Babylonian era. The second temple was built by Zerrubabel, fourth in descent from king Yehoiachin who had been deposed in 597 BC and who died in 560 BC, having been taken into exile in Babylonia with some eight thousands prisoners. Yehoiachin's brother and successor, king Tsidqiyah, would also lose the crown, again to the Babylonian in 586 BC, would see all his sons killed in front of his eyes and would be blinded afterwards. Only two members of his family would survive, two daughters, one by the name of Tamar Tephy, who, with the prophet Jeremiah, would reach Ireland, where Tamar married Eochaid the Great, ancestor of the Dalriadan house, which would rule Western Scotland from AD 498. Jeremiah, by the way, happens to also be the son of Hilkiyah, the last Zadokite high priest of the first high priesthood of Jerusalem.

This archeological conclusion is not new. In 1999, Professor Ze'ev Herzog of Tel Aviv University declared that after seventy years of intensive archeological research and digging in the Palestinian region, nothing from the forty years wandering in the desert and the military conquest in Canaan, including the division of the promised land among the twelve tribes of Israel, could be historically proved. Except for a handful of pottery shards from a period going back to the days in question, little if nothing proves that the Jewish kingdom of David and Solomon was ever there. While the Bible claims that monumental architectural buildings were built, no archeological evidence, no stone foundations or remains fitting the picture as given in the Old Testament have been revealed. In the view of this Jewish academic, the biblical empire, which supposedly stretched from the Egyptian border to the Euphrates "was probably much poorer and a smaller state than what one is taught to believe."

In fact, nothing tangible proves that empire ever to have been in Palestine in the first place. Needless to say, the Jewish religious hierarchy in Jerusalem disagrees. Rabbi Shalom Gold, dean of Jerusalem College for adults, questioned the academic interpretation of Professor Herzog. "Pots and shards could not out-weigh the living evidence of a living people transmitted for four thousand years," said Gold. The Jews, he claims, had been celebrating every year for 3,500 years their forebears' great march out of Egypt, and he is not ready to say that they have all been fooled, that it was all a lie. But what if the event was not a lie? What if the places in Jewish history just aren't where everyone thought they were?

While traveling down the Red Sea, the Templars found remnants of ancient cities bearing near identical names to Jewish cities in the Old Testament. These were found in western Arabia, between the coastal area stretching from the port of Jiddah to that of Jizzan. What were Judaic names doing in Arabia? The discovery of these Jewish names in western Arabia is nothing new. Lebanese professor Kamal Salibi wrote about it in 1985. This finding was ridiculed by Israel as utter nonsense. But is it? Very little in Palestine proves it to be the promised land of Moses, even less that of the kingdom of Solomon. In fact, unknown to most, the place names in the Old Testament were set in Palestine in the nineteenth century by Christian so-called scholars, and most of that placement was based on very little archeological evidences. And the archeological evidence produced since then is so flimsy and confusing that it cannot be enough to present us with a historical *fait accompli*.

Nor should we take for granted the idea that Jews were the slaves who built the pyramids or Egyptian temples. The truth is that Jews had never been slave builders to pharaohs. In the year 2000, the graves and houses of the people who built the pyramids and temples were found in Egypt. The archeological evidences of their lifestyle proved that they were housed, fed and cared for to a better standard than the rest of the population living in the area at the time. The archeological findings and DNA tests made on the recovered bones show that the entire workforce was, actually, Egyptian. No Jewish slaves were used to build the pyramids. Never at any time in Egypt's history did pharaohs and the Egyptian priesthood put the building of temples in the hands of foreigners.

Furthermore, the Jewish claim relating to a biblical exodus from Egypt to Judah taking forty years makes no sense whatsoever, particularly if one takes into account the fact that the Jews originally resided in the Egyptian city of Zarw (as Eighteenth Dynasty records show), near the Mediterranean coast. Making one's way to Jerusalem from Zarw, even by foot, would not take more than a few months. You d simply follow the coastal road rather than go into the desert. The Old Testament, however, informs us that the Jews sojourned forty years in the desert. What desert? There is also the fact that the Middle Eastern regions were quite well known to the people living in the area. Maps showing the area from south of Yemen to the Mediterranean Sea in the north, from Central Africa to Jordan in the east, together with roads to Qadesh, Canaan, Megido and Lebanon (Phoenicia) were available to travelers. The question that the Templars had to ask themselves was: did the Jews, following their Babylonian exile, go back to the right area of origin or did they simply choose a new area to settle? The simple truth is that none of those Jews who "came back" to Jerusalem after 539 or 519 BC (scholars are still arguing the exact date when the Jews left Babylon) had been born in their place of origin. All of them, including Zerrubabel (whose name actually means "born in Babel"), were born in Babylon. In all probability, Zerrubabel and his people were told by the Persian king Cyrus or Cambyses where to settle.

The displacement of an entire people is nothing new. The Americans did it to the American Indians, the British with the native South Africans, the Germans under Adolf Hitler. Keeping some of the place names of the country of origin is not uncommon. Place names tend to migrate with displaced communities. This is what happened to the forty thousand Jews following Zerrubabel when they were told to resettle in Palestine by the king of Persia.

Further, and this most people have historically forgotten, only two tribes were allowed to leave with Zerrubabel, those of Benjamin and Judah. The rest, so most encyclopedias would have us believe, would be scattered all over the Persian Empire or assimilated within the ethnic environment in which they had settled. As such, only the descendants of the tribes of Judah and Benjamin, due to the fact that they both produced a royal line, have survived today as Jews because they were allowed to leave Babylon and settle in what has been claimed ever since to be their homeland. I always find it very strange that people are unaware that the "kingdom of Israel" only lasted for three generations and kings. Saul, David and Solomon consecutively ruled over a unified kingdom for ninety-nine years, from 1021 to 922 BC. These three kings ruled over twelve unified tribes. In 922 BC, the kingdom had split in two, with an independent kingdom of Israel, comprised of ten of the twelve tribes, ruled by a new dynasty in the north, and a kingdom of Judah, represented by the Solomonic dynasty in the south. Those writers claiming the tribe of Benjamin to be missing simply are unaware of the historical truth of the matter. In 721 BC, the Northern kingdom was conquered by the Assyrians, which, gradually, assimilated the ten tribes living in the area. The ten tribes, so the *Encyclopedia Britannica* informs us, disappeared from history.

Actually, the ten tribes did not disappear at all as claimed by some biblical scholars. They are alive and kicking today, and their descendants are still living in their country of origin, the area of Asir in western Arabia. However, they are no longer Judaic in essence but became Arabic over the millennia. Some did cling to their old-fashioned monotheism and survived till the days of Muhammad. In fact, there are still Jews in western Arabia even now. The Templars found this Jewish population during their trip to Ethiopia. Not only did they find the tribes, they found the original Jerusalem, by then a city reduced to the status of a village.

What struck them most was the fact that surrounding villages still bore the names of the various fortification gates that surrounded the original city of Jerusalem, as mentioned in the Torah and the Old Testament. Gates such as those of Benjamin (Jeremiah 37:13, 38:7; Zechariah 14:10), Corner (2 Kings 14:13; 2 Chronicles 25:23, 26:9; Jeremiah 31:38; Zechariah 14:10), Dung (Nehemiah 2:13,3:13, 14, 12:31), East (Nehemiah 3:29), Ephraim (2 Kings 14:13; Chronicles 25:23; Nehemiah 8:16, 12:39), fish (2 Chronicles 33:14; Nehemiah 3:3; Zephaniah 1:10), Fountain (Nehemiah 2:14, 3:15, 12:37), Horse (Nehemiah 3:26; Jeremiah 31:40), Inspection (Nehemiah 3:31), Middle (Jeremiah 39:3), Jeshana (Nehemiah 3:6, 12:39), Prison or Guard (Nehemiah 12:39), Sheep (Nehemiah 3:1, 32, 12:39), Upper Benjamin (Jeremiah 20:2), Valley (2 Chronicles 26:9; Nehemiah 2:13, 15, 3:13), Water (Ezra 8:1; Nehemiah 3:26, 8:1, 3, 16, 12:37), Shallecheth (1 Chronicles 26:16), Sur (2 Kings 11:6; 2 Chronicles 23:5), Joshua the governor of the city (2 Kings 23:8), Potsherds (Jeremiah 19:2), New Gate of Yaweh (Jeremiah 26:10), Upper Gate of the house of Yaweh (2 Chronicles 27:3), the gate behind the two walls (2 Kings 25:4; Jeremiah 39:4, 52:7) and that of the gate behind the guards shall guard the place (2 Kings 11:6).

One of these trips actually took place between 1165 and 1170. From Palestinian Jerusalem, the Templars traveled to the coastal port of Aquaba and boarded ships. They then made their way down the Red Sea and landed in the port of Lith. From there, they traveled by land to Al Madinah (Medina) to finally cross the mountain ridges and the highland of the Asir region of western Arabia. After investigating the region and its history, they then made their way to the coastal strip of Jizan, boarded ships again and made their final sea journey to Ethiopia. What became transparent to them through this first trip is the fact that all biblical Old Testament place-names could be found in western Arabia while these names were missing in Palestine.

When reaching Taif, the Templars then made their way to the city of Makkah in order to touch the stone in the holy temple. Entering Ka'bah, they were then faced with three pillars. The Templars must have realized that what could not be found in Palestine, could be found in Arabia. Thus, the present tradition in Palestine must have been transposed from western Arabia to Palestine via Babylon. (Genealogically, both Arabs and Jews are Semites.) The Templars found more Jews outside Palestine than within Palestine. Even with the Roman genocide of AD 70, this made little sense. In Ethiopia, they found several tribes containing strong elements of Judaism. (In fact, as late as 1990, an entire Jewish tribe, the Falasha, was airlifted from Ethiopia to Israel because of civil war and a drought. The Israeli government did not want the tribe members to suffer and so decided to repatriate them to Israel. Those who had no "Jewish" connection were left to die of thirst.)

Traveling to Medina, the second holiest city within Islamic tradition, the Templars then found the tomb of Aaron on the highest peak of Mount Uhud. What the blazes is the tomb of the first high priest of the Jews doing here? Actually, who on earth was the historical Aaron? The answer to that is: Pharaoh Smenkhare, whose full name was Smenkh-ka-ra-on ("victorious is the Soul of Ra"). Smenkhare was Pharaoh Akhenaten's (Moses') cousin, son-in-law and successor. Smenkhare's father and one-time minister of Egypt, also succeeded the Egyptian throne.

It soon became evident to the Templars that there were two facets to the Old and New Testaments: the religious aspect (that is faith), and the facts that equate with "history." The first can seldom prove the second, but the latter can shed a tremendous amount of light upon the former. Further, if Aaron was buried in Medina, where was Moses (Akhenaten)? His remains, surely, would be found in a site that would have been venerated since his death. Would Makkah fit the bill? The answer to that is yes. The whole area abounded with names of Judaic origins, older in origin than many of the names to be found in Palestine.

Moreover, the Templars believed they had found both the Garden of Eden and the tree of knowledge (of good and evil, Genesis 2:17, 3:3) and the tree of life (Genesis 3:22). They most probably also found the birth place of

Abraham, "wr ksdym" (Ur Kasdim), in the Wadi Adam, and his resting place (the biblical wood of Mamre, also referred to as Moreh) in the Dharan region of the southernmost highlands of Asir in western Arabia. And pigs can fly I hear you say. Like it or not, the cult of sacred groves was disseminated worldwide, even unto premedieval Britain, Europe and America. It applied to both Egypt and Arabia as well, particularly to the Asir Highland region of the Wadi Bishah in Western Arabia. We are talking in terms of large oases, of course, the "God of life" and "God of knowledge" respectively. The Templars became aware that the geography of the region, with its rivers, mountain ranges and place-name connotations, even in its Arabic version, actually fit the history found in the Old Testament. This area included the exact volcanic locations of Sodom and Gomorrah, which archeologists are still unable to find in Palestine. When they found Mount Zion in western Arabia, the reference to Bakka (Makkah) in the Old Testament (Psalm 84) thus started to make perfect sense.

On reaching Ethiopia, where they actually set up upon the throne Prince Lalibela, younger brother of King Harbay whom the Templars simply swept aside. They then proceeded to build Templar churches (most are to be found below ground). Graham Hancock, in his book *The Sign and the Seal: A Quest for the Lost Ark of the Covenant*, heavily researched the subject. While there is conjecture as to where the ark may be hidden today, there is no conjecture whatsoever with regards to the fact that Templar church structures, dating back to the twelfth century, are to be found in Ethiopia. The ark was that of Akhenaten. It is a mistake to believe that the ark is historically Jewish. Before the Jews claimed a monopoly on it, the Egyptian pharaohs were using an ark as well. And no, it was not the ritual barge processed at the funeral of pharaohs, as some people believe, but a proper box, gold plated and shining with esoteric and hermetic designs that only the pharaoh, together with the high priests of Thebes and Heliopolis, would have been able to decipher. It is believed that the key to activate the ark was the "word" (most probably a magical formula) and gave the user superhuman psychic powers. Even the history relating to Solomon in the Koran tends to prove this as it mentions him practicing magic and being able to command genies to do his bidding. The temple that Solomon had built had no other purpose than to house the ark. Once a year, the high priest entered the temple's holy of holies, where the ark was housed, plugged into it, so to speak, and then decided the political and religious courses of action to take for the year. The ark was an oracle and only one person, the high priest, had access to it, though the king, on occasion, could also consult it. This tradition is wholly Egyptian and it came down to Solomon via his ancestor Akhenaten who carried it out of Egypt from his capital city of El Armana.

Many people will have a problem accepting the fact that the original Jerusalem is to be found in western Arabia. However, think of the following within the Scottish equation. There are two towns of Perth, the original in Scotland and another one in Australia. Edinburgh, capital city of Scotland, is also known by its pre-Anglicized name of Dun Edin in New Zealand. There is a Paris in France and a Paris in Texas, USA. A York in England and a New York in the USA. There are numerous Oxfords outside England. While there is a Moscow in Russia, there is also a Moscow in Scotland! The world abounds with place-names whose original uses are to be found somewhere else, even across oceans and deserts. To think that Palestinian Jerusalem is a daughter city called after its original in western Arabia, where all the biblical place names can still be found while only a handful can be traced in Palestine today, makes perfect sense. Herodotus informs us that the Phoenicians originally came from a western Arabia region bordering the Red Sea before some of them left for the Mediterranean. The idea of this small exodus was to improve on the trade routes and thus to expand to a larger area of trades on their own behalf. Phoenician place names found their way to the Mediterranean area. The Phoenicians created a second kingdom in the Mediterranean with place names that had their origin in western Arabia. One is also reminded of those Irish Scots of Dal Riata who left County Antrim in AD 498 to settle in the western coast of Argyllshire in Scotland, where they created the kingdom of Dalriada. By AD 835, this distinct Irish-Scot community had more or less unified Scotland as a single national entity with a role to play in Europe.

So the true treasure of the Templars was threefold.

Firstly they found records pertaining the Essene community of the pre- and post-Christ era (200 BC and the first century AD, respectively). This gave them the key to understanding the New Testament in its proper context. It was written in a code that only the Essenes would have understood. According to this code, based on words for those with eyes to see and ears to hear, it showed Jesus Christ as being a man, not divine, to have been a husband and a father, a possible pretender to the crown of Judaea and the leader of a political faction. Like the Koran, it mentions the fact that he did not die on the cross. This to them, was nothing new. Our nine original Templars had genealogies taking them back to biblical times of Jerusalem. As far as they were concerned, they were not only part of that great Jewish "diaspora," they also belonged to the desposiny, the family of Jesus.

The particular records detailing the genealogical links of the various Templar families were kept at the commandery of Kirbet-Qumram (in Palestine) from the year 1142, when three knights, Raimbaud de Simiane, Balthazar de Blacas and Pons des Baux, set up the commandery. Interestingly, the commandery of Kirbet-Qumram was built on top of an ancient Roman fort that had been itself built upon the foundation of an old Essenian monastery. It is on this site that the ancient Visigoth Spanish archives of the

Aryan Church were housed for safety. They had been brought from Cordoba so as to be hidden from the clutches of Rome. It is also here that the archives of the first Christian Ebionite communities in both Jerusalem and Rome were housed in the commandery's scriptorium. To these early records was added the proof that Christ survived the Crucifixion. Indeed, the same records, which also showed that Christ had visited the city of Arles in AD 50 under the name of St. Trophime, were sent to Kirbert-Qumram, together with an original copy of Suetone's (AD 69–125) "History of the Caesars' and Flavius Josephus's Hebrew Antiquities." Both books detail the life of Christ after the crucifixion. Moreover, the true location of the tomb of St. Peter in the district of Verdon, in France, was also known to the Templars. The idea that Peter, supposedly the first pope of Rome, regardless of the fact that the title of pope was not used till the end of the fourth century AD, is buried at the Vatican is totally spurious. And our Templars could prove it (just as they knew that the papal throne was nothing more than the throne of an Arabic potentate that had been stolen and brought to the Holy City).

Secondly, the Herodian temple records, which the Templars found, like those of the Essene Church, gave them the precise location of the gold, the temple tax, which the Jews from the then-known world had sent to Jerusalem. Gold, even today, is power. The more gold, the more power. But what is more, through the Gnostic Church of the Mandeans in Palestine, one of the Templars early allies, they were able to acquire more gold. The Mandeans, although of Persian origin, are said to be an early Christian Gnostic sect. (At least, this is what the Church of Rome would like us to believe.) However, the Mandean priesthood was much older than Christianity: its lineage goes as far back as the Egyptian priests of Karnack and the Egyptian metallurgists dealing with gold. Some alternative historians claim that the Egyptians were able to transmute selected metals into gold but the Egyptians had a perfectly natural way of extracting gold in vast amounts from river deposits in Africa. Those very mines provided the eighteenth Egyptian dynasty with an unparalleled wealth. And it was the locations of those very mines that the Mandeans presented to the Templars, who, over the next two centuries, would manage to mine the equivalent of four hundred million pounds sterling in gold.

These mines were not like modern mines as excavated today. The way the ancients extracted gold was by wells, bored into the ground through rock (preferably near a river), and lined with masonry. Then, by hundreds of slaves, the rock was brought to the surface and given into the keeping of other slaves, who would grind the rock into dust. It would then be washed with water and the gold separated from the rock dust. When too much water was seeping back into the well, they simply filled it and bore another well some few feet away, following the strike of the reef. Mines like these could span a distance as long as a mile and a half, and would be six feet wide and at least fifty feet deep. Opened rock trenches, on the other hand, would be hacked with adzes of iron and iron wedges pounded into the grain of the rock with stone hammers. If the rock was too hard to resist this method, the ancients then built fires upon it and poured water mixed with sour wine on the heated surface to shatter it. From this hole, lumps of gold quartz would be removed, packed into raw baskets to be brought to the slaves who would then separate the gold from the rock. Altogether, an estimated seven hundred tons of fine gold from mines spread over an area of three hundred thousand square miles of central and southern Africa was removed. To this must be added vast quantities of iron, copper and tin. So while transmutation is appealing, and notwithstanding the fact that the Templars did indeed have alchemists among their ranks, it was their golden wealth from Africa, brought by their secret caravans, that helped them built cathedrals in Europe. Yet, to this day, no one has ever asked how the Templars were able to build for themselves the biggest gold reserves in our medieval history.

The Jewish "tax" gold that had been recovered was kept by the nine knights in trust, while the Essenian records were sent to Europe, to Bernard de Clairveaux, the Cistercian leader, to be secretly translated. By 1128, Bernard de Clairveaux intimated that all the literary works that "could be found had been found and all that could be translated had been translated." "The work," stated Bernard de Clairveaux, "has been done." In 1128, Bernard de Clairveaux called for a council to be held in Troyes. The pope, Honorius II, acceded to Bernard's every desire.

Thirdly, the Templars realized that the Jerusalem of their day may not be that of Solomon. From an archeological point of view, everything pointed to Islamic Makkah and western Arabia to have been the Jewish people's original pre-Babylonian place of origin. However, there was no use to think of reclaiming it since it had become the holy of holies of Islam.

Chapter 8

Rex Devs, Ismaeli and Nvsayri

The Cistercian equation is one that, for some odd reason, has never been dwelt upon by many religious historians. In fact, it is something they avoid doing like the plague. Discussing the various religious concepts of this order is something that we must do if we are to understand the Templars, even Freemasonry, in its proper perspective. Truth be told, to be a Templar meant to be a Cistercian and to be a Cistercian meant to be a Templar. Moreover, it is Bernard de Clairveaux's relationship to Hugues de Payens that is the key to it all. To define Bernard de Clairveaux is quite difficult. Was he a fanatic, a politician or a visionary? Personally, I would say the latter, though his vision was already quite old when he set out to put it in motion.

A Cistercian is described in most dictionaries as a "member of a Roman Catholic monastic order founded in 1098 in Citeaux by Robert de Molesme." Citeaux happens to be situated near Dijon, in the dukedom of Burgundy. Molesme housed a group of Benedictine monks who, apparently, were dissatisfied with the lax observance of their abbey. Wanting to live solitary lives under the stricter rule of St. Benedict, they simply excused themselves, walked out of Molesme and founded Citeaux. Citeaux's third abbot, Stephen Harding, was the real organizer of this new order. Its rules and regulations insisted on severe asceticism, rejected all feudal revenues and reintroduced manual labor for monks.

The aristocracy and landed gentry throughout Europe dedicated some of their lands to this order. The Cistercians, with this addition of devolved estates together with an unpaid new labor force, were able to develop all branches of farming, in the same manner as the Muslims were able to do in Spain. Without the hindrance of manorial customs, the order managed to reclaim marginal land, increased production, especially of wool, and came to play a large part in the economic progress of twelfth-century Europe. Like the Muslims, they put into practice the various techniques of marketing. If they were indeed religious and praised God through both chanting and pure meditations, they were also recognized as the new public-relations people of the day. The order was also free from interference of the pope and local bishops.

Most books will tell you that the family of Bernard de Clairveaux, born in 1090, was of minor Burgundian nobility, but this is quite untrue. Both his parents were in the major league of the established Burgundian hierarchy. His father was Tescelin le Saur, lord of the castle of Fontaine and Viscount of Dijon. Tescelin's mother was a de Grancey by descent, thus Tescelin was connected to the de la Ferte family. A de la Ferte would become, during the early days of Hugues de Payens in Jerusalem, Latin patriarch of Jerusalem. In fact, this is the patriarch who signed the charter recognizing the Order of the Temple of Solomon with Baudouin II of Jerusalem in 1118. Bernard's uncle, Andre de Montbard, was a founding member of the Templars with Hugues de Payens. Bernard's mother was Aleth de Montbard, which connected him directly to the Count of Champagne. Seemingly, Andre de Baudemont, seneschal of Champagne, was also a founding member of the Order of the Templars. Andre's wife was Agnes de Braine and their line would ultimately marry within both the royal houses of Navarre and Bourbon-France. Through her mother, Aleth was descended from the Merovingien comtes de Tonnerre, who had been dukes during the Merovingien administration. Tonnerre (thunder), as a minor title, was one that this family had chosen to bear as descendants of the "Thunder" Judaic Essene high priest Jonathan Annas. That Annas traveled to Europe, there is no doubt, as we find mentions of him in the Roman records of the early emperors. The heiress of Tonnerre, Ermengarde, eldest sister of Humberge, wife to Bernard, Count of Montbard (father of Aleth and Andre de Montbard), married Guillaume I of Nevers and their line would culminate with the eastern Latin emperors of Constantinople, the imperial royal house of Courtenay. If anything, they knew very well which families would become prominent in world politics.

However, the most obvious thing about the genealogy of Bernard de Clairveaux is that it is, in effect, wholly royal. It encompasses no less than four royal families: the Merovingien, Caroloringian and Capetian families of France and the family of Saxon England. The de Montbard family, for example, is very important as well. Bernard de Montbard's sister, Gundrada, was also the daughter of Tescelin le Saur's aunt. Gundrada married Thibault III of Champagne and their grandson, Thibault IV, would be the one who supported Bernard de Clairveaux's calling for a church council to sit at Troyes in Champagne. In other words, Thibault IV, Bernard de Clairveaux and Hugues de Payens, whose mother was Helie de Montbard, aunt to Bernard de Clairveaux, are all related within a very close degree.

Bernard had several brothers and sisters, and all had been educated at St. Vorles, once upon a time a Celtic church center par excellence that had been set up by a monk of the abbey of Iona in the eighth century. Charlemagne had given St. Vorles a new impetus by granting it a charter. This relict Celtic school was to be of prime importance to the agenda that various Burgundian families had created between themselves. Not only did it promote the concept of Celtic Christianity, but it also produced a tremendous amount of spiritual students who would strive to create and make the Cistercian order one of the most powerful religious entities in medieval Europe. At the age of twenty-one, in 1111, Bernard decided to become a monk at Citeaux. This Cistercian proto-monastery was only a few miles from the family home and run by a prior who was a cousin of Bernard.

Interestingly, Bernard persuaded several members of his family, uncles, brothers (married) and his married sister, Humbeline, to follow him to Citeaux. (Humbeline, by the way, was the direct ancestress of Philippa of Hainault, wife of Edward III of England.) By 1115, a mere four years after entering his spiritual vocation, he was sent to Clairveaux, in Champagne, to found a house to which his entire family and friends became fully fledged members. By 1118, he started to found daughter-houses that would come under his unique authority. Actually, sixty-eight foundations, extending across Europe, from Portugal to Scandinavia, from Scotland to Central Europe, answered to him by the time of his death in 1153. A tremendous amount of men left military careers in order to enter the order and take up a cloistered life. Few people are aware that each house counted up to a hundred people, so that well over 6,800 souls came under the authority of this one man alone.

The one thing that springs to mind when looking at the Cistercian Order is how terribly similar to the Celtic Church this so-called Catholic institution happens to be. In fact, it isn't just similar, it is practically identical. While preoccupied with modernizing Europe, it, too, drew upon education, art and literacy. The Cistercians were not just copiers of old works, but they also were able to translate the various literary works coming to them from outside the frame of accepted Christian tenets. Indeed, the Cistercians are those who first translated the Koran into Latin, using Muslims to aid them in this task. There is no doubt whatsoever that the Cistercians drew their spiritual lore and asceticism from the surviving but struggling Sufis of Muslim Spain and from the remnant of the Celtic Church of Ireland and Scotland. There is no doubt that the Cistercians adopted their white mantle from the Celtic monks who, once upon a time, roamed the confines of Europe, liberating Christians from the dogmatic constraints and liturgical nonsense imposed upon all by the Pauline

Roman authorities. Of notable interest is that these Celtic monks were also known as "The Militia of Christ," which is what St. Columba and his twelve apostles were known as when they crossed from Ireland to settle in Iona in AD 563. This, we must keep in mind as it is quite important.

Bernard de Clairveaux was also the promoter of the cult of Mary, a cult not of the deified virgin but rather of womanhood. This cult of womanhood had been originally founded by Islam and practiced in Islamic Spain. What Bernard did was modify the Islamic cult and Christianize it, centering its aspect around one of the most prominent women of the Christian faith. Had Bernard not done this, the feminine aspect of the deity would have been lost forever. While he borrowed from the Muslin concept, Bernard de Clairveaux never did revere the mother of Jesus Christ as the "immaculate conception" as promoted by the Council of Ephesus in AD 431 and subsequently forced upon Christianity by the Church of Rome.

It is Bernard de Clairveaux who also brought the architectural concept of God. Writing about God, Bernard actually defined him in terms of "width, length, height and depth." Indicative of Bernard's power over Rome is the fact that he was never chastised for taking a different view on the matter.

This brings us to a subject that has been debated rather a lot lately within the history of the Templar Order, that of the Rex Deus families. Did they truly exist and are they active today? The ideal of the "king of God" (from which derives the term "by the grace of God") was Merovingien in concept and started with Theodoric IV of the Franks. Loosing one's kingdom, as Theodoric IV did, is never easy, even when offered an alternative one, such as Septimania, as a consolation prize.

The Merovingien empire had been vast, but so was the membership of its family. Unfortunately, all Merovingien males, from one generation to another, wanted a piece of the cake. As such, each was given a portion of the empire over which he happily ruled. Partition and fragmentation, however, means loss of power and political influence. Add to this the fact that the Roman Catholic Church grew to believe it had the God-given right to rule and dictate to individual kings what to do and what to say, and you have a recipe for disaster.

The Merovingiens were partly Judaic in their royal practices and, yes, they were descended from Jesus Christ and the Magdalene. In fact, the cult of the Magdalene was of great importance to them as a counter-balance against the growing power of the Church. It is a mistake, however, to believe that this house disappeared from the face of the earth in the eighth century. In fact, it is alive and well, and, indeed, politically active on several levels of the European social strata. Nevertheless, I must stress here that both the succeeding houses in France, the Caroloringien and the Capetian royal families, are wholly Merovingien by male descent as well. On taking over the reins of the kingdom of the Franks, they simply assumed the name of an individual of the family, as the Merovingien family originally did. But they are all the same family divided into one main branch and two cadet branches.

Theodoric was king by God's wish and was dethroned by a cousin of his. From then on, the ideal of the Rex Deus family was born. In the main, anyone descended from the original line was a member of it. When the house of Charlemagne lost power to their cousin the Capetians, it joined the Rex Deus families as well. Descendants from both the Merovingien and Caroloringien lines, which, from then on, intermarried with one another on a regular basis, made several marital alliances with the Capetian house and produced altogether no less than twenty-three queens of France. This reverence of the marital power that these women held over their partners was part of the Rex Deus philosophy. The house of Hapsburg, however, did not come within that equation until Maria Theresa of Austria, daughter of Charles VI, married Francis of Lorraine, a Rex Deus descendant, in 1736. From then on, and only from then on, do they become accepted members of the Rex Deus order. In fact, before that time, every house belonging to Rex Deus avoided marrying into the Hapsburgs as if they had the plague. Only the original house of Austria, the House of Babenberg, belonged to the Rex Deus. Other houses, among many, with Rex Deus ancestries were those of: Flanders, Champagne, Luxemburg (old), Bourbon (the original one, that is), Bavaria (old), de Coucy, de Gueldres, de Nevers, de Courtenay, Brittany, Tuscany (old), Toulouse, Barcelona (old), d'Avesnes de Hollande, Normandy, d'Anjou, Lorraine (old), Stewart of Scotland, Portugal and Navarre.

The Rex Deus was, actually, divided into two memberships. Those descended from the Judaic/Christian side and those with a Christian/Islamic descent from either the Umayyad royal house or from Muhammad, the Seal of the Prophets. Within this latter category came the de Payens family and his Order of the knights Templar, together with the various Rex Deus families ruling the crusader states of Jerusalem, Edessa, Caesarea, Sidon, Tripoli, Cyprus and Oultrejourdain. The Rex Deus minor family is quite extensive: on the Templar list of Rex Deus members can be found names such as: de Laplace, de Boeli, de Cugnieres, de Peraudo, d'Arblay, de Frenecourt, de Vasiniac, de Trecis, de Annonia, de Thaton, de Lechun, de Boucheurs, d'Oysemont, de Troyes, de Tournon, de Camborin, de Gonaville, de Taverni, de St. Just, de Gisi, de Brencourt, de Rumprey, de Masvallier, de St. Benoist, de Mont-Lodat, de St. Jore, de Lagni, de Grumesnil, de Madic, de Buris, du Plessis, de Santoni, de Corneilles, de Raineval, de Brali, de Somerens, de Novions, de Ervival, de Marseille, de Villars, de Sanzet, de Roche-Abeille, de Masvalier, de Mursac, de Liege, de Canes, de Ville Parisis, de Ville Mostrue, de Serra, la Chassanades, du Puy, Theobaldi, Charneri, Harnery, de Puiset and de

Bonnefort. Those are but a few. The families with royal connections were, among others, those of Bigorre, de Lara, Montdidier, Rameru, Montpellier, Toulouse, Urgel, Savoy, Provence, Flanders, Besalu, Vermendois, Beaudement, Champagne, Poitou, Brabant, Hainault, Aquitaine, Coucy, Dreux, Bruce, de Braose, Gueldres, Guise, Brittany and Barcelona. The Islamic allies of the Templars were the Idrisids of Fez and the Ismaili and Nusayri heads of families descended from the sixth imam of Islam, Ja'far as-Sadiq, a descendant of Muhammad the Prophet. It is interesting to note that the doctrines of the Nusayri order involved a deification of Ali (son-in-law of Muhammad the Prophet) within a trinity akin to that of the early Christians, and the Nusayris enjoyed an eclectic group of holidays, some Islamic, some Christians. Their interpretation of the five pillars of Islam, requiring Muslims to pray five times a day, is purely symbolic. This means that the practices of Islamic duties, according to this order, are not required by law but are left opened to the conscience of the individual.

In 1128, Bernard de Clairveaux, a member of the Rex Deus, a descendant of the royal houses of France and England, the new leader (albeit not the head of it) of the Cistercian Order, called for a church council to sit at Troyes. There was no precedent for such a move. No one has ever thought to ask by what authority did this one man, admittedly the leader of his own religious community, have to require a pope, the supreme leader of the Roman Catholic Church, to call for a council to take place in Champagne at all. Bernard is no more than an abbot, not a bishop. However, from a Celtic Church point of view, the abbots had supremacy over the bishops. The latter were accepted as those imbued with the right to ordain priests and other bishops while the former took care of the administration and education of the clergy, the ministry and the overall population living within their spiritual jurisdiction.

Interestingly, St. Malachy, Celtic bishop of Down, left his vestments to Bernard de Clairveaux. (It was St. Malachy who wrote the papal prophesies that predicts the ending of the papacy in the twenty-first century.) The Celtic Church was of paramount importance to Abbot Bernard and this is why he behaves in the fashion of a cleric belonging to the Celtic Church rather than one belonging to the Roman persuasion. And the pope, Honorius II, readily gave in by giving Bernard the responsibility to organize the council at Troyes, without knowing quite what this council will discuss, debate and finally stamp and deliver. This is unparalleled in the history of church councils. No other orders were ever funded and recognized through a church council. The Templar order is the only one. Honorius was a follower and the successor to Callistus II, a relation to Henri of Burgundy, ruling count of Portugal. Indeed, Callistus' real name was Guy of Burgundy. They do say that blood is thicker than water and this certainly applies to the various people concerned.

Taking part in the Troyes council were Matteo, bishop of Albano and legate of the pope (formerly Mathieu, superior of St. Martin-Des-Champs in Paris, and is thus a Frenchman); Rainault de Martigne, archbishop of Rheims; Henri le Sanglier, archbishop of Sens; the bishops of Chartres; Goscelin de Vierzy of Soissons; Etienne de Senlis of Paris; Hatton of Troyes, Jean of Orleans; Hugues de Montaigu of Auxerre; Burchart of Meaux; Erlebert of Chalons; Barthelemy de Vir of Laons and Beauvais; the abbots Renaud de Semur of Vezelais; Hugues de Macon of Pontigny; Gui of Trois Fontaines; Ursion of St. Rhemy of Rheims; Erbert of St. Etienne de Dijon; Stephen Harding of Moslemes and of Citeaux, Maitre Aubry (of Rheims); Maitre Souchier, Guillaume II, Count of Nevers; Thilbault de Champagne; Andre de Baudemont (senechal of Champagne); Bernard de Clairveaux; and a scribe by the name of Jean Michel. Invited to participate to this council were Hugues de Payens, Archambault de St. Amand, Payens de Montdidier, Jeffroy Bissot, Godefroid de St. Omer and Roland Guizot, all members of the Order of the Temple of Solomon under the leadership of Hugues de Payens, an order under the protection of the crusader king and the Latin patriarch of Jerusalem. What, of course, stands out straightaway is that this council is altogether a French affair. Most of the participants are related to one another and make this so-called religious council, condoned by the pope, a family thing with an agenda unprecedented in any way within the history of the Catholic Church.

The Council of Troyes did something that had never been done before. It formally recognized the sovereignty of the Templar order under Hugues de Payens and allowed Bernard de Clairveaux to present the order with the gift of a rule consisting of no less than seventy-two regulations. It allowed the Templars to receive gifts of land and money and to set commanderies both in the West and the East, the properties and incomes of which could not be interfered with nor be taxed by the various kings within whose kingdoms these commanderies had been set up. Further grants would allow the Templars the use of mercenaries whenever deemed necessary and gave the various chaplains of the Templars the right to give anyone excommunicated by the church communion once a year. It made the Templars answerable to the pope alone and only in extreme cases. The Templars were known under three different headings: the Poor Soldiers of Christ, the Knights of the Temple of Solomon and the Militia of Christ (in the same manner as those Celtic abbots from the sacred kindred of Iona descended from the leadership of St. Columba).

The Templars would be divided in three distinct categories. There were those who prayed, that is to say the Cistercians themselves. Then, there were those who built, that is to say the workforce that would build their abbeys, templar castles and cathedrals. finally, there were those who fought, the knights Templars themselves. The knights requirements were also threefold. A series of three vows were expected of them: poverty, purity and chastity (in view that so many of them were married, we have to wonder why) were required. They had to partake of communion three times a year, had to hear mass three times a week, had to adore the cross three times a year, had to eat meat three times a week and had to fast three times a year. They had to own three horses and could not flee from three enemies facing them. Multiple trinities were what it was all about.

The knights were entitled, in the East, to employ Muslim jurists and translators. It is a fact that certainly in the Middle East, the Templars were divided equally between a Christian membership and a Muslim one. Most Templar masters were close friends to the Sultan of Cairo, and it is even claimed that Caliph Saladin himself had been invested within the Templar order by Hugues de Tabarie in 1187. Many people have wondered at the reason for Saladin's knighthood, but this is resolved when one realizes that he was, maternally, a grandson of Hughes de Puiset, the lover of Alix of Jerusalem and a knight Templar himself. It is strongly assumed that Richard the Lionheart was a knight Templar and that this was the reason why Saladin's brother, Malik al-Adil, sent Richard a horse to replace the one that had died under him during a skirmish between the two armies. It may well be the reason that when Saladin was besieging the Syrian city of Massiaf, the Order of the Assassins gave him a warning rather than just plunging a knife in his back. (Saladin understood the warning perfectly well, since he simply left the city.)

As for the Order of the Assassins, it must be remembered that the colors of their order were, surprise, surprise, white and red for their cloaks and white and black for their standard. The Order of the Assassins also functioned on the concept of a double hierarchy, with a secret core known to but a few and an outer one known to all, just as the Templars had set up for themselves. Moreover, the Order of the Assassins was allowed, by order of the Templars and with the support of the crusader count of Tripoli, to consolidate itself in what is today Lebanon. As I said previously, the origin of the word "assassin" has little to do with "Hashish" as some historians would like us to believe but rather in the Arabic word "assas," meaning "guardian." The fact is that the Order of the Assassins was an initiatic order in the East imbued with a hermetical doctrine. Interestingly, when the Order of the Temple of Solomon was pursued in Europe from 1307 onwards till 1314, contemporary records found in the National archives of both France and Spain state that rather than give up the right to knighthood, many Spanish knights Templar became, overnight, Muslim knights.

The Council of Troyes also confirmed that the master of the order had the right to wear the red robe and hat of a cardinal of the Roman Catholic Church without going through the required ordination within Catholic priesthood. In effect, Hugues de Payens and his successors were recognized as "high priests" in their own right, members of a high priesthood residing permanently in Jerusalem. As in the old days of the kings of Judah, the private guards of the crusader kings of Jerusalem (but in reality looking after the interests of the counts of Tripoli) would be the militant priests of the temple. In fact, since the order's recognition as a sovereign entity, the master adopted the style of "by the Grace of God." In the earliest Templar cathedral of St. Denis in Paris, this elected royal dignity was portrayed in stone as an abacus of an exact measure, surmounted by a square platform on top of which sits a sphere. Seen in profile, it looks very much like the Egyptian ankh. Another insignia of the Templar master as the master of the East holding in the left hand a whip (a replica of the Egyptian flail) with three strands divided by knots. The three knots denoted the Islamic understanding of a triune God to be "Allah, God the One; God the ever self-subsistent; God the eternally ever-living." The right hand, pressed against the heart, holds a small octogonal pillar. As in the old days of the Solomonic kings of Judah, the head of this militant priesthood wore the white and red colors of his high priestly office. As in the old days of the kings of Judah, this high priesthood was sovereign. This is important. The concept of the messiah was twofold and the word meant nothing more than "anointed one," that is to say "king." But Judah, and later Judaea, had always two kings and both were hereditary. One was the typical hereditary king, who held a "temporal" rule over the people, the other was the hereditary high priest of Jerusalem, who held the spiritual rule over the Jewish tribes. Both lines were connected to one another. Both dynasties had a straight pharaonic descent through Nashon, from whom both the Davidic line and the high priests of Jerusalem traced their ancestry.

What the Council of Troyes did, under the leadership of Bernard de Clairvaux, in other words, was to create an independent sovereign entity within the kingdoms of Christendom. The spiritual patrons of the Templar order were to be the succeeding Cistercian abbots of Clairveaux, the very order promoted by Bernard de Clairveaux and his family. The knights, like the monks, were to wear a white robe of the Cistercian order and were to be referred to as "the Militia of Christ" and as "the Monks Militant" by the Cistercian hierarchy. Years later, during the rule of Pope Eugenius III (originally a Cistercian monk by the name of Bernard de Paganell whose family was very much involved with alchemical esoterism), they were given the right to wear a red cross pate on their mantle. Further bulls would entitle them to allow criminals, excommunicates and heretics to enter the order on a fee of three denaris per year and to bury within their own cemeteries usurers, adulterers and excommunicates—power indeed to rival that of the church.

A Templar/Cistercian connection with Scotland rests with the de Paganell family. Pietro Bernardo de Paganelli, Pope Eugenius III, son of Fulk de Paganell, had a sister, Agnes, who married Robert de Bruce, lord of Cleveland and first lord of Annandale. Their eldest son, Adam, succeeded as heir to the English estates (from whom came the de Braose family) while the youngest, Robert le Meschin, succeeded to the Scottish ones. Robert le Meschin would be the direct ancestor of Robert the Bruce, hero of Scotland's war of independence.

Little has been written about the cross pate by Templar historians. The symbolism of it is hardly Christian and rather refers to the Islamic zodiac related to the number twelve. Actually, it encompasses all the numbers between one and twelve: the four cardinal points (south, north, east, and west); the four elements of fire, water, earth and air; and the twelve body openings. In fact, the cross pate relates to both the microcosm and the macrocosm of mankind. Further, it represents the measurements of the Dome of the Rock and is a design that was used throughout Islam by the Sufis. But it is disguised. This symbol can also be found in a particular Cistercian monastery.

Although they are missing in Europe, Templar architectural symbols can be found in Cistercian monasteries in Scotland, all daughter houses founded from Clairveaux. Although Cistercian monasteries, in Europe, are extremely simple in terms of architecture, this is not the case in Scotland, particularly with the abbey of Melrose where the cross-pate was intrinsically added to the abbey's iconography on the vaulted ceiling over the presbytery. As the saying goes: the proof of the pudding is in the eating!

That the Order of the Templars was as much an esoteric body as it was a military one, there cannot be any doubt. In fact, it is this knowledge that, until the year 1307, would make the order one of the most successful organization in the known world, gaining an ascendancy that only long-term planning by a few visionary could have envisaged.

The Templar order ruled over areas that spanned over the water, both in Europe and the Middle East. These areas were referred to as "provinces," and in the East comprised Jerusalem, Tripoli, Antioch and Cyprus in the East. In Europe, it comprised several royal territories. France included northern France and the present-day Netherlands. Normandy and Burgundy were later added. The European province also included Auvergnes, Poitou (in fact all of ancient Aquitaine) and Provence (engulfing the Languedoc). Further west, the order held vast tracts of land in Castile, Portugal and Aragon-Catalonia. The North had provided them with lands in England (engulfing Scotland, Wales and Ireland as separate entities but under the same tongue). This also applied to Italy (also at times referred to as Lombardy hence northern Italy), Pouille or Apulia (southern Italy and Sicily) and Hungary (for central Europe).

Following the fourth crusade, the order added the extra province of Greece, occasionally referred to as of the Morea.

The order was not, though most books will tell us otherwise, for unmarried men only. Quite a few were actually married and had sired children. In fact, some of the early knights married native women, be it Jewish or Muslim, and their offspring were known as "Poulin." Most of them remained within the order and quite a few reached the level of the inner circle. The records show that, by the thirteenth century, the order had no less than thirteen thousand poulins in its rank, either sons of or descended from Templar knights. As such, like the married knights, they wore a black mantle instead of a white one and resided in separate quarters. Few people are aware that prior to 1129, the order also had women Templars, sisters who were in charge of education. Although some of the bishops attending the Council of Troyes were quite against this feminine involvement, this "sisterhood of the Temple" would survive well into the fourteenth century. They, like the rest of the men, followed the Cistercian rule. So whoever within the academic world believes that the Order of the Templars was just like any other military/religious order is depicting something that is quite unlike the historical records shows the order to be. Nothing follows the norm when we talk about Templarism, and it is about time that historians were aware that most people are well aware of this.

Part Two

CHAPTER 9

BETRAYED FOR THE SAKE OF A DEBT

By the beginning of the fourteenth century, the Order of the Knights Templar, although no longer in power in Jerusalem, held an unsurpassed amount of power over kings and governments. All owed the order money. The lands the order held within these various kingdoms could not be taxed, and the knights residing within the commanderies and preceptories of the order in Europe could not come under the various kings' laws. In fact, the knights Templar were a law unto themselves. Though they owned nothing as individuals, the wealth held in common, which could be seen by visiting monarchs, was staggering. The worth of gold, silver plates and cups secured within their walls, the financial revenues from their banking or from the lands they held, even the amount of horses and weapons the order possessed, was more than the kings of France had ever owned. It is known that by 1180 the knights Templar were masters to no less than eleven thousand commanderies. Over a period of fifty years, they had largely paid for the erection of sixty Cistercian abbeys (mostly those coming under the leadership of the abbots of Clairveaux) in Europe, each peopled by one hundred monks. To this was to be added the building cost of eighty cathedrals in Europe.

Moreover, together with the Cistercians, the Templars had transformed Europe into something that had never been seen before. Twelfth-century Europe experienced what I would call the birth of a new monetary economy. Unlike other religious institutions, who based their wealth upon farming, the Templars administered their estates with regards to yielding revenues in cash rather than the harvest that would derive from the land. Not that money had not been used in Europe before then. In fact, since the days of Charlemagne, the common European monetary unit used had been the silver penny (known as the denarius). This, however, would be replaced by new twelfth-century Templar mints to cater to the emerging concept of independently trading city-states.

Banking activities had already been established since the days of Pope Sylvester II and were by now firmly established in cities like Siena, Lucca and Florence. As such, to say that the Templars invented banking, as some previous writers have claimed, is rather far fetched. It would be more accurate to say that the Templars improved banking credit and payment techniques and by so doing increased the volume of money in circulation in the then known world.

In Palestine, the Templars monetary system was based on three different kind of currencies. The gold Arab dinars, which was their principal currency in the Middle East, the Byzantine hyperpera and the silver drachmas. It is this proficiency in currency dealing that made the order the foremost expert in all precious-metal economy. Add to this their mercantile posts in every ports and the fact that they owned their own fleet of ships, it is not surprising that each knights received their feudal income in cash—cash that they kept in their own banking houses.

By the end of the 1200s, the Templars were also the protectors of many trends of philosophy that the Roman Catholic Church had declared to be heretical. The principal groups they protected in Europe were the Albigensis, Cathars and Bogomils. The church of the Albigensis and Cathars was mentioned as far back as 1020 by Raoul Glaber, a monk from Burgundy, who was based in Orleans. He is rather scathing about them and claims that, as well as worshipping the devil, they held secret orgies whereby any children born from that union were burned to death and their ashes ingested. (Raoul, if anything, had rather a sick mind.) This sudden rise in the Languedoc of this not-so-new faith took place during the immediate aftermath of the fall of the Umayyad empire of Cordoba, when the pro-Catholic kings of the Asturias were gaining some ground on the now-fragmented enclave of the Islamic world in Europe. That the Cathars were powerful is in no doubt. The Duke of Aquitaine, William IX, protected them and most of the southern French nobility very quickly joined their rank. The Cathars formed a group of protesters against the corruption of the Roman clergy and its lack of toleration towards both Muslims and Jews.

The confessor of Constance of Provence, third Rex Deus queen of Robert I of France, was actually a priest of the Cathar Church, a church well organized, well supported and well established in the South of France. Rome took fright and called for a crusade against this sect of heretics. Robert I, second Capetian king of a dynasty still struggling to establish itself in the eyes of the papacy, was called to act by the papacy and had the fourteen principal heads of the Cathar Church arrested. Following a mock trial, all except for one, who recanted, were convicted to be burnt to death proclaiming their faith. The first

Cathar martyrs died. Later, in 1119, the Roman council of Toulouse ordered, in vain, that the secular powers assist the ecclesiastical authority in quelling the heresy. A subsequent pope, Innocent III (1198-1216) tried to force Raymond VI of Toulouse to put down what the pope called an infectious disease. This ended in disaster, with the papal legate murdered, some believe, on the order of Raymond himself.

So why were these people seen as incarnation of the devil on earth? Their faith was based upon, among other traditions, the ideology of Manicheism, which believed in the concept of dualism. In fact, St. Augustine of Hippo (AD 354 to 430) had been a member of the Church of Manes in North Africa before abjuring it in order to become a Catholic. From then on, Augustine became a fanatic and the sworn enemy of Manicheism.

History claims that the roots of the Cathars can be traced from the eighth century Paulician sect first founded in Armenia. In the ninth century AD, the Paulicians penetrated the confines of Europe, particularly the Balkans area, where they became known as the Bogomils, the translation of which means "friends of God." From Bulgaria, they travelled to the north of Italy where they were known as "Patarins," and then to France, to the town of Albi, which then became their principal fief. The Languedoc thus became privy to a new tradition. Or did it?

I have my doubts as regards to a Paulician link with the Cathars. However, a direct link with a trend of Islamic/Judaic belief from Cordoba, where many faiths flourished and evolved together over three centuries of tolerance, makes much more sense. Also, since the counts of Toulouse held their territory from the caliphs of Cordoba, resettling in the Languedoc would be perfectly natural. Moreover, "friends of God" can also be translated as "Cele Dei," a remnant of the Scottish Celtic Church who had evangelized all over Europe, including in Islamic Spain.

In Greek, "catharos" means "pure," and that is precisely what the members of the Cathar Church, known as "perfects," called their leaders. Their priests, who wore black and proclaimed the ideology of charity, usually traveled in pairs and preached the concept that the world as we know it was merely a battlefield between good and evil. Mankind, physically that is, is part of evil. The spiritual soul of each individual, however, belongs to that divine light, which, through constant transmigration, helps the physical towards a liberation of the carnal need to reproduce. In other words, good always wins over evil. Tolerant of other faith, these "pure" priests observed an asceticism few could follow.

Their baptism was simple but effective and took place not in churches but in the homes of those who wished to become perfects. After the individual was enlightened on the tradition, effect and spiritual nature of the baptism he or she was about to receive, and the hard work expected from the said individual, the individual was asked the question "Do you have the will to receive this holy baptism of Jesus Christ under the form revealed and given to you, to keep it for the whole of your life with purity of heart and spirit, and never to fail its expectations no matter the reason?"

The first phase of initiation within the Cathar Church started with the recitation of a prayer called "Pater." Within their tradition, this prayer was that recited by the angels before their fall from grace. Fallen angels had lost the will to recite this prayer, and so the recitation of it by Cathars perfect and pure was the first step towards these angels' reintegration into their original spiritual world. Again we are faced with a concept of an Essene concept of angel-Christology.

The second phase was then that of baptism, with the Cathar priest holding over the individual's head the book of the Gospels (opened at the Gospel according to St. John), while the perfects, one after the other, held their right hand over it. Why St. John? Simply because the Jesus of St. John is understood to be based on the prophetic, and because of the fact that St. John was one of the very few who had interpreted the true meaning of Jesus' initiatory rites. To the Cathars and the initiated church, St. John is solely concerned with Christology as a direct witness to the meaning of Jesus' works. Within the whole, the symbolic aspect of death and rebirth was also enacted. The Cathar emblem, a white dove, is still to be seen within the arms of the town of Toulouse. (The dove, the emblem of the Celtic Church stolen by Rome to represent the Holy Spirit. The dove, a spiritual Muslim emblem denoting the universal soul of mankind.) Like their fellow Muslims, Cathars refer to Jesus as "the prophet of God, the sign of God and the servant of God," in the same manner as the Koran refers to him. The disciples of Jesus were referred to as "the helpers unto God."

Nothing remains today of the Cathar religion in the Languedoc. The Cathar Church has been totally eradicated through a crusade the papacy called against it. Genocide, big-time genocide, over several centuries, made sure of its disappearance. We have, of course, archeological vestiges of its ancient and wise passage in time. The "spoulgas," or natural caves, actually used by the Cathars as places of refuge and as their temple are still to be seen today. That of Ornolac is particularly interesting because there the Cathars carved a pentagon into the wall. Walking backwards, one can actually step into it and thus find oneself representing the symbol of Hermes Trismegitus. Within the Cathar tradition, this was referred to as "the cross of life." This was also the way they portrayed Christ upon a cross, not crucified, as per the Roman Catholic dogma, but rather within an esoteric concept. The number of caves amount to over forty and all of them are similarly orientated, axed towards the magnetic North Pole where many ancient religious traditions claimed a "king of light" had come from.

Montsegur, long before it became their last place of defense before falling to the army of the papacy in 1244, had a hidden secret in its architecture. An astronomer could easily point out at various time of the year the exact position of the sun rising in the horizon. In fact, exact measures from twelve different points within the structure of the castle were taken and proved that the rising of the sun and its entry within each sign of the zodiac could be calculated with total precision. Montsegur is both religious and astronomical in concept, just like Stonehenge in England and Callanish in Scotland. Within the name of "Montsegur" can be found the Celtic root "egu," meaning "sun," and one can find vestiges of megalithic structures of sun worship. The belief in "spiritual light" was the very tenet followed by both Manicheism and Catharism.

This religious and astronomical architecture can be found in most Cathar castles, as demonstrated in the castle of Queribus. Queribus's principal cylindrical pillar is offset by seventy centimeters towards the southeast, so that its base can be precisely orientated to the four cardinal points. A small vaulted room adjacent to it was built upon a plan showing, only on the winter solstice, the rising sun fitting perfectly within the square window facing it. Queribus is a solar calendar that works only one day a year, the day of the resurrection of the sun, the day when Christians celebrate the birth of Jesus Christ, the day of Mithras.

The Templar order never fought the Cathars. Historically, the Templars protected them and were privy to their rituals and beliefs. It is understood that many Templars were also perfects and that the church of the Cathars was a recognized branch of the Templar church. On being required by the pope to speak against them in 1147, Bernard de Clairveaux does so only half-heartedly. In fact, following rather one very mild speech, unusual for one of the greatest religious and political leaders of his day, Bernard retired to bed, claiming to be unwell. For a while, this one major individual within the hierarchy of the Catholic Church was left alone, forgotten by his peers, and traveled from one Templar commandery in the south of France to another, meeting some very strange people. Two in particular, Isaac the Blind and Joseph Gikatilla, met with Bernard de Clairveaux within the county of Montpellier, and both had their roots with the ancient caliphate of the then defunct Islamic kingdom of Cordoba. So the influx from that part of the world is obvious. Bernard not only met key figures in the Cathar hierarchy, he listened to them, worked with them, and created a new religious concept that would become acceptable to all, a kind of West meets East. Rome, of course, was unaware of this new development. This is when Bernard required the pope to issue a new bull, allowing excommunicates, thieves and other undesirables to join the Templars. This move made sure that the Cathar Church survived, that its traditions and beliefs would add to the Templars hidden paths and strengthen the order.

This was also when a new architecture was added to Cistercian abbey, the square walk, often referred to as "the cross-road of the winds" and the "rhythmic walking path." The very same had been practiced within the Sufic schools in Spain and was linked with the paths of the cabala. Bernard was behaving, to say the least, very much like a heretic himself. There is, however, the fact that for a period of eight years, from 1145 to 1153, the papacy was held by one of Bernard's Cistercian colleague, Eugenius III, originally born Bernard de Paganell, whose family had been involved within the art of alchemy for years. Eugenius' call against the Cathars was hardly taken seriously. Bernard has literally a free hand and could do what he wanted. This link will help the Order of the Temple of Solomon, following the loss of Jerusalem in 1187, to secure a stronghold in the South of France.

Over the years, the Templars reformed the finances of Europe by improving Pope Sylvester II's banking system and introducing the letter of credit, which had been used by Middle East bankers for generations. It is a historical fact that one could put money in, say, a Templar commandery in Scotland, get a receipt, and travel to anywhere in Europe or the crusader kingdoms of Jerusalem, Tripoli, Antioch or Edessa. On arrival to his or her destination, the individual would then present the said note and retrieve from whatever Templar commandery the very amount that he or she had originally paid in Scotland, less the actual expenses of the trip.

The Templars set up the basis of the insurance company by allowing families, from the lowest to the highest, to pay the order a yearly sum. This sum was different from one individual family to another and related to the family's social circumstances, so that, should its circumstances change for the worst, the order would support them. Anyone excommunicated, no matter his or her station, could be sure to receive communion once a year by a Templar priest, usually at Easter so as to keep the requirement of observing "Easter duties." Most of the cathedrals in the West were designed and paid for with Templar cash and erected by Masons, together with their apprentices, and bricklayers linked through the "*Confrerie Templieres de Francs Metiers*" to the order. These confreries had the right to hold a general assembly to discuss matters pertaining to their particular trades. Only members could attend.

By the beginning of the fourteenth century, the master of the knights Templar counted no less than fifteen thousand knights proper and an overall two hundred and sixty thousand souls under his wing. The lands for which he was responsible amounted to no less than 10 million hectares in the then known world. The order, till 1307, was the richest, the most successful, and biggest corporation that ever lived on the face of this planet. By the beginning of the fourteenth century, it was also considered, by some, to be the most feared and the most despised organization in Christendom. By then, it had defied popes and kings, had betrayed Christian princes by allying itself with Islamic potentates, betrayed some of those as well and altogether had played some against the others. What the order actually introduced in Europe was high-caliber politics that none but itself could master. Theirs were long-term policies that would be curbed from time to time following analysis of the known world stage as it changed.

Within their ranks stood alchemists, theologians, scholars, mystics (of the western and eastern persuasions), guild apprentices, mercenaries and excommunicates (which the order was given the right to enroll by papal bull), and thousands of monks. Among the order's hierarchy were those who prayed, the Cistercians; those who built, the operative masons (four hundred of them per cathedral built) with their apprentices and companions; and those who fought, the militant monks, the knights Templars themselves. They, in turn, were composed of knights proper, sergeants, ecuyers (squires) and servants. They would fight on behalf of kings but only if they saw a political expedient for the order and the royal family of Jerusalem (in reality that of Tripoli). Jerusalem was regained by Islam in 1244, when the Templars then moved to Acre, which fell, in turn, to Islam in 1291, after which the Templars moved to Cyprus. It was not just the crusader kingdoms that were fighting for their survival.

By the beginning of the fourteenth century, Scotland was in turmoil over the claim of suzerainty put forward by the English king Edward I, while the king of France, Philippe IV le Bel, was in debt to the order to the tune of over one million livres. Philippe was a bad debtor and, notwithstanding the fact that he did not have the way clear to pay the debt, did not wish to repay it anyway. The only way out for Philippe was to eradicate the order totally within the confines of his kingdom and to persuade his brother kings and the papacy to do likewise. From 1305, a plot was devised by the king and his financial minister, Enguerrand de Marigny, to do just that. It almost worked out as Philippe thought it would, just not quite as expected.

The twenty-fourth master of the order was, at the beginning of the fourteenth century, Jacques de Molay. He was the son of Jean de Longvy (buried in the Church of St. Jacques de Doles, in Franche Comte) and the daughter and heiress of Mathe de Rahon. Molay itself, in terms of the property name, is situated in the diocese of Besancon, France. Around the year 1265, Jacques became a knight Templar at Beaune, becoming later a prior and finally succeeding as master in 1298. During the baptism of one of king Philippe IV of France's son, prince Robert (born after 1295), Jacques de Molay acted as the boy's godfather. In other word, not only was Jacques de Molay extremely well connected family wise, but his standing with the king of France, prior his becoming Master of the order, was also on a sure footing. But in 1298, all this would change when the responsibility of running the sovereignty of the order fell upon him. Each of the previous masters had been of the Rex Deus families. Out of the twenty-four Masters, twenty-two were French, one was Italian and another one was a Syrian Christian. All were related to each other.

Master	Years Ruled
1. Hugues de Payens	1118–1139
2. Robert de Craon	1139–1147
3. Eberhard des Barres	1147–1151
4. Bernard de Tremelay	1151–1154
5. Bertrand de Blanchefort	1154–1169
6. Philippe de Naplouse	1169–1171
7. Odon de St. Amand	1171–1180
8. Arnould de Torogo	1180–1185
9. Jehan Thierry	1185–1187
10. Gerard de Riderford	1187–1191
11. Robert de Sable	1191–1196
12. Gilbert Roral d Eralie	1196–1201
13. Philippe du Plessis	1201–1217
14. Guillaume de Chartres	1217–1218
15. Pierre de Montagu	1218–1229
16. Arnold de Grospierre	1229–1237
17. Armand de Perigord	1237–1244
18. Guillaume de Rochefort	1244–1247
19. Guillaume de Sonnac	1247–1250
20. Renaud de Vichy	1250–1257
21. Thomas de Beraud	1257–1274
22. Guillaume de Beaujeu	1274–1291
23. Theobaldo Gaudini	1291–1298
24. Jacques de Molay	1298–1314

There had been many moves, not least from the quarters of the papacy, to reduce the power of the Templars. In 1291, the Synod of Salzburg wanted to unite the various orders of the Templars, Teutons and Hospitallers into one body. Pope Nicholas IV died before a decision was reached on the matter, and the Templars' sovereignty was saved. But everyone knew that the days of chivalric bodies, as known in those days, were numbered. In effect, the Templars and the Catholic Church had parted company a long time before, during the Magistry of Pierre de Montagu, who ruled the order from 1218 to

1229. The new patriarch was not a member of the "family" and de Montagu declined to recognize his authority and, by so doing, he thus declined to recognize the authority that Pope Honorius III held over the order. Pope Alexander III, who ruled from 1159 to 1181, had the order censured at the Lateran council held in 1179 for weakening episcopal authority, burying excommunicates and improperly admitting them to the sacraments of the church, as well as receiving private churches from lay persons. The papacy had finally come to understand that it had a monster in its own cloisters. Both bishops and popes were feeling antagonized, as the order eroded their powers, and legally at that. Previous papal bulls gave them those rights and helped the order to grow into its own hybrid of Christianity.

Years later, Etienne de Sissi, the order's great marshall, would be excommunicated by Pope Urban IV (1261–1264) for his support in a total break away from the papacy. The order simply took arms against the pope and declared war on the papacy. Urban, it is said, died of fright. His successor, Clement IV, dutifully absolved the Great Marshall and the order resumed its usual business. In fact, as early as 1154, complaints from successive Latin patriarchs ended on successive popes' desks. In 1279, the king of Portugal stood against the Templars, as had done Emperor Frederic II of the Holy Roman Empire. The latter fought the Templars when they took arms against the prince of Antioch and sacked Thessalonica and the Peleponese and pillaged Athens. However, all Frederic II had confiscated from the Templars was returned to them by order of Pope Gregory IX. The might of the order was felt by all at all times and places.

However, without the support of the papacy, France's king Philippe IV could not achieve the order's destruction, and his standing within that particular quarter was none too high anyway. He had fallen out with Pope Boniface VIII, who had claimed authority over all kings. Philippe, enraged on hearing this, sent troops to Rome, intending to have the pope brought to him in chains. Boniface's humiliation was so complete that he died of shock on October 11, 1303. His successor, Benedict XI, died on July 7, 1304. There would be no pope to succeed to him for eleven months, till June 5, 1305, when Bishop Bertrand de Got, French by birth, was finally elected and crowned in Lyon. By then, Philippe had astutely put the exceedingly good-looking daughter of the Comte de Viane in the lap of Bertrand, now Pope Clement V, who fell head over heels for the girl. So much so that he established the papacy in Avignon, France, where it was to remain for seventy-three years, which are referred to as "the Babylonian Captivity." A further six popes of French nationality would succeed to Clement V, supporting French policies.

There is no doubt that Bertrand de Got was elected pope due to the support he got from Philippe, and one of the main reason for Philippe's support had been a written extraction from Bertrand that said he would help the king of France destroy the Order of the Templars. In fact, Philippe says so in a letter he wrote to the Comte de Flanders. Having the pope in his pocket, the plan of Enguerrand de Marigny could then be put into action. Marigny's plan was twofold and dated as far back as 1300. Time is what gave the game away. Originally, the plan had been devised by a Norman lawyer by the name of Pierre Dubois. Suppressing the order was, to him, of paramount importance since it would give Philippe of France the right to plunder the French Templar treasury. The capture of Constantinople, to be ruled by Prince Charles de Valois, also came into this plan, as did Philippe being proclaimed "Bellator Rex" of Jerusalem. Phase one was to remove the Jews, all of them, from France, by force if need be. This was de Marigny's idea. Their goods, their money and their assets were confiscated in the king's name and for the king's coffers. What Philippe forgot was that, as far as the Order of the Templars was concerned, those diaspora Jews were subject to the titular king of Jerusalem, then the king of Cyprus.

While Henry II de Lusignan, king of Cyprus, gave little thought about Philippe's move on his exiled Jewish community, Henry's brother, Amaury, certainly saw it as a threat, so much so that the brothers fell out. The order definitely took Amaury's side in the argument, but had to consider the fact that Cyprus was now their only base in the East. But there is no doubt that Philippe's move was noted and the political repercussions dissected. In the early months of 1306, Jacques de Molay, then in Cyprus, and the master of the order of St. John of Jerusalem, received a letter from Pope Clement V inviting them to join him and the king of France at Poitiers on June 6. The letter asserts that they were to advise the pope with regards to sending aid to King Leo of Armenia and the king of Cyprus and to discuss the recent idea of a union between the two orders. It also required de Molay to bring only a nominal amount of knights. Jacques' reaction is to send two separate memeranda to Pope Clement. The first dealt with the proposal of a new crusade and the second dealt, at length, with reasons not to unite the two orders (which the master of the Hospitallers readily agreed that it would do both institutions no good). De Molay also put together a fleet of ten ships and sailed to La Rochelle, bringing with him money that he thought the king wanted to borrow from the order. The sum, in gold bullion, was astronomical and, following his arrival in Paris, was housed in the treasury chambers of the temple. The master of the Order of St. John also came with his own fleet to the port of Marseille.

Few historians have ever realized that to sail from Cyprus to La Rochelle, the latter admittedly a Templar port, makes no sense. These ships should have sailed to Marseilles rather than make their way through the pillars of Hercules, both sides of which were then still in the hands of the Moors. But, again, few historians, save again Frenchman Jacques Rolland, ever mention the fact that the relations between Jacques de Molay and the Muslim hierarchy in Baghdad, Cairo and Jerusalem were extremely cordial. Imagine, the year is 1298, and Jacques de Molay, then based at the only remaining Templar castle in the East, that of Ruad (situated on an island two miles off the coast from Tortosa), together with an army consisting of merely two thousand Templars, enters Jerusalem which, under the terms of a Templar/Muslim treaty, he has held for no less than three years. At that time, the master of the order, Theobaldo Gaudini, dies in Cyprus. De Molay simply leaves Jerusalem, makes his way through Palestine to the port of Tyre, crosses to Cyprus, where he is elected master of the order, and makes the return trip to Jerusalem without being stopped at any point by the Islamic hierarchy, be it Turkish, Saracens or any other Arab followers. Not till 1301 would de Molay and his two thousand Templars leave Jerusalem and travel, unmolested, back to Cyprus.

While it makes no sense for a Christian fleet to travel through Islamic territories, it makes perfect sense if it has a treaty of nonaggression. As a port, La Rochelle is, of course, a safer haven than Marseilles, since from La Rochelle, which the order owns outright, one can flee to kingdoms where the rule of Rome is still not all powerful.

Coming to France, the Templar master realized that something was afoot, but as for rumors of betrayal, Jacques de Molay simply ignored and laughed at them. The father of his godson would never dare. Further, the wrath of the pope would fall upon Philippe. Not everyone was convinced. Knights were sent out of Paris to various commanderies and preceptories. The money that de Molay had brought with him was sent back to the fleet, kept in readiness, just in case. Moreover, the knights Hospitallers kept the same arrangements and were seen to leave France on the very same night as the Templar fleet. The only thing that was left in the treasury room of the Temple in Paris was the king's treasury that was housed in the building, nothing more, nothing less.

Obviously, the plan did not remain secret from the Templar hierarchy in France. James II of Aragon knew about it from Christian Spinola of Genea, who told him, "I understand, however, that the pope and the king (of France) are doing this for the money (of the Temple), and because they wish to make of the Hospital, the Temple and all other military orders one united Order, of which the king wishes and intends to make one of his sons the king. The Temple, however, stood out strongly against these proposals and would not consent to them." Jehan de Clinchamp, lord of la Buzardiere, also became privy of the king's plan against the order through his chaplain.

At the manor of la Buzardiere, several knights Templar friends of the family, were spending some time and were told of the plan that was being fomented by Philippe IV against their order. Pierre d'Aumont, Gui de Montanor, Gaston de la Pierre Phoebus, Pierre le bon de Lombardie, Richard l'Anglois (a member of the English commandery), Yves Lancel de l'Ysle, Louis de Grimoard, Pierre Yorilck de Riveault, Cesar Minvielle and Jean Marie de Senectaire, together with their servants, galloped their way back to Paris and informed the Templar hierarchy of the plot against the order. Clearly, something was done, since the Templar fleet and many knights, on the eve of Friday, October 13, 1307, sailed away to better and safer ports from La Rochelle. Interestingly, the Hospitallers fleet sailed away from Marseille, master included, on the same night. Also, for those doubting Thomases, in the archives of the Vatican are lists of Templars who fled before the arrival of the king's guards. This alone proves that the papal ploy had failed and that most Templars were able to escape before they could be apprehended.

In the early hours of Friday, October 13, 1307, seventy-two Templars, of which fourteen knights were Templar, including the master of the order, three priests, twenty serving brothers and others unidentified, were arrested in Paris and throughout France on charges of heresy. Clement V, influenced by the king of France, ordered all Christian rulers to arrest all Templars on their territory, and instructed the inquisition to extract confessions from the knights through the use of torture. Their detractors, a Frenchman and an Italian, were two ex-Templars who had been expelled from the order. At once, Philippe IV found himself faced with the fact that not all in France were willing to obey him.

In Metz, the authorities neither got confessions from the knights, nor were the knights harmed in any way. In Nismes, nothing could be proved against them. The cities of Boulogne and Ravennes actually absolved them. In Brittany and Provence alone, although the knights insisted on their innocence, would they be condemned to death. In Paris, one hundred and forty knights, including de Molay, would be accused of every sin under the sun. One hundred and thirty-two witnesses appeared against them, of which forty were ex-Templars who had been expulsed for bringing disrepute against the order. The Templars were allowed, for their legal defense, the use of two priests of the order, Freres Renauld d'Orleans and Pierre de Boulogne. The judicial know-how was provided by Renauld de Pruyn, Guillaume de Chambonnet, Bertrand de Sartiges, Guillaume de Foux, Jean de Montreal, Matthieu de Cresson, Essart, Jean de St. Leonard and Guillaume de Guirissac.

The charges that they suddenly had to answer were divided into three very distinct criteria. The first stated that the members denied Christ, God, the Virgin, or the saints during a secret ceremony. The second that the members committed a variety of sacrilegious acts on the cross or the image of Christ.

The third stated that the members practiced obscene kisses. It did not stop there. Further charges were laid to the Templars door, such as that the members encouraged and permitted the practice of sodomy, that the priests of the order did not consecrate the Host, that the members did not believe in the sacraments, that the Templars practiced various sorts of idolatry and that the master, or other dignitaries, absolved brethren from their sins. Altogether, the number of charges amounted to a staggering 177.

Thirteen knights admitted to the charges against them but later recanted. fifty-four were burned to death behind the abbey of St. Antoine in Paris. Others were sent to Benedictine cloisters where they ended their days as unwilling monks. But what to do with de Molay was still a dilemma. On October 16, 1311, the Council of Vienne, to which no less than 300 members of the clergy had been invited but to which a mere 114 took part, started proceedings against various individuals belonging to the Order of the Temple of Solomon. It is during this council that the papacy dissolved the order "not by law but by provision." On August 14, 1312, the council decided that the possession of the order should pass into the hands of the Hospitallers.

Finally, on March 11, 1314, during the hours of Vespers, Jacques de Molay, master of the order, Geoffrey de Charny, preceptor of Normandy, Hugues de Peyraud and Mahaut d'Auvergnes, were burnt to death, together, in Paris. Of those four people, as of the other fifty-four who died by fire, nothing would be left. In fact, the remains of their bones were pulverized into powder and their ashes were simply thrown into the River Seine. Yet within the history of Freemasonry, particularly that of Sweden, the belief of an actual grave for Jacques de Molay persists. All previous masters had been buried outside France, first in Jerusalem and then, following Jerusalem's fall to the Muslims, in Acre. finally, when Acre fell to Islam, in Cyprus. Jacques de Molay is the only master to have died on mainland Europe. Today, a plaque, by the side of Notre Dame's cathedral, commemorates the death of Jacques de Molay and his colleagues.

Among the many charges against them, one claimed that the Knights Templar worshiped a head. The inquisitors made quite a play of it when they extracted under torture so many "facts" under their obscene way of providing evidence. The ordinary knights were never really privy to the ritualistic goings on that was performed by the top Templar hierarchy. The notion, however, that the head of Baphomet was that of either John the Baptist or that of Christ (or of any other male individual) must be put firmly into the realms of fantasy and wishful thinking by some misguided writers. The word is merely a coded one from a cryptographic system that had been used by the Essenic/Nazorean Church to disguise theological concepts or names of individuals. This cryptographic system had been earlier on used by those who wrote the scrolls found at Qumram. Subsequently, the system was decoded by Dr. Hugh Schonfield.

According to Dr. Schonfield in his 1984 book *Essene Odyssey*, the word "Baphomet" when decoded translates as "Sophia," which is the Greek equivalent for the Judaic name of "wisdom." Wisdom has always been religiously related to the female aspect of the godhead. The head was thus a physical reminder that though the order came under the aegis of the male dominated Roman Pauline Christian orthodoxy, it nevertheless acknowledged that wisdom came from the female aspect of the deity, that which had been worshiped long before an all male form of worship had raised its ugly head. Wisdom is referred in Genesis as "she who flies over the waves of the waters."

In effect, this one piece of information made the order more of a Gnostic body than a Roman Catholic–related one. The Templars would have been termed heretics, and this was the basis for the dissolution of the order. It also proves that they followed Judaic/Hellenistic and Islamic thoughts rather than Christian ones. Wisdom, within the frame of Judaic belief, is feminine. The "word," as in John's Gospel, is definitely masculine. Wisdom, whether you call it Sophia, Mary Magdalene, Helen, Cybela, Athena and so on, finds its roots with Isis, herself an emanation of the old Sumerian goddess Inanna. The entire concept is Essenic and has roots with a school of thought set up by Tuthmosis III of the Egyptian Eighteenth Dynasty, from which both the royal house of Judaea and the hereditary high priests of Jerusalem were descended via both Akhenaten and Smenkhare. As protagonists of the god Aten, hence Adon, as in Adonai, that is to say "The Lord," they both lost power over Egypt and ended up in exile. Their descendants would rule over Israel as the Judaic kings from which both Jesus and John the Baptist could trace a direct ancestry. For those interested in linguistics, it is a fact that the Egyptian sound T changes to that of D in Hebrew. The Egyptian sound E becomes an O sound in Hebrew.

The Gnostic concept is kept going within the order when one finds out about the order's particular use of iconography. It used the crescent moon of Islam on many of its seals. This symbol has, of course, many meanings. On the one hand, it is a female attribute of virginity as well as pregnancy and birthing. Further, the Islamic calendar is a lunar one, the word "luna" being feminine. It represents both Artemis and Isis. In Islam, it symbolizes simultaneously openness and concentration, referring to the victory of eternal life over death. Even some Islamic countries used a "red" crescent, reminiscent of the red cross of the Templar order.

The order also used the emblem of the lion. Some historians think that the lion represented England (never mind the fact that the heraldic symbol of England is three leopards, while that of Scotland is the lion), but in fact it relates the order to both the sun and the old royal house of Judaea. The lion also represents the rising and the setting of the sun, east and west, yesterday and today, and, of course, it is an astrological symbol. Within the iconography of the Templars, the feminine and masculine, the crescent and lion, are used, and reflecting the fact that the Templars' understanding of religion was quite unlike that taught by the dogmatic and narrow-minded Church of Rome. Also, notice that the order never used the Catholic cross, but rather the lamb and the fish, the earlier symbols of Christianity that were changed by Rome to a cross showing Christ crucified. The Templars also had their own icon of Christ, which might have been what is now known as the shroud of Turin.

Did the Templars reject Christ as a deity as one of the charges against them claims? Hugues de Payens, first master of the order, was of both Christian and Muslim origins. He is descended from both a brother of Christ, the Shadow of God, and Muhammad, the Seal of the Prophets. Moreover, the order had, among its archives, proofs that both Christ had not died on the cross and that St. Peter was not buried in Rome. All successive masters of the Temple, including Jacques de Molay, belonged to a wider genealogical family that had the same origin with that of the first master. Considering these facts, the deification of Christ must have been one concept they would have, secretly, rejected.

Was the inner hierarchy of the order masters of alchemy? Their immediate early links with the Moors of Spain, together with the Sufis, Nusayris and the Assassins in the Middle East can only show that many esoteric and hermetic works and ideals would have been available to them. This is how they were able to introduce the concept of beneficial windows that negated ultraviolet rays as the light enters their cathedrals. Their first workshops producing this new kind of glass were first based at Citeaux and St. Denis in France and were originally run by Persian alchemists. Were they the masters of those masons who built their new style cathedrals? The answer to that one can only be a resounding yes since it is the Order of the Knights Templar who gave that workforce its rule. But it is a workforce that was first trained in Jerusalem and by no less than a Muslim one. No one else in the known world could work stone and wood like a Muslim mason. A trip to Cordoba will prove that simple historical fact.

Did they perform homosexual acts? We are on shaky grounds here. This was, in the main, an all-male-dominated military order. Homosexuality has always been practiced within the army (though this would be strongly denied by our military leaders, even today), but it has many levels: that which is practiced physically and that which is practiced mentally (the latter concept is accepted by the Roman Catholic Church). The rape of women was often avoided during the aftermath of battle with soldiers that preferred their own male company to that of the female sex. In the Middle East, certainly in those days, homosexuality was common, almost expected. In Europe, it was referred to as the "Greek" vice. Poetry, both Greek and Arabic, was written about it, and it certainly was not seen as either obscene or against nature. That does not mean that I believe that the Templars were homosexuals—simply that some, merely by the nature of the thing, may have been.

There is, however, the fact that the esoteric members of the order practiced sexual magic as based on the Gnostic writings of Epiphanes, bishop of Constantia in AD 370. At age eighteen, Epiphanes moved to Alexandria, in Egypt, where he came in contact with a Gnostic group of sabyrite known as Barbelites. Among many of its rituals, this unconventional Christian sect practiced group sex, the women collecting the ejaculating sperm of men in their hands, which they then raised to the sky saying, "We offer you this gift, the body of Christ." When women were menstruating, the men would collect the blood and offer it as "the blood of Christ." It was, in the true antique rituals of Eleusis, Cybela and Attis, a carnal communion.

As Gnostics, the Templars were also aware of the secret gospel of Thomas and the mention of a bridal chamber and sexual initiation. The Roman Catholic Church, since the days of the second-century theologian Clement of Alexandria, associated sexual intercourse with guilt and argued that it could only be justified by the obvious need to reproduce. Clement even believed that the human soul fled the body during a sexual climax. St. Augustine concluded that the male semen contained the new life and transmitted Adam's original sin from generation to generation, a concept totally rejected by the Celtic Church. As such, the Roman Christian Church considered that sex for pleasure or as a ritual for magic was nothing else than satanic practices.

In fact, this charge was not a new one. Previously, two popes mention, by letter, to the Templar master of France that they were rather put out by these practices within the order. Innocent III (1198–1216), writing to the grand visitor of the order, said, "The crimes of your brothers pain us deeply by the scandal that they provoke in the Church. The knights Templar practice the doctrines of Satan." Gregory IX (1227–1241) mentions the fact that he knew that the Templars practiced the act of homosexuality and occult sexual magic under a secret new rule established by Roncelin de Fos (later master of Tortosa and Syria) in 1240. This new rule was written in a Templar book known as "the book of baptismal by fire." Interestingly, Roncelin de Fos was married to Mabile d'Agout, with whom he had four children.

Was the order heretical in nature by the standards set by the papacy? The answer must be "guilty as charged," but only in the eyes of the church, not that of the Templars.

What transpired, however, during these seven years of hell for the French Templars is that few of them were actually put on trial and murdered than originally believed. This can be seen in the archives, now in Paris, that deal with the trials. Though extensive, the archives deal time and time again with knights going from one trial, admitting the charges, recanting and being tried all over again till the inevitable is done to them—death by burning. This is what happened to 638 of them, not the thousands as claimed by various historians.

There is also the fact that, in view of the matter that Templar properties did not come under the laws of the kings of France and so did not come under the French land tax register. It is a mistake to believe that the French authorities knew where these hundreds of commanderies were situated throughout France. And the secret archives of the Vatican do have lists of Templars who escaped. So what happened to the rest of them?

Chapter 10

Scotland

a Kingdom in Need
and a Safe Haven

The end of the thirteenth and the beginning of the fourteenth centuries were years of upheavals for Scotland, years when dynastic successions were engendering an opening for Edward I to assault Scotland in his territorial wish to own it. Alexander III of the Scots had died in 1286. His two sons had predeceased him, and his only surviving grandchild was a girl, Margaret, the daughter of Eric II of Norway and of Margaret, Lady of Scotland. In 1290, Margaret, Queen of Scots, died on her way to her ancestral kingdom when reaching the Orkneys. Scotland was without a monarch, a situation it could ill afford with England ruled by the territorially obsessed Edward I. Guardians were elected to look after Scotland while a council looked into the succession problem. There would be altogether thirteen claimants, the number of which would then be reduced down to two names: John Balliol, who owned one third of the lordship of Galloway, and Robert Bruce, referred to as "the Competitor," who owned the lordship of Annandale. Both were lawfully descended from Prince David, Earl of Huntingdon, through his daughters. Bruce, years before, had already been chosen heir presumptive by Alexander II, but this decision had been discarded following the birth of Alexander's son, the late Alexander III. The Scottish council was in a bit of a quandary.

Bishop Fraser of Glasgow, God only knows why, decided to send a delegation to London, to Edward I, in order to ask his opinion on the matter. Edward I at once sent an army north, entered Scotland and required that all fortresses should be handed over to him. As for the succession matter, he had brought with him the best brains that English law could muster and declared, by the way, that whoever was to succeed to the Scots throne would do so under him and was expected to swear an oath of fealty to Edward I.

In 1292, John Balliol, whose wife and Edward I shared the same great grandmother, succeeded under Edward I, to whom he gave his oath of fealty. What Edward I had extracted from Scotland was fresh troops whenever needed and, of course, food. By 1295, Scotland could and would no longer afford Edward's arrogance, and John I of Scotland had allied himself with Edward's enemy, Philippe IV of France, with the signing of a mutual treaty of military help to one another. The "Auld Alliance" between Scotland and France had been born and would last till the year 1906. It would prove the longest treaty ever practiced between two nations on this planet and would be the bane of England for centuries.

By 1296, Balliol had abdicated, though Edward would claim to have deposed him. Balliol was held in the Tower of London for a while and then was sent to France, where he would die in 1318. Edward I, once more in charge of Scotland, believed that all things would go back to normal. He was in for a surprise and a disappointment. Within months, Scotland was whispering the name of a Scotsman who had just come back from France where he had learned the craft of warfare at the court of Philip IV. The name was that of William Wallace, younger son of Malcolm, Lord of Ellerslie in Ayrshire and Auchinbothie in Renfrewshire. Further, the male members of the Wallace family had been knights of the household of the lord high stewards of Scotland, Stewarts by name, and Sir James Stewart, high steward of Scotland, was one of the regents of Scotland in the first and now second interregnum. Moreover, the high stewards, on successive generations, had endowed the Order of the Knights Templar with an incredible amount of land since 1128 onwards. Sir James, within the later Scottish and French Masonic traditions, was considered a Templar master, if not the Templar master for Scotland.

Walter fitzAlan, first high steward (*Dapifer Regis Scotia*) was a benefactor of the Templar order in Scotland. He founded the Cluniac Priory of Paisley in 1164, an order that, like that of the Cistercian, had separated from the Benedictines. His son, Alan, had followed Richard the Lionheart to Jerusalem. Alan's son, Walter, third high steward, raised Paisley Priory into an abbey. Alexander, Walter's son and successor, was also a crusader. When Alexander married Jean of Bute and Arran, of the line of Somerled of the Isles, the lands engulfing the Cistercian Abbey of Saddel, situated on the Mull of Kintyre on the west coast of Scotland, came within the Stewart family. Alexander's son and successor, Sir James Stewart, fifth high steward, had supported the claim of Robert Bruce, the Competitor, from day one. William Wallace was a knight of his household. We know that in 1295, Jacques de Molay acted as godfather to Prince Robert of France. The court was invited to the baptismal proceeding. William Wallace, a household knight of a Templar Scottish family, would have attended. A discussion between the knights and Wallace would have been of the norm. In fact, Wallace's way of fighting the English forces of Edward I in Scotland were based on Middle Eastern tactics of hit and run, proving that he was aware and privy to the Templars various ways of fighting. Indeed, we must recall that Wallace was a trained knight when he came back to Scotland.

It is now that most historians miss the point in this interesting part of Scotland's most fascinating history. Most of them will tell you that Wallace acted all by himself. That, however, cannot have been the case. Wallace's loyalty lay with the most prominent family of the land, the Stewarts. This family held the coffers of the exchequer of Scotland and owned a piece of Scotland that could only be acceded from the sea, Saddel Abbey, then a Cistercian monastery, and thus belonging to the Order of the Knights Templar. Wallace's loyalty totally lay with pro-French Sir James Stewart, fifth lord high steward of Scotland, co-regent and guardian of the realm of Scotland and supporter of the Bruce's claim to the crown of Scotland. While William Wallace's name is absent from those on the Ragman Roll of August 1296, that piece of paper by which all signatories gave allegiance to Edward I, that of Sir James can be found on it. Sir James Stewart, as co-regent and guardian, greatly believed that the Auld Alliance treaty had to survive at all cost and would have been privy to English policies and movements in Scotland. Information could easily have been past on to Wallace, who would accordingly have acted upon them.

What is not generally known is that all the major protagonists, Balliol, Bruce, Stewart, John Comyn and Wallace, even Sir Andrew de Moravia (Moray) were related to one another. They are all cousins. Wallace has a direct relationship to the high steward of Scotland via his mother, who was descended from the Boyd family, a scion of the Stewart dynasty, and had an extra link to the Stewarts via the de Craufurd of Crosbie family. Sir Andrew Moray, a military colleague of Wallace, is himself the nephew of John Comyn. Family connection was an important part of Scottish life, and no upstart would have been given the right to lead an armed force.

The battle of Stirling Bridge, which Wallace and de Moray's army won in 1297, gained Wallace both a place on the regency council as well as the title of guardian of Scotland. This can only be seen as the culmination of a well-orchestrated plan that can only have been engineered, Templar style, by the Bishop Wishart, Bishop William Lamberton of St. Andrews, and Sir James Stewart. This organized resistance movement would be the root of Scottish nationalism that would culminate in the Scots voting in 1997, seven hundred years later to the day, for the reinstatement of a Scottish parliament in Edinburgh. The strangest thing yet is that Scotland, when Wallace was made guardian, was held in name on behalf of John Balliol. Stranger still was the fact that none of the regents and guardians made any move to bring Balliol back to Scotland. Balliol, by then, was in France and residing on papal property. Even more incredible is the fact that Wallace, who in 1299 traveled to France and to Rome, avoided meeting Balliol altogether (despite what some writers have written on the matter) and never brought up the subject of Balliol's kingship with Pope Boniface VIII at all. Although the kingdom was held on Balliol's behalf in theory, the truth is that, in practice, Scotland was held by Bishops Wishart and Lamberton for Robert Bruce, then Earl of Carrick and grandson of the Competitor, who had died in 1294.

The reason that the young Earl of Carrick could not be brought forward just yet was simply because his father and namesake, the Lord of Annandale, was still alive and was a ward of Edward I. While Annandale was alive, Carrick, even had he been proclaimed king of Scots, could still have been blackmailed by Edward I with Annandale's life. Robert Bruce's crossing between the Scottish and English camps was not one of expediency, it was merely due to his being brought to the Plantagenet heel whenever he overreached himself when fighting for Scotland. Few people are aware, for example, Bruce's grandfather, the day following Balliol's recognition as king by Edward I, resigned both his lordship of Annandale and his claim to the Scottish crown to his son, Robert Bruce's father. Two days following his succession being read in parliament, which was sponsored by Sir James Stewart, high steward of Scotland, Robert Bruce's father resigned all his titles and rights to the Scottish crown in favor of his son. Again, Sir James Stewart is involved in the proceedings of transfer.

The year of 1305 was to be a crucial year. Actor Mel Gibson will be remembered forever for shouting "freedom" in his epic film *Braveheart* and for his wonderful performance of William Wallace. As the film depicts, Wallace was hanged, disemboweled and castrated; his heart taken out of his chest while he was still breathing, and finally he was beheaded. His head was set on a spike on London Gate while the various pieces of his body were sent to various towns throughout Scotland. If Edward thought to teach the Scots a lesson, he got one himself. This action inflamed the rebellious spirit of Scotland even more. Their hero, in the prime of his life, had been cut to pieces, and none north of the border would take this national slight lying down. With Wallace out of the picture, his place had to be filled in by the man that Wallace had asked many times to make his bid for the crown. Robert Bruce, Earl of Carrick, whose father had finally died in 1304, could officially enter the scene and succeed Wallace.

As soon as his father had died, Bruce had signed the bond of Cambuskenneth with Bishop William Lamberton of St. Andrews. From that year, Wallace, who had taken a step backwards in favor of Bruce, together with the Scottish clergy and several magnates were backing, openly, the rights of the Earl of Carrick to succeed to the crown of Scotland. Nevertheless, Bruce needed the backing of one man, Sir John Comyn, whose claim to the crown was just as good as his. A deal, somehow, had to be reached. A meeting was arranged to take place on February 10, 1306, within the holy precinct of the Church of the Friars Minor in Dumfries. Whatever happened, Bruce ended up committing the most sacrilegious act on holy ground. He drew his dirk and dispatched Sir John Comyn to his death. The church stood within the diocese of Bishop Wishart, and he simply forgave the act committed by Bruce.

On Friday, March 25, of the same year, Bishops Lamberton and Wishart, together with the earls of Atholl, Lennox, Menteith and Mar, crowned Robert Bruce king of Scots at Scone. He went through a second coronation ritual on Palm Sunday when Isabella of fife, sister to the Earl of fife (the traditional crowner), then in London, and wife of the pro-English Earl of Buchan, deposited a circlet of gold upon Robert I's head. It was said that the coronation took place with the full consent of the entire community of the realm. Truth be told, Bruce's position had been hailed by only 135 landed gentlemen, 42 hailing from south of the Forth and the Clyde, most of them from the southwest. Only fifteen were from the Borders, and none at all were from the Lothians. The rest of Bruce's support came from the Highlands and the islands—quite surprising when one realizes that Bruce's Celtic blood was pretty thin.

And what of his army and the financial assistance, which he would suddenly gain after the death of Edward I in July 1307? That inauspicious year, Bruce had been a "king in the heather" for over a year, and the Templars in France were arrested and put to trial. Scotland, her nation, clergy and her king had been excommunicated a year earlier by Pope Clement V, previously Bertrand de Got, archbishop of Bordeaux, a city then under the control of the English King Edward I. We have here a pope stretched between two kings, Edward I of England and Philippe IV of France, who are enemies to one another (yet related by the marriage of their children, Edward, Prince of Wales, and Isabella of France).

In 1307, the Templar fleet at La Rochelle suddenly, in the middle of the night, on Friday, October 13, set sail and divides in three sections. The first section sails to Portugal, the second back to Cyprus, the third, possibly the most important, carrying the order's archives and the Temple of Paris's treasury, sets sail for the one kingdom that is facing the wrath of Pope Clement. Under the leadership of Pierre d'Aumont, it sails for Scotland, for the Mull of Kintyre and the Cistercian abbey of Saddel—the Cistercians who are the order's spiritual leaders. Saddel could only be reached by sea in those days. There the fleet rests, lies low, and recoups, and the knights Templar in Scotland regroup. They also get in touch with the excommunicated king of Scots, Robert Bruce. This, these knights Templars are perfectly entitled to do.

The order may be in trouble, but it is not yet under interdict, nor has it yet been suspended. An excommunicated king is not a problem for them to deal with since they can, through an earlier papal bull granted to them, engage excommunicates as knights Templars.

It is interesting to note that the Scottish clergy also ignored the papal whim of excommunication. Marriage, baptism and burial rituals, including holy communion, are being performed in a country where no such things should be taking place. But with the Templar/Cistercian equation, we have to remember that Scotland has a clergy that can function outside a bull of excommunication. It is also an equation that, in any case, being a sovereign entity outside the laws of the kingdoms of Europe, can step in and literally take charge. There was nothing more to stop the order throwing its might behind the one man and the one kingdom that had given them a safe asylum. By the end of 1308, two thirds of Scotland would be under the control of Robert Bruce.

Survival of the Fittest

Scotland, the northern tip of Europe, was the most ancient kingdom in western Christendom. Its royal family was older than Christianity itself and was a kingdom where the Templars owned a great amount of land, providing the order with a yearly revenue of no less than 30,000 merks (equivalent to £20,000, a fortune in those days). The order owned a port on the West Coast, then administered by the Cistercian monks of Saddel Abbey. It owned lands in the principal port of Leith, in the shire of Edinburgh, in the constabulary of Haddington, in the shires of Stirling, Peebles, Lanark, Annandale, Dumfries, Kincardine, Linlithgow, Aberdeen and Banff, in the county of fife and in the Stewartry of Kirkcubright. It was the single largest landowner in Scotland, where it owned no less than 550 properties. In 1308, the knights Templar in England were arrested and their lands confiscated in favor of the crown. In 1309, Bishop William Lamberton of St. Andrews, within the precincts of the Augustinian abbey of Holyrood, questioned two Templars, both Englishmen and the only two that could be found in the kingdom, and declared them innocent of all charges.

There is something fundamentally obscene with historians obstinately telling us that the Templar support that Robert Bruce gained from 1307 is nothing more than wishful thinking. The fact speaks for itself. The largest estate in Scotland could hardly be administered by a mere two people. For once and for all, let us be quite plain about this. A large contingent of knights Templar came to Scotland to escape the wrath of the king of France and a French pope. Just as it had helped the Count of Portugal by marriage, Henri of Burgundy, consolidate a kingdom for himself in 1094 under the leadership of Hugues de Payens, the Templars, coming to Scotland under the leadership of Pierre d'Aumont in 1307, did the same for Robert Bruce.

Without the Templar support, the tenants on Templar lands could not have joined the army of either Wallace or Bruce. The lack of documentation proving this is not a problem. The order's political activities were always played secretly, and its objectives were always reached through secret treaties. Further, the Roman Catholic hierarchy has always admitted that Templarism survived in Scotland after 1312 to evolve, many years later, into a Masonic entity. Indeed, the *Catholic Dictionary* of 1884 is quite emphatic on the subject of Freemasonry. It states that "the suppressed order of the Knights Templars, too, has been taken to have been the source of the sect; and this theory may have some countenance in the facts that a number of the knights in Scotland illicitly maintained their order after the suppression, and that it was from Scotland that Freemasonry was brought into France at the beginning of the last century."

Roman Catholicism is superb at keeping its historical records, even those secret ones. Few people are aware that the Vatican, in its archives and secret archives departments, is in possession of documentation that is no longer extant in the various kingdoms and republics of Europe. All entries of baptism, marriage and death were originally duplicated and sent to Rome, every year. Political-analysis reports were sent to Rome by the bishops to keep the papacy abreast of what was going on in the confines of Christian Europe. We know that Bishop Lamberton of St. Andrews kept in constant contact with the papacy in order to improve the papal relation with Robert Bruce and sway the papacy in his favor. So who were the knights in charge and why did they come to Scotland at all? Indeed, what was so special about the Scottish royal family?

Quite simply, Bruce, Scotland's patriot and warrior king, was a member of the family that once upon a time ruled over the crusader kingdom of Jerusalem. Hugues de Payens visited the Scottish court in 1128 and had been entertained by David I and his wife Maud of Huntingdon. She is the link that brought the Scottish royal family into the Templar equation from day one. Most historians have Maud as an Englishwoman, the richest heiress of England and the heiress of Northumbria. That she was those things is quite correct. But she was not so much English as she was Flemish. She was Godefroid of Bouillon's full cousin. She was of the Davidic dynasty more than anything else. Related to both Godefroid and Maud were Seir de Seton and Walter de Lindsey (now Lindsay) whose descendants would become knights Templars, together with members of the Sinclair family. With her marriage to David, then prince of Strathclyde, later to succeed his brother as king of Scots, trades with Flanders, and particularly with Brugges, became opened to Scotland. Scotland became part of a family trading monopoly that would sway between western Europe and the Middle East, the Baltics, even Russia.

Brugges' maritime trading ally was Venice, and the Venetian fleet was partly loaned from the Templar one, which was the largest single fleet in Christendom. It can thus be said that the order had a port not just in La Rochelle, which the order owned, but in Cyprus and Venice, in Brugges, and in fife, Leith and Saddel in Scotland. Even during the reign of Alexander III, Scotland had been a refuge for the royal family of Jerusalem in exile. In fact, Alexander's widowed mother, Marie de Coucy, had married Jean de Brienne, titular king of Jerusalem, following the death of her husband in 1249. The link between Scotland and the crusader kingdom went back a long way.

As for the Templar fleet that came to Scotland in 1307, it was lead by a Templar knight by the name of Pierre d'Aumont. The bay into which the fleet sailed, and site of Saddel Abbey, was ideally situated. Saddel was far away from the prying eyes of the English king and was part of the vast territorial ownership of Sir James Stewart, high steward of Scotland. From Saddel Abbey, the fleet could sail to and from the Scottish mainland, to lands that were within the ownership of Stewart. In 1312, the knights convened a meeting and elected Pierre d'Aumont to be in charge of their contingent until Jacques de Molay could be freed from Philip IV of France and the clutches of the Catholic inquisition. Following de Molay's death in 1314, they reconvened, and in 1315 d'Aumont was elected master of the Templar group residing in the excommunicated kingdom of the Scots.

From Saddel, the Templar fleet could also sail to Ireland, where the Templars were endeavoring to establish Edward Bruce, younger brother of Robert, as king. In this particular instance, the Templars would be successful. Edward Bruce died king of Ireland in 1318. From 1308 onwards, Ireland began to help Scotland by sending arms, paid for with Templar cash, and Scottish troops would be trained by Templar masters at arms. From then on, Bruce would go from strength to strength. By 1312, most of Scotland had been regained from the English and incursions into northern England were taking place. Rather than see their cities destroyed by fire, the bishop of Durham advised everyone to give in to Bruce's terms. They were to pay 2,000 merks, in installments, for a truce that would last till Midsummer's Day of 1313. When Cumberland failed to pay, it was ravaged by a Scottish army led by Edward Bruce in April 1314.

On St. John's Day, June 24, 1314, three months following the death of Jacques de Molay in Paris, Edward II's army met Bruce's troops on the battlefield of Bannockburn. The might of the English army, by far superior in strength and number, was humiliatingly defeated by Scotland's smaller one. Near the end of the confrontation, a contingent of some hundreds of mounted soldiers appeared out of nowhere and charged against the might of Edward II. Edward, on seeing this new military force fighting for the Scots, wearing the emblem of the red cross pate, and carrying the black and white banner of Beauseceant, fled the scene. That army was the brothers of those knights he had had arrested in 1308 and who now languished against their wish in English prisons and Benedictine monasteries, the members of the Templar order whose properties he had confiscated.

Scotland had finally regained its lost independence, Bruce was for once and for all king of Scots, and the Templars had rendered Scotland a favor that would never be forgotten. Moreover, the death of William Wallace had been avenged. Prior the battle, Walter Stewart, sixth high steward of Scotland, had been knighted. Surviving the 1314 battle, he married Bruce's daughter, Marjory, Lady of Scotland, that same year. Their son, Robert II, would succeed David II as king of Scots in 1370 and would be the founder of the Royal House of Stewart.

It is interesting to note that the Scottish relics brought onto the battlefield of Bannockburn and to which the Scottish army prayed to were not those of St. Andrew, the Roman Catholic patron saint of Scotland, but those of St. Columba, a Celtic saint with no links to the papacy. Worth remembering is the fact that the title of pope was actually stolen for the Roman Church hierarchy by St. Siricius in AD 384 from the Celtic Church in Ireland, which had a "papa" (Celtic for father) since its inception in Britain in the first century AD. Furthermore, the Celtic Church, as previously stated, was also connected to the Alexandrian and Syrian Christian churches, both of which were well known to Templars, and had chosen the Cistercian Order as its spiritual successor.

There is another proof that the Templars were active in Scotland at that time, and it lies with the cathedral of St. Andrews. After October 1307, cathedral building temporarily stopped in Europe. If one looks at the records in Europe, no major church building was erected for eleven years after that date. In fact, all work stopped save in one country, Scotland. It took 150 years to build the cathedral of St. Andrews, and even during the wars of independence work went on, regardless of the political situation. In 1318, the cathedral was finally finished and consecrated; Bishop Lamberton officiated the service, even though the king, the clergy and the nation were still under interdict of excommunication, which would not be lifted till 1323. It is also a historical fact that most, if not all, of the stonemasons belonged to the "*Confreries Templieres de Francs Metiers.*" They were part of the 260,000 souls coming under the aegis of the late Jacques de Molay as master of the Order of the Temple of Solomon. This applied to bricklayers, compagnons and apprentices as well. The records, throughout Europe, show that the building of a cathedral took no less than 400 stonemasons plus their companions and apprentices.

Once a year, this confrerie would meet to discuss business, the plans and designs of new buildings, and the rate of pay. The expenditure providing the site for a religious building, be it a priory, a church, an abbey or cathedral, fell upon a land donation from a magnate. The buying of material, quarried stones, wood and so forth, would land on the burgesses, while the lodgings for the workforce would fall upon the church. The salaries of the workforce, on the other hand, was always taken care by the Templar treasury. In eleven years, between 1307 and 1318, nothing of a spiritual nature in stone was either built or even finished in Europe. Only the Cathedral of St. Andrews in Scotland was finished and consecrated in 1318. It is a significant fact of history totally ignored by historians.

But there is more. In 1317, a remnant group of Templars traveled from Scotland to Avignon under the guise of "The Elder Brethren of the Order of the Rosy Cross" and met with Pope John XXII. This is exactly at the same time that two Templar orders (see chapter 11) were reconstituted in Spain and Portugal. The remnant Templars were received by the pope, who agreed to recognize this new order as long as his nephew could be grand master. The pope's nephew was readily accepted, only to die a few weeks later, thus putting the election of the next grand master of the order back into the hands of the Scottish contingent who traveled back home. In 1662, one of its satellite institutions would be the Royal Society (previously working towards the Stewart restoration of Charles II under the guise of the "Invisible College"). It was led by Viscount Brouncker, its first president; Robert Hooke, its first curator; and King Charles II, its first hereditary royal patron. In 1318, six months after St. Andrews Cathedral was consecrated, Robert Bruce held a parliament at Scone that was, to say the least, very much avant-garde. This parliament was well ahead of its time. It was aimed at curbing the might of the papacy and the advantage that the Order of St. John, the Hospitallers, which had fought in the army of Edward II at Bannockburn, was gaining over the Templers all over Europe. The Scottish parliament passed various acts "for the honour of God and Holy Mother Church, the amendment of the land and the defense of the people." An excommunicated clergy has no right to adjudicate on Roman Catholic Church matters, but Bishop Lamberton ignored all the rules. His clergy, we must deduce, must be above the laws of the papacy. Having granted the Scottish church parliamentary statutes for its protection, this parliament went on regulating ordinances to establish equality for all Scots before the law. It then laid down legal procedure to which all had to conform, regulated a strict control of Scotland's fishing industry and the conduct of Scotland's armed forces. The most important bill was that which forbade the export of both money and goods outside Scotland. It kept the Hospitallers, who had fought for Edward I and Edward II against the the Scots, at bay and made sure that Templar revenues could never be used to favor, through the Order of St. John or the territorial greed of England.

CHAPTER 11

SECRET TEMPLARS AND HIDDEN ORDERS

When historians claim that the Order of the Temple of Solomon does not exist today, that is not altogether true. There are many Templar orders in Europe recognized by both states and the Catholic Church. Moreover, they all follow the same Templar rule, and all, certainly in theory if not so much in practice, owe their allegiance still to the Cistercian Order of Citeaux. Furthermore, it is a mistake to believe that Templar knights were not allowed to survive the events of 1312. Clement V actually tried to make some kind of reparation when he published his bull "Considerantes dudum" on May 6, 1312. He decided that Templar leaders would come under papal judgement, but the ordinary brothers would be judged by provincial councils. These councils delivered, as a whole, very lenient decisions. Those Templars who were found innocent or who willingly submitted to the rule of the church were allowed to reside on former Templar properties, from which they would draw a pension.

As such, Templar knights were still living in Aragon in their own houses in reasonably large groups till the mid-fourteenth century. Twelve former Templars were drawing pensions in England till 1338 (by which time, presumably, they died). Up to 1350, Beranger dez Coll was still living at the preceptory of Ma Deu in the Roussillon. So for over thirty-seven years, the irder survived in a contained, underground existence. Templars commanders who survived 1307's royal and papal onslaught on their order founded various orders. So under which guises did these Templars make sure that the order would function within Europe to this day? The records are quite emphatic and very explicit.

In Portugal, the Order of Christ suddenly made its appearance in 1317 and had as its first grand master a former Templar commander by the name of Don Giles Martinez. It would follow the old Templar rule that Bernard de

Clairveaux had originally given to Hugues de Payens and would be under the protection of the crown of Portugal. Having gained that protection, it was also recognized by Pope John XXII. All original Templar lands came under the tenure of the new Order of Christ. Until 1522, its grand masters were elected from within the membership, but it was then decided to invest the royal house of Portugal with the grand magistry of the order in perpetuity. In effect, it became the national order of Portugal and would admit only Portuguese nationals. The ritual of knighting individuals was based upon the same ritual used till the demise of Jacques de Molay. So this is one order, though under another name, which was set up by Templars who had survived and regrouped after 1307.

What of Aragon and Castile? (Spain was still a divided territory under the kings of Aragon, Castile and Navarre, notwithstanding the Islamic city-states still surviving in Spain.) Let us deal with Aragon and the Order of Callatrava. King Jaime II of Aragon had always disliked the idea of an order set within the confines of his kingdom but owing allegiance to a grand magistry situated in Castile. This was the case with the Order of Callatrava. By 1317, Jaime II founded the Order of Our Lady of Monteza, choosing as its first grand master a former knight Templar by the name of Guillaume Erilli. Again, the very same Templar rule of Bernard de Clairveaux was officially adopted by this new order, which answered only to the abbot of Citeaux. Again, all former Templar lands came under the authority of the new order's grand master. During the reign of King Felipe V, the grand masters became officially the succeeding kings of Spain. In Castile, several knights joined the Order of Callatrava, but, in the main, decided to join their Muslim brothers down south and became, overnight, *Fatas* (Muslim knights).

With France, we enter a difficult phase in Templar history. The only thing that we have stating that the order survived under a true Templar leadership is the Larmenius Charter. which claims the magistry passed from Jacques de Molay to one Jehan Marc Larmenius of Jerusalem. Larmenius, who is referred as grand master in the charter, is believed to have received his magistry from de Molay in 1313. There is, obviously, a problem with this, inasmuch that Jacques de Molay was very much alive in 1313, though in prison and half starved. Further, the order never had had grand masters, only "masters" of the Temple. It could not have been until after the last master's death in 1314 that a a new master could have been chosen. Some believe that the Larmenius succession was spurious and an elaborate fraud. The debate still goes on about it, mostly because the charter was written in a cipher based on designs said to relate to the cross pate.

I do believe there is a case for fraud since, in the charter, Larmenius claims to have been elected by a "Supreme Council of Knights." But traditionally knights had no say in the election of a master; only a chapter of twelve brothers called in by the grand commander of the order could elect a master, and only at the death of the previous one. It is interesting to note that the Scots knights Templars are claimed to be schismatic by the Larmenius contingent. In matter of fact, the Larmenius contingent emphatically refused to have anything to do with the Scottish Templars. Indeed, Scotland's Templars are perceived by the Larmenius gang as being nothing less than upstarts. As Shakespeare says, "The lady doth protest too much, methinks."

I believe that the Larmenius "Order of the Temple" was no Templar order at all. It is nothing more than an elaborate eighteenth-century fabrication created by people desirous to gain power, political or financial, and using the order's history and name, thus gaining for itself both a pedigree and a certain kind of respect. Naturally, it never gained recognition from the papacy, nor would it ever use the Templar ritual of knighting, not being privy to what the ritual consisted of in the first place. Nor would it be acknowledged by the Order of Christ in Portugal, the Order of Our Lady on Monteza in Aragon, or the Order of the Elder Brethren of the Rosy Cross in Scotland, although all three of these orders were headed by former Templar commanders and used the Templar rule of 1128.

In 1705, this newly created Templar body gained ascendancy under the leadership of Prince Philippe, Duc d'Orleans. Succeeding as grand master, the duc reconstituted the order under the aegis of the French crown and with new statutes that were ratified at Versailles that year. This was a twist of history organized by the Jacobite movement in France in a bid to restore the Stewart monarchy, then in exile in Paris, and which would both follow and support their leadership over many generations.

Until 1941, the Larmenius succession was meticulously kept within a French hierarchy, when its magisterial archives were transferred from its Brussels headquarters in Belgium, which by then had been invaded by the German troops of Hitler, to Portugal and Switzerland, which were then neutral in the World War II conflict. Count Carlo de Souza Fontes, based in Oporto, acted till his death in the 1970s as "prince regent" of the order and was then succeeded by his son Fernando under the same title. Certainly, until then, its grand masters bore the best names of France and had even gained recognition from Emperor Napoleon III.

Interestingly, it was not till after World War I that this pseudo-Templar order started to branch out throughout Europe by creating national grand priories, including one in Great Britain after World War II. By 1978, the Larmenuis order had split into two separate grand priories of England and Scotland, when Francis Andrew Sherry, grand prior for Britain and a Scottish nationalist, decided to come back to Scotland. He rightly pointed out that Scotland, as an independent entity, needed to be catered for separately from England. The Grand Priory of the Chivalric Military Order of the Temple of Jerusalem was born.

From then on, under Sherry's leadership as grand prior of Scotland, the order's philosophy was pro-Scottish, very much nationalist and would draw its membership mainly from the Scottish Nationalist Party and those people with pro-Jacobite tendencies. By the mid-1980s, it became infiltrated by neo-Templars, members of a quite different group that dated back to Hitler's occult interest in the order. It became quickly obvious that the involvement of several individuals with the order was simply to plot the downfall and promote the concept of a restored Royal House of Stewart in Scotland within the order's membership. From 1978 till 1985, the order annually celebrated Bannockburn Day by laying a wreath and openly marching to commemorate those ancient brothers who had died in 1314 fighting on the side of Robert Bruce. Although never powerful, the order was seen as a committed organization whose interest was mainly historical, academic and literary, commemorating those battles upon which Scottish armies fought and either won or lost against the common enemy Scotland and France shared, England. Once a year, the order would award a medal to the "Scot of the Year" and hold a "Joan of Arc" dinner in the Glasgow City Chamber to celebrate the Auld Alliance between Scotland and France.

However, following internal struggle for the leadership, the order fell into disarray. It had also been infiltrated by pro-British establishment agent provocateurs. The order was said to be under close investigation by MI5 (the United Kingdom's security intelligence agency) during the heyday of the conservative government. Innuendoes and a whispering campaign of the worst kind made the members feel rather uncomfortable. The perpetrators were kicked out of the order, but for several weeks afterward, Grand Prior Francis Andrew Sherry received frightening phone calls in the early hours in the morning and threatening letters through the post. The stress would take its toll on the man that had reintroduced a Templar order in Scotland, and his health would soon decline to such an extent that he became paranoid that his life was actually in danger. Following a breakdown, senility set in, and Sherry ended his life within the walls of a closed psychiatric ward. The order soon became a shadow of its former self and has today split into various separate entities.

The situation was further exacerbated when, during the 1980s, Count Fernando de Souza Fontes started to use the prefix of "grand master," even though no election had ever taken placeand even though in the 1960s, his father, Count Carlo de Souza Fontes, had recognized Switzerland's Anton

Leuprecht as "chef mondial" ("world head") of the Larmenius order. Leuprecht had an interesting history. During World War II, one of his brothers was an archbishop of the Roman Catholic Church, while the other worked for the Nazi Party in Austria. Before he died in the early 1980s, Leuprecht decided to appoint Francis Sherry as his successor to the office of chef mondial. While I never met Leuprecht in the flesh, I met the younger Fontes in Edinburgh in 1983. (Actually, he and I are related, although distantly.) I soon found out, through private talks, that Fernando had a personal problem with Sherry taking over from Leuprecht. Fernando had hoped that the style and office that had been set up by his father would die out with Leuprecht, thus giving him, Fernando, full reins on the organization. Most of the priories, however, felt that Fernando was encroaching on their autonomy. The organization became schismatic in the extreme all over Europe, even in the United States, where it managed to gain some support from people believing that this order was the only true Templar order.

The other interesting note about the Larmenius succession is its insistence that it has no link whatsoever with Masonic organizations. It is, in essence, a chivalric entity and claims to draw nothing, either esoteric or ritualistic, from Freemasonry. This is where, of course, the Larmenius order fails in its understanding of Templar history. The Templars played a huge role in bringing into Europe an Islamic infrastructure that would modernize all those ancient kingdoms, where the original Order of the Temple of Solomon held sway. Moreover, when one talk about Templarism, one has to talk about Freemasonry, albeit a Freemasonry that was quite different from what it is today and that was definitely consolidated in Scotland after 1312.

Scotland is, of course, the key, the cornerstone, the kingdom where Templar knowledge, philosophy and politics would evolve into a secret service intended to look after the interest and safety of its royal family. It also perceived that the law of the land and the sovereignty of the Scottish nation and people would need to be safeguarded at all cost. It would help Bishop Lamberton and the abbot of Arbroath Abbey, Bernard de Linton, draw up Scotland's written constitution of 1320, better known as the Declaration of Arbroath, which would afterwards influence all eighteenth- and nineteenth-century constitutions in the Christian world, including that of the United States of America. Scottish exiles would later export the Scottish Templar concepts of "liberty, fraternity and equality under the law" to France, Italy, Portugal, Spain, Sweden, the Netherlands, the United States, Canada, Russia, Australia and New Zealand.

Despite Scotland's masonic achievement, few people are aware of the real roots of Freemasonry. All most people are told is that it started in 1717 when, out of the blue, England claimed for herself a grand lodge. This followed the advent of the House of Hanover and the decline in exile of the Royal House of Stewart. England's grand lodge would claim and gain ascendancy over all lodges worldwide. To believe the English claim is to accept a political abomination, and it can be quite easily refuted both on historical and philosophical grounds. Time, I think, for truth to prevail and for the soul to be enlightened.

Chapter 12

Let There Be Light

While the Order of the Templars in 1307 counted about 260,000 people, the number of actual knights amounted to about 15,000, including sergeants, squires and servants. Historically speaking, the European records clearly show that less than 2,000 were tried in 1307 and that most of them survived, save the few hundreds in France who were burned to death or left in their cells to die of old age. While the order lost its entire territories in Europe to the greed of the papacy, its kings and the Order of St. John, the membership it embraced is another matter.

The greater part of the Templar force was still in the Middle East and looking after the safety of Cyprus against the territorial advances of Turkey. This is a fact. In view of the Turkish threat to Cyprus, coupled with the problems it was also facing from maritime powers such as Venice and Genoa, Henri II was well aware that his power of this last bastion of the crusader kingdoms depended upon the support of Templar Knights. Henri, despite pressure from both France and the papacy, refused to entertain the idea of falling in with Philippe IV of France's plan. He refused to let the papal bull be read within the confines of his kingdom. Cyprus had been ceded to the Templars in 1191 before being ceded in turn to Guy de Lusignan in 1192 following his deposal as king of Jerusalem. Templar presence upon the soil of Cyprus had helped the de Lusignan family keep its hold over the kingship.

The Templar order and its fleet survived till Cyprus fell in 1489—177 years after the order's dissolution in 1312. So much for the sway of Philippe IV of France and Clement V in that part of the world. What happened to these Templars after the fall of Cyprus is a mystery. It may be, as some historians tend to think, that these Middle Eastern Templars finally joined the Order of St. John, then in Rhodes, but in view of the enmity between the two orders, I have my doubts. The mystery might, one day, be found in the archives of the Ottoman Empire and the reign of Sultan Beyezid II, "the Just." He may have made a deal with the Templars of the Middle East and integrated them within his imperial forces, which would, during the reign of his brother Selim I, "he Grim," conquer Syria, Palestine and Egypt, making the Ottomans supreme in the Arab world and wealthy as never before.

Templar philosophy was too deeply embedded into the lifestyle of western European society to be able to get rid of it. Portugal and Aragon saw to it that it would survive as mentioned earlier. Scotland would be the one country where Templarism would evolve in quite a separate entity than those countries' sovereign orders of Christ and Monteza.

Scotland, as a kingdom, has always been the exception within the monarchic concept of Europe. Its system of government was based on the cooperation between all concerned, the king, church, people, burgesses and barons. All depended upon one another. The king of Scots represented them all equally under the laws of the realm. Though, once upon a time, the understanding and regulating of those laws were of an oral nature, it was written down in statutes at the Parliament of Scone held on December 2, 1318, and finally confirmed and proclaimed for ever in the Declaration of Arbroath in 1320. The pope, then residing in Avignon, and all the rulers of Christendom were sent a copy of the declaration in order to be well appraised of the Scottish situation and its uniqueness.

While the Declaration of Arbroath is quoted galore in Scotland (since it is the *raison d'etre* of the little kingdom), no other people in Europe were told about it at the time of its publication. In fact, the entire paper was kept secret by the various kings and the pope it was sent to.

There are several reasons as to why this was done. The first was that serfdom had been re-established following the Templars demise, and the rule of kings was now firmly imposed upon society, which, for almost 200 years, had been exempt from it. Instead of the Scottish concept of equality under the law, Europe came under the abject absolutism of kingship to which all had to conform. Plus, in Scotland, the power of the papacy was more often than not defied. And unlike the rest of Europe, Scotland also had the remnants of a church, the Celtic Church, which once upon a time had held sway over that of Rome, and which was still functioning, albeit in a very minor way, in the days of Bruce and the successive Stewart kings. (Following the rise of reformation, it would then go underground when the last Celtic Abbot of Iona, John Mackinnon, died, sword in hand, in 1555.) All of these factors would make the kingdom of Scotland unlike any other in medieval Christendom.

Where does this leave the Order of the Temple of Solomon after 1314? According to most historians, the Order of St. John of Jerusalem inherited the properties of the Templars after 1312. This is not quite true. In France, the properties had been taken over by Philippe IV, and the Hospitallers had to buy these from Philippe's son, Louis X, for an astronomical sum. In England, Templar lands had been taken over by the crown. In Spain and Portugal, they had been regranted by their kings to newly founded Templar orders. The idea of the Hospitallers taking over all of Europe from the Templars can be thus dismissed as wishful thinking and historically incorrect. Further, the Templar workforce, the *Confreries Templieres de Francs Metiers* (masons, quarriers, wrights, carters, sledders, barrowmen, pioneers, boatmen, smiths, sawyers, slaters, plasterers, roughlayers, wallers, causewaymakers, carvers, painters, carpenters and glaziers), was still active and definitely not functioning under the Hospitallers.

And here comes the crunch. These confreries, under whose aegis the guilds would later be formed and recognized, with a structure borrowed from the Middle East and disseminated throughout Europe by the Order of the Knights Templar, were also given something else, something secret, something that made them unique in their own right. I am not just talking about the confrerie of masons, but all the others as well. They were given historical allegories that would add spices to their practical knowledge, some of which would mostly connect with the Old Testament and sometimes, though seldom, with the New Testament. Since most of these craftspeople traveled far and wide—basically sent throughout the Templar empire by the order—they all needed someway to recognize one another during their travel. Moreover, the hierarchy of the order had to recognize them too.

Actually, truth be told, these travelers collected data, news, gossip, any information that kings and potentates did not wish the Templars to be privy to. In other words, the confreries were the Templars' unofficial secret services. In order to pass on the collected information, special sayings would have been of the norm. Like the Templar order, the confreries held meetings which only their membership could attend. The opening and closing of the proceedings consisted of a ritual to which no one else was privy. Members discussed everything that related to their trades. New projects and failed ones, latest theories and new requirements, disciplines and the matter of salaries. Those who had cause for concern or cause for complaints could also make this known and an adequate solution found to solve the problems. Neither the church nor the kings had any say upon this workforce. Like the Templars, this vast group of people was out of their reach and became, to both authorities that saw them as nonconformists, something to crush, particularly in Europe. In 1326, fourteen years following the dissolution of the Templar order, Pope John XXII would excommunicate the members of its confreries. It was this very move that would see Templarism evolve into a masonic entity in Scotland.

For some odd reasons, the year 1326 is hardly ever mentioned by historians, despite the fact that it was, for Scotland, a momentous one. At Corbeil, King Charles IV of France and Robert Bruce of the Scots reiterated the 1295 treaty of military help between the two kingdoms. Bruce, now well established as the king of Scots and recognized by the pope, decided to have several new palaces built. Cardross, his new residence, would be fitted with windows of colored glass (something unheard of in fourteenth-century Scotland), decorated paneling and tapestries, the latest luxuries available. He then had another royal castle erected on a hill in Tarbet, in Argyllshire. He modernized and reinforced the old castles.

And who was doing the work? The Templar confreries, which were, once again, at a standstill in Europe due to their having been excommunicated. They could be found in Scotland, fully active and working on the king of Scots' behalf. Once again, one would find them in the peninsula of Kintyre. In 1326, Walter Stewart, high steward of Scotland, widower of Marjorie, Lady of Scotland, and son-in-law of Robert Bruce, died, leaving as his successor a boy of eleven. This child would then be proclaimed the heir presumptive of the kingdom, after the two-year-old Prince David Bruce. In 1326, Edward II found himself displaced by his estranged wife, Isabella of France, and her lover Mortimer, who took the power of the crown on behalf of her son, soon to become Edward III.

In 1326, in all probability, and certainly not before then as some historians have claimed, the Order of St. John and the remaining Templars became, in Scotland only, a combined entity. From then on, Templar properties would be administered by the Hospitallers preceptor of Torphichen, where the remaining knights Templar would take up residence in the tower designated "the Templar Tower." Those knights would, in succeeding charters granted to this new combined chivalric entity, be separately named. To those who may doubt this, it is interesting to note that all charters (issued in Latin) concerning the Order of St. John are made in fifteenth century Scotland to "the Knights of St. John of Jerusalem and the Brothers of the Order of the Temple of Jerusalem." The last royal charter using this phrase was signed in 1488 by King James IV. This particular state of affairs between these two orders only applied to Scotland. Nowhere else in Europe was the Order of St. John (the knights Hospitaller) referred to as being combined with that of the knights Templar. Scotland is the exception to the rule. By 1488, the preceptor of Torphichen was made a lord of the Scottish "Three Estates" under the title of Lord St. John and would vote on Scottish bills as the master of the Hospitallers and Templars in Scotland.

But what, then, of the confreries? What of the workforce engulfing these trading monopolies and upon which Europe had grown into a military power and a modernized Christendom of the West? What indeed? In Scotland, these Templars confreries were regularized under the crown, while being allowed to keep their distinct traditions and allowed to meet, as of old, once a year, under the leadership of a dean of guild from the early fourteenth century. This is a fact that is confirmed in *A Dictionary of Scottish History* by Robert S. Morpeth and the late Professor Gordon Donaldson. Further, the dean, head of the merchant guild, had his own court to which these guilds could take and settle their disputes. Incredibly, this entity would survive in Scotland until 1975 when the Labour Party abolished it. By then, its function was confined to superintending building operations, and it would be the precursor to the new planning authorities. Few people were aware of the long history this local council department had in Scotland. Certainly, none remember it now. It has long been forgotten in the struggle of bringing this Templar medieval organization to governmental conformity of Westminster and its blinkered political outlooks.

Which brings us to the fact that, in medieval days, there was more than one trend of masonry. Templar masonry was divided into three distinct branches. There were the Children of "Maitre Jacques" whose signature in Templar cathedrals was the oak leaf. They dealt specifically with pagan motifs and sculptures. The Children of Solomon, whose seal was the great seal of Solomon (actually a sun sign, the up-turned triangle depicting the triangle of the gods and the odd numbers one, three and five, while the down-turned triangle depicts the triangle of men and the numbers two, four and eight), dealt specifically with esoteric motives of Islamic and Judaic origins. finally, the Children of Father Soubise, whose signature was the companion's knot, dealt purely with Christian topography. While society today tends to think of Freemasonry as something that evolved from stonemasons through the introduction of nonoperative members into their organizations, that is not altogether the case.

What is true to say is that stonemasons, having a trade that would take them to the far confines of the kingdom, were better placed for their secrets and traditions to survive the ravages of time. While Scottish towns, villages and burghs would be invaded and burned to cinders by the armies of the succeeding kings of England till the days of Cromwell (from 1296 till the eighteenth century Scotland would be invaded by England some 84 times), masons would come and go through the kingdom, escaping the destruction brought by wars. There were always enough of masons to rebuild what had been desecrated.

One has to realize that being a stonemason was more than just being a stonecutter. Within the same criteria were to be found architects as well as sculptors. Most houses, today, are built like square boxes and have few artistic features of interest, but hundreds of years ago, architecture and stone cutting were applied from a certain geometric philosophy and artistic understanding. To build a castle, a town house, a priory, a church, a cathedral or a monastery, geometry and mathematics were put to good use. All buildings of a religious kind were constructed not merely to amplify the words spoken into them, but also to enhance the music that was sung into it. The windows particularly were extremely important. The rose windows, an Islamic inheritance that could be found in practically every religious buildings, would give those initiated into the esoteric aspect of religion all that could be understood from the Christian and all other current and past faiths, and the key to a particular truth. The glass embedded into these windows, colorful as it was, made sure that the ultraviolet (UV) rays of the sun could not enter the inside of the building.

In other words, Persian alchemical practices were used knowingly in the erection of places of worship to make the inside of the structure safe from the harmful molecular aspects from the outside world. But what's more, within the designs of the rose windows, with a circumference usually connected to the golden number of Pythagoras, can be seen the squaring of the circle, or rather the squarings of the circle, while showing, albeit veiled in Christian iconography, the Islamic numbers relating to Middle Eastern mysticism and the zodiac pantheon. The sites for these sacred Templar structures were specially chosen so that the energy forces at crossing ley lines could add to the spiritual adventure on entering the structure. Inside, the intricate carvings, rising into the air, showed beasts, flowers and plants, strange faces and gargoyles. These, together with the colored glass windows showing biblical scenes, were to teach a well-defined school of thoughts and a religious history that had little to do with Roman Catholicism. To the noninitiated, however, it would look as if it conformed to church dogmatic teachings.

In truth, all Templar cathedrals were built on special mathematical, hermetic, Pythagorean, Manichean, Judaic, cabalistic, occult, Persian, Egyptian and Celtic traditions. This is particularly the case with the Cathedral of Notre Dame in Paris. In addition to the fact that the whole edifice is built atop an underground chamber containing a megalithic standing stone some forty centuries old set at the crossing of tellurian current, the cathedral is offset to follow this beneficial current to 47 degrees northeast. Notre Dame, a purely Templar built cathedral, does not face the right way. Furthermore, the great square, which could be found at the crossing of the transept and the choir, was linked by its proportions to the king's chamber of the great pyramid of Cheops.

Add to this the dimension of the "rosace," or rose window, reaching almost thirteen meters in diameter, and you find yourself looking at the golden number of Pythagoras. Through the multicolored rosace, the divine and beneficial light, known as truth, would fall within these gothic spiritual sanctuaries, themselves built within an architecture that was aerodynamic, with "ogival" pointed arches. The architecture itself differed from that of gothic Christianity, being drawn from Middle Eastern designs, the church and cathedral towers superseding the minarets of Islamic mosques. Islamic architecture was adapted into a concept that would not offend the Christian mind. Church bells replaced the physical calling for worship. The whole edifice became an especially made garden to communicate with the divine—not God, mind you, but the divine—and the oratory was the laboratory where this could be achieved. Those who understood this, who gained the key to enlightenment, would soon find themselves in touch with Jewish cabalism and would soon come to understand the duality of this divinity. From then on, the female aspect of the divine would be restored within their lifestyle. Interestingly, though all guilds in Scotland choose a male saint to represent them, they also prayed to a female one. This was a requirement, the acceptable duality by Rome's standard, but those practicing guild members knew better and were much wiser.

CHAPTER 13

From Operative to Speculative

Stonemasons and lay people alike have been wondering for the past four centuries why people with no obvious link to the stonemasons' trade were allowed to join the various lodges that could be found in the major cities of Scotland from the late days of King James III. In order to find the answer, we have to look in the accounts of the lord high treasurer of Scotland and the Scottish records of the master masons and masters of works to the crown of Scotland. A list of names of the people in office will soon point out the one thing most of these masters had in common: a genealogical connection to Scotland's aristocracy.

To think of them as commoners would be quite wrong. Aristocrats held offices, which were purely administrative in purpose, as a way to keep the king aware of both the expenditure and how any of the particular building or repair projects were faring at any time. However, it wasn't only the king who was employing masons; the aristocracy also spent money on new projects. The one thing that English invasions provided Scots masons with was constant work. Whenever the English went home following one of their usual incursions (the last major invasion of Scotland that spread devastation to abbeys, castles and royal residence took place under Cromwell), masons would be called by both the king and the aristocracy to repair the damages.

Over the years of direct involvement with the masons, a move was made by the very people paying the bills to become, somehow, part of the craft. For many years, the aristocracy and the monarchy took a deep interest in the craft and the architecture of the new residence being built for them and the design of the various curves that would make their home unusual. This is when non-operative masonry, later referred to as "speculative Freemasonry," was introduced within an elitist system, which, till then, had been free from outside interference. Somehow, to have their patrons involved with their trade must have made sense to the operative masons of Scotland, and by the sixteenth century, the move to include patrons in the mason organizations was implemented. This, needless to say, gave rise to two an exchange of thoughts within these two very different hierarchies. One must understand that each of these sections of society was as old as the other, since both the arts of nobility and the crafts of masonry were hereditary, passing from father to son in both cases. If anything, this shared antiquity merely added spice to the idea of sharing knowledge that was so different to the norm.

By 1598, William Schaw, master of the king's works and as such in charge of all the masons in Scotland, produced the first draft of his new statutes for masons. A second draft was produced and ratified by King James VI a year later. Actually, the 1599 statutes were referred to as a constitution. This is, needless to say, a move of paramount importance within one of Scotland's most ancient institutions. For the Scots masons to gain a constitution, fully recognized by the crown, is indeed unique. Moreover, it gave the craft a new impetus, a focus that had been missing for some thirty years.

Few people are aware that following the exile of Mary, Queen of Scots, in England (where she died in 1587), building work in Scotland was, to say the least, rather restrained because of the austerity of the newly recognized state kirk of Scotland. Mary lost her throne in 1567, and her son, then thirteen months old, was not really able to take proper control of the kingdom till his marriage to Anne of Denmark in 1589. This means that an entire generation of masons was unable to practice its craft freely and creatively. The kirk prevailed on all things spiritual and temporal, and objected to any religious imagery in any kind of buildings being newly built. The Highlands had remained predominantly Catholic, but the Catholic Church did not prevail, and for many masons looking for worthwhile and challenging commission being unable to find work for a long time.

When John Knox, the leader of the reformation party, died in 1572 (James VI was only then six years of age), a move was made by the Catholic Church in Scotland to gain the ascendancy. The idea was to help James VI over a period of years to restrain the policies of the kirk over those of Parliament. The Presbyterian parliament, resentful of Catholicism (which had been declared "independent" from the pope in 1471 by King James III, did its best to counteract the Catholic party. The parliament truly overreached itself in 1592 when it sacked, but did not demolish, Roslin Chapel. This was the second church that the Presbyterians had tried to destroy; the small chapel at Scone was the first to be destroyed, on the order of John Knox.

James VI had, by then, been working behind the scenes and created the Scottish Episcopal Church, Catholic in essence but not Roman as such. It was

James who acknowledged, against the wishes of the kirk of Scotland, the style of bishop within this newly established religious institution. This, of course, meant new churches and new residences to house these Episcopelian priests and bishops needed to be built. Roslin Chapel, seemingly, is now an Episcopalian chapel where worship is still being practiced today. Which brings us to the Sinclair equation within the masonic persona of Scotland.

Again, it is William Schaw, James VI's master of works, who is involved with the proceedings. However, when reading the chart, now known as the Sinclair Charter, one thing is quite evident. There is no mention of the Sinclairs of Roslin being termed "hereditary grand masters" to the masons, as many books on the subject claim. What the charter does state, however, is that "the Lairds of Roslyn has ever been patrons and protectors of us and our privileges—like as our predecessors has abeyit and acknowledgit them as patrons and protectors." This takes us back when, years before, the various aristocrats were brought into the mason organizations as nonoperatives. The artisocrats were all "patrons and protectors" of the masons working for them, but none of them were "hereditary grand master" and could never be so without the king's consent. There are, of course, two Sinclair Charters, the second one having been written some thirty years following the one that was drafted by William Schaw. It is the second charter that most writers on Masonic subjects claim establishes the Sinclairs of Roslin as grand masters.

Again, all are mistaken in this belief for the charter states only that the masons of Scotland

> in the name of our hail brethren and craftsmen agree and consent that William Sinclair now of Roslin for himself and his heirs purchase and obtain at ye hands of our Sovereign Lord liberty freedom and jurisdiction upon us and our successors in all times coming as patrons and judges to us and the hail professors of our craft within this realm.

Note the word "purchase." In effect, what the masons had done was to vest the offices of master of works and master mason in a hereditary manner within one prominent Scottish family. What set the Sinclairs of Roslin apart was the chapel that William Sinclair, Earl of Orkney and Caithness, had commissioned to be built in 1446 at Roslin and which would prove to be the architectural apotheosis of Templar iconography and symbolism, together with Oriental and Celtic traditions, set in stone from floor to ceiling.

Roslin Chapel, originally dedicated to St. Matthew, is a small church, which, over the years, has become one the most renowned buildings in the Masonic world. Many writers have connected it to Freemasonry. To some, it is a reproduction of the Temple of Solomon, but this cannot be true. first, the four successive temples—the first built by Solomon, the second by Zerrubabel, the third by Onias IV in Heliopolis and, finally, the fourth by Herod the Great—were actually a vast conglomeration of buildings housing the high priest, his subordinate priests and the temple guard. Second, the gothic architecture used in Roslin Chapel would have been totally alien to the Jewish religious faith, which was required to keep its temple plain and free of "godly" images of any kind. Roslin Chapel has even been claimed to be a reproduction of the temple's "Holies of Holies," However, no one knows what the Jewish Holy of Holies looked like. Only the high priest and the king could view the very *raison d'etre* of the Jewish nation, and there has never been a description of the Holy of Holies anywhere. Thus, to most people, Roslin (which got a royal charter from King James II in 1456), remains a mystery.

The chapel was built due east to west at the top of a village that was itself built in the shape of a cross. From the very first step you take into the chapel, you quickly realize that the concept of life and death was of paramount importance in the first carvings. They start with the vine of life, and a line of foliage starts around the inside of the outside walls, emerging from the mouth of the head of a green man. What's more, these heads are not specifically European in look, but also Eastern and Asian. Incidentally, the north door was the one used by men to enter, while the south door was used by women, as the congregation was actually separated during the ceremony of the mass. You would not find seats in the days of Catholic Roslin, as all had to stand during any services. Only the lame had the right to sit on the stone seats around the walls (hence the old saying "weak to the walls").

Now for some interesting numerology. From the chapel's north view can be seen seven pinnacled buttresses, five of which have flying buttresses connected to the main choir. They appear to hold part of the weight of the building, but, in fact, they are purely decorative and hold no weight at all. At the springing of the roof, there are twenty-six shields, each alternating with a letter or a number and an engrailed cross. There are symbols of Tyler and sword before entering the north door, and equilateral spherical triangles with three gothic points above the south and north doors. The chapel is divided into five parts, namely the main choir, two aisles, a retro choir or Lady Chapel, and the lower or first part of the building. It was within that lower part that the masons originally carved the sculpted stones that can now be found adorning Roslin. Supporting the main choir are thirteen pillars, forming ten arches, five on either side. In the two aisles, north and south, the pillars on the outside walls are separated by architraves, which are built in nine hollow sections. Nine, of course, is the number referring to the angelic hierarchy of seraphim, cherubim, thrones, dominions, principalities, powers, virtues, angels and archangels.

To the left of the north door, one can find the carved depiction of the crucifixion, while to its right can be seen curtains being drawn opened for St.

Helen in the Holy Sepulchre, revealing the "Agnus Dei" or "Lamb of God" with a Templar cross in the middle. On the next architrave is a carving of a blind man and his dog. In the southeast corner, both the seven acts of mercy and the seven deadly sins are to be found. Next to these, we then find, written in the Lombard tongue, the saying "Wine is strong, a King is stronger, women are even stronger but truth conquers all."

Look up to the roof of the main choir, and you will see five separate sections, the first representing the creation of heaven with a sun, a moon, stars, guardian angels, Christ, a dove (for peace) and a cornucopia. The second section shows roses, meaning the love of Christ; roses are also understood to be a reference to the goddess Ishtar and her resurrecting son, Tammuz. The third section shows flowers open to the sun in adoration. The fourth section shows lilies for purity and the Virgin Mary.

Situated at the east side of the chapel, the retro choir has four separate altars dedicated to St. Matthew, St. Andrew, St. Peter and the Virgin (the latter being used by lepers). Look for the large pendant keystone, with the eight-pointed star of Bethlehem, around which is carved a representation of the expulsion and redemption from the Garden of Eden as well as the Madonna and child. The keystone also contains the "dance macabre" or dance of death, the first ever sculpted in stone in the world. Look at the east wall and you will see the fallen angel Lucifer ("Bringer of Light") hanging upside down. Look closer and you will see the death mask of Robert Bruce.

The three pillars refer to Wisdom (the master mason, represented by an Ionic column), Strength (the journeyman, a Doric column) and Beauty (the apprentice, a Corinthian column). The latter, being also known in Cistercian architecture as "Solomonic," was carved over a period of three to four years while the master was away to the continent (looking for better designs) by his apprentice. Seeing that the apprentice had surpassed the master, the latter lost his temper and hit him on the forehead with a mallet, killing him. The chapel had then to be reconsecrated (still showing the signs of it today with the cross of St. Julian in and out of the building) a second time. This murder at Roslin Chapel is commemorated in the third degree of Scottish Freemasonry. The apprentice pillar has eight serpents (a reference to the uroboros as a symbol of infinity, of eternal recurrence, of the descent of the spirit into the physical world, and as an alchemical symbol for change) carved at the bottom of the pillar with the vine of life coming out of their mouth. It also has four strands of foliage winding round in thirty-three segments each. There are no fruits on the vine, and it is said that the serpents have sucked all the goodness out of it, allowing it to grow in its purest form. Interestingly enough, the apprentice pillar detracts the attention from the real secret of the chapel. In other words, the pillar is no more than a beautifully carved decoy placed there to make it harder to decipher the visual riddles. Carved among this section of the chapel are a number of musicians with their instruments—the lute, bagpipe, fiddle, mandolin and flute—and little square boxes, hanging from the ceiling, each denote a particular musical note.

Roslin is not so much a mystery as the history of Scotland, of a family, of a connection with past and contemporary faiths encoded into stone by the last Templar masons before they became engulfed under the authority of the crown. Look at the architectural cross section of the chapel, and you will be faced with the Dome of the Rock as depicted upon many Templar seals, including that of the grand master. Look up to the roof and you will see the starry firmament, as you would see it in the Templar chapel of Montsaunes, in Provence, though the latter shows stars with eight branches instead of five, as in Roslin. Interestingly, you will find the same starry firmament and the same pentagram stars connected with the afterlife of Osiris within the Great Pyramid of Unas.

Everything, when it comes to iconography, has a meaning, and the pentagram star has connection with many faiths. To Pythagoras, it was the perfect number of man the microcosm. He explained it as being the unification of two plus three, by which is meant the symbol of marriage and synthesis. It is the number representing the five senses of sight, hearing, touch, taste and smell (the microcosm), while pertaining to the five elements of ether, fire, air, water and earth (the macrocosmic). To the Christians, it was seen as the symbol relating to the five wounds of Christ, and to the Muslims it was understood as representing the five pillars of piety. It also had a relation to the world of the alchemist, being seen as the fifth element, known as the life-generating and life-sustaining spirit. Within the dimensions of Roslin can be traced the cross pate, the personalized iconography of the Templar chalice (often referred to as the Grail) based on the Islamic number eight, the Star of David, the squaring of the circle. Within the actual stone carving is shown the history of the Sinclair voyage to America (alluded in the carved Indian corn and aloe cactus) that took place some one hundred years before that of Christopher Columbus. A Christlike head situated above the altar blesses not the grail, but rather the vessels holding wine and host to be shared with the congregation during communion.

Another part of the ceiling is checkered and is symbolic of the black and white Beausceant flag of the Templars (now used by Freemasons as their checkered black and white floor). There is much more, but this book is not one on Roslin Chapel. One thing, however, is sure. Although Roslin is not the only chapel to contain Templar iconography and symbolism, it is the only chapel that contains so many in such a confined space. Roslin is a reminder of a forgotten ideal and of the fact that many concepts in life are older than Christianity. But above all, it is a monument to the hope in the survival of knowledge brought from as far as the Middle East and from within the country in which Roslin was built.

It is the architectural prominence of this chapel that brought the Sinclairs, an ancient line of lairds, which was connected to the family of the order's first grand master, Hugues de Payen, into Freemasonry. It was for this reason alone that the masons of Scotland choose the lairds of Roslin to physically hold the responsibility and the care of their ancient rights. That the Masonic organizations fell into abeyance is not surprising. Most stonemasonstoday are taught their trades through government schemes and the guild of master masons, and few hold their trades in a way that can be called hereditary. The fact that the building trade is used for profit rather than aesthetic does not help much, nor does the fact that the aristocracy of Scotland, mostly English educated in institutions such as Eton, Cambridge and Oxford, hotbeds of status quo, has forgotten the ideals for which its ancient ancestors stood.

CHAPTER 14

James VI

I, the Solomon of Britain

Thanks to the late historian-novelist Nigel Tranter, most people remember James VI as "The greatest fool in Christendom." But this is what the Cromwellian propagandists said of him. In his day, James was considered to be quite an intellectual and was referred to by his contemporaries as "the Solomon of Britain." He was also a Freemason and had been invested in Scone. For those people who have their doubts about this, the Grand Lodge of Scotland, situated at the west end of George Street, Edinburgh, does possess the actual documentation proving it. (Should you wish to consult it, I am sure that Bob Cooper, the grand lodge's librarian, will accommodate by showing it to you.) James VI became a nonoperative (few people like the word "speculative" in Scotland) mason prior to his succeeding as king of England following the death of Queen Elizabeth I in 1603. James' active involvement in operative masonry dated to the years before when he decided to have the Chapel Royal of Stirling Castle redesigned for the baptism of his son, Prince Henry Frederick, Duke of Rothesay.

The trend of "Freemasonry" practiced by James VI, however, was quite different from that practiced today and was divided into several schools of thought. Freemasonry was not just about sacred buildings, but also about ancient sacred geometry and native history. It was completely oral, and what was practiced was the art of memory, as it would have been found in pre-Roman Britain. Only the law was written in pre-Roman Britain. It is a Roman emperor who forced a Druid to write the lore of their faith down onto paper. Again, this same oral tradition was taken over by the Celtic Church in Britain, Ireland and Brittany although, admittedly, Celtic monks spent a great deal copying books pertaining to both the Old and New Testaments. The Celtic iconography in these works of art are of both of Middle Eastern origin (most individuals, for example, are shown to have two left feet, depicted Egypt, with some reference to the hermits belonging to the ancient Order of St. Anthony) and native to Britain, the latter hinting to ancient Celtic heroes and lore. Most of it was based upon both an oral tradition and interpretation.

There is one thing that is clear when one looks at Celtic Christian iconography. It is a mix between Eastern and northern Western traditions, between early Christian and what would be referred later by the Church of Rome as "pagan." This is understandable when one realizes that, till the year AD 371, it was the pagan world that prevailed in Europe, not the Christian church. While Constantine the Great called the Council of Nicea to vote in favor of Jesus Christ being declared "God incarnate upon earth," he himself did not convert to the Christian Roman faith till he found himself on his deathbed. And though the Christian church had been officially recognized, for political reasons rather than spiritual ones, as the Roman state eeligion, the pagan world was less than enamored and fought it tooth and nail. But the Christian faction won the day, and the "art of memory" had to go underground.

Subsequently, this underground tradition was promoted by the Celtic Church. Being far away from the rule of Rome, it was well aware of what could be lost if this particular culture was terminated in Britain. The Council of Whitby, held in 665 AD in Northumbria (thirty years after the fall of Jerusalem to the power of Islam), grandly declared the end of the Celtic Church. That, however, can hardly be credited as fact when one realizes that the Celtic monks of Northumbria simply packed their cases and removed themselves to Scotland. There, they survived very well indeed into the twelfth century, being mentioned in the records of King David I as the Church of the Culdees. Moreover, like Islamic art, none of the Celtic crosses, prior to the Council of Whitby, depicted Christian scenes but, rather, depicted nature and/or geometrical designs.

In fact, Catholicism per se would not be introduced in Scotland till ten years after the death of King Macbeth in 1057. It was Margaret Aetheling of England, the second wife of King Malcolm III, who strove to extinguish the Celtic Church, a church she did not approve of or understood. By 1124, her son David I had introduced the Tyronensian Order into Scotland. This was followed by the introduction of the Cistercians, who had many denominators in common with the declining Church of the Culdees. The latter elected to amalgamate with the former, and most Cistercian priories and abbeys were built upon a former Celtic Church settlements.

With the rise of Presbyterianism, which, despite what some may say, was nothing more than a political expedient for the Knoxist Party in Scotland to take over the lands of the Catholic clergy and those various religious orders in Scotland, the art of memory, once again, had to go underground.

There were, actually, two arts of memory. The oral one and the one represented in symbolic iconography, that is to say one of "riddle" or "message" set in stone (as in Roslin Chapel). Mary of Guise Lorraine, for example, was much versed in both arts, but then her family had a claim to the crusader crown of Jerusalem and a lineage going back to Rene of Lorraine, a sovereign prince who delighted in this tradition. While queen regent of Scotland, she fought as hard as she could to make sure that this tradition would not die.

When her daughter came back to reign over her ancestral kingdom in 1560, she was well versed in many things, including the tradition of the "art of memorie." Mary, Queen of Scots, is seen too often as a "femme fatale" or the "scarlet woman" of Knoxist propaganda. What should be remembered is that she was the most educated woman in Europe, a princess whose sponsor was Diane de Poitier, King Henry II of France's cousin and mistress and a woman whose esoteric knowledge was the most accomplished in her days. Diane wanted to make sure that she would have a successor worthy to carry on her work and her choice fell upon "Marie" of Scotland and "Margot" of France, who would marry Henri III of Navarre, later to succeed to France as Henri IV of Bourbon. As well as teaching Mary several languages, such as Spanish, Italian, Latin, Greek and French, Diane made sure that within the entourage of her pupils would hover both Jewish cabalists, together with Greek and Eastern teachers. It only takes a look at the French records to see for one's self that the French court entertained, sometimes for years, foreign people it understood to be the best in their crafts. Moreover, both the late Francis I of France and his son Henry II were allied with the Turks against the growing expansionist threat of Charles V of Spain, which is why Muslims could be found at the French court.

Not only do the records show Mary declaiming poetry, but we can also see her, like her father before her, writing her own poetry, a tradition into which her son would follow. Their poetry sometimes included the most unfathomable riddles imaginable. It was imbued with Hermeticism, occult understanding and pre-Roman esotericism, that is to say, drawing upon an Egyptian tradition. James IV, Mary's grandfather, had already been heavily involved with esotericism, particularly with the lore of alchemy. James IV's court abounded with geniuses, like Desidarius Erasmus, the foremost philosopher of his days, who was the tutor of James' natural son, Alexander, who gained the archbishopric of St. Andrews and the title of Duke of Ross. The art of memory had been practiced first in Egypt by each pharaohs when entering the temples that housed the various gods and goddesses of the Upper and Lower Kingdoms of Egypt. As they followed the prescribed route that took them to the inner core of each temple, the pharaohs of Egypt had to recite the prescribed liturgical text. It was extensive, and only the word of mouth from the mind was used. In order to keep them on the right track, the route would take them to a different imagery painted on the temple walls. The images would trigger the right formula to be expressed verbally at the right time. In other words, it was the visuality of the scene that did the trick but, foremost, the liturgical text it was believed to be imbued with magic.

The same was applied in the art of memory in Scotland, but instead of using an actual visual mode, it was mental visualization that was used. Basically, so that they could memorize a speech or a formula, initiates were trained to think of a particular mental architectural framework and create a complex, templelike building with an array of rooms that were furnished with images and symbols and that would trigger the memory of whatever they were supposed to say in reality. As the ancient pharaohs of Egypt, many initiates believed that this art had occult properties closely linked to spiritual enlightenment. Even today, those using this particular traditional lore as a ritual feel that they act as a priestly embodiment for the greater good of mankind. There is both a liberation (from the clutches of mainstream religious bodies) and intoxication within this phenomenon. But it is not new. Far from it. That Scotland's early kingship was imbued with this tradition, there is no doubt. It existed throughout many European countries, had been imported from Egypt into Europe and had been used by both the Cistercians and Templars in their rituals.

Some will say, "Rubbish"; others might be thinking, "He may be right but can he prove it?" Yes, I can. Unlike the rest of Europe, the royal house of Scotland draws its roots from Egypt (Eighteenth Dynasty), Greater Scythia and Solomonic Judaea. Pharaohs were the physical embodiments of gods and their principal wives that of goddesses. When the line came to settle in the West, principally in Ireland and Scotland, my kingly ancestors also physically embodied the gods that local people worshiped. Let us look, for example, to Erc, king of Dal Riata, whose three sons, Loarn, Fergus and Aonghus, settled in Argyllshire in AD 498 and from whom Scottish kingship can be traced. A quick look at a book written by the late Sir Iain Moncreiff, *The Highland Clans*, will soon tell you about the god and goddess connections in the genealogical sections. My ancestor Erc, for example, is described as "formerly pagan sacral Ulidian or fir-Bolg royal house descended through the semi-legendary 'Peace-King' Conaire Mor from the ritual incarnation of the Celtic god-spirit of the sun, Eochaid (the horseman of the heavens), equated with a male manifestation of the ancient Belgic Goddess—spirit of lightning, Bolg."

Moncreif describes another of my ancestors, King Ingiald, the "Ill-Ruler," of Norway, as being "last of the Frey-born Yngling pagan sacral 'Peace Kings' of Uppsala in Sweden, associated with human sacrifice of Royal victims from within their own dynastic family, and descended from ritual incarnations of the male manifestation of the ancient goddess-spirit Nerthus, 'Mother-Earth', whose emblem was the moon-crescent shaped galley." Not until the days of St. Columba, who inaugurated Aedan MacGabhran "King of the Scots in Dalriada" (Argyllshire) in AD 574, was kingship in Scotland Christianized in its ritual of crowning. Till then, all kings and queens embodied physically the emanation of tribal gods and their female counterparts. But each had to be initiated into this godly embodiment before kingship, just as pharaohs had been before them. When Christianity overtook the pagan traditions of kingship initiation, it borrowed it and weaved a ritual whereby any anointed king or queen in effect was made priest-king or priestess-queen of the people.

This, in Scotland, happened secretly on the eve of the actual coronation when the king/queen to be was ritually purified and ordained. It happened to all Scots kings, from Aedan to Charles II, the last Stewart king to be crowned with the Honours of Scotland in 1651. It is a fact that princelings belonging to certain royal houses were trained from an early age as initiates into certain mystery schools. This is were the grail stories came into their own, grail stories taking us as far back as the foundations of Islam, but Christianized along the way in the process of translations.

The biggest problem that the Stewarts, as esoteric initiates, had to cope with is that they all died too young. Mary died in 1587 in her prime at the age of forty-five; her father was merely thirty years of age when he gave up the ghost after the defeat of the battle of Pinkie in 1542. His predecessor, James IV, was forty when he met his maker following the battle of Flodden in 1513 (though it now looks as if he died four years later), and his father, James III, was thirty-six when dispatched to heaven following the battle of Sauchieburn in 1488. James II died at agethirty during the siege of Roxburgh in 1460 when one of his canon exploded and tore him to pieces, James I was merely forty-three when he was assassinated in Perth in 1437 during a failed coup to put a cousin of his on the throne. Only Robert II and Robert III, grandfather and father of James I, respectively, reached great ages; the latter died in 1406 at age sixty-nine, and the former died in 1390 at the age of seventy-four.

This means that by the time their mind had been formed to cope well enough with their esoteric heritage, they never were given an opportunity to put it into practice. Each of these kings, when one defines the achievements of their reign, dealt with a specific issue, which helped create the Scotland we have today. James I dealt specifically with the law. The legal system as we have it today in Scotland dates basically to James I's modernization of a system dating from King Macbeth. James II dealt specifically with strengthening the armed forces of the kingdom, thus father and son gave us the concepts of law and order. James III became the royal patron of art, music and architecture, thus welcoming new aesthetics in Scotland. James IV introduced the education bill, an early concept of trade unionism, and the concept of the royal navy in Scotland.

With James V, we reached the point where Europe was facing the religious crisis of Catholicism, and the Protestant Church was gaining ground in its bid for recognition. With James V doing his utter best, but failing to stop the Machiavellian plots of Henry VIII against Scots policies, Scotland experienced a religious division it could have well done without and which brought the country to a standstill. The one achievement we can boast for James V was his awarding the Gypsies in Scotland equal rights to the Scots. As a mark of respect for his decision and to thank him for granting them civil rights and liberties in Scotland, James V was proclaimed "King of the Gypsies" by the very people he had granted freedom to. With Mary, Queen of Scots, having a mere six years to act as Scotland's proper ruler, things took a turn for the worst. Her son James VI, on the other hand, as would his lawful successors, would be given the chance to try to finish the "Great Work," the Magnus Opus pertaining to their distinct genetic lineage.

The Oxford Illustrated Dictionary defines philosophy as "love, study, or pursuit, of wisdom or knowledge, esp. that which deals with ultimate reality, or with the most general causes and principles of things." The Stewarts were perfectly aware that one need not be a philosopher to wish the best and offer the best opportunities to one's people. Stewart philosophy provided Scotland with a legal system considered to be the best in the world today. Their code of law and order, which, had it not been infringed upon by Westminster, made Scotland to a country with a low crime rate. They believed in a science that related the perception of beauty to the geography of the kingdom. They promoted a system of education that was tolerant of diverse opinions and showing Scotland to have its own, very individualistic tree of knowledge. Scotland was recognized as a republic of letters and languages. The Stewarts enlightened minds would be the precursor of the era of Scottish enlightenment and the country's literary proficiency. It was the Stewart belief in these particular principles that would help Scotland survive the throws of English political domination.

Born in Edinburgh Castle in 1566, James VI was thirty-seven years of age when he became king of England. What is not altogether known, even in Scotland, is the fact that James VI had been, since 1590, the grand master of the Order of the Knights Templar of St. Anthony. This reconstituted order, under the leadership of the Scottish crown, was based on former lands in Leith, where a Templar chapel was built. The chapel is now known as Trafalgar Place and houses Lodge Robert Burns 1781, of which I am a member. There, the Templars were required to build a new hospital that bore the king's name. King

James' Hospital lasted till the 1800s when it was pulled down to make place to new tenements. In 1616, on King James' order, the hospital was transferred into the keeping of South Leith Presbyterian Parish. The records explicitly show that when the Catholic government of Marie de Guise-Lorraine fell following her death, the new Presbyterian parliament decided that all Catholic institutions had to disband, including the Order of St. John of Jerusalem and its preceptory of Torphichen. One David Seton addressed the Scottish parliament and made a case that the Templar order and properties that were administered by the preceptor of Torphichen could not possibly come under this new Scottish ruling since the order had been suppressed since the days of Pope Clement V. The parliament readily accepted Seton's argument and allowed the order to remain dormant rather than being declared extinct under Scots law. This Templar Order occasioned an interregnum of only thirty years before it was revived in 1590 by King James VI and put under his authority and that of his descendants. This is the third legal Templar order in the world to be a direct successor of the original order that was suppressed in 1312. Like the Order of Christ in Portugal and that of Our Lady of Monteza in Spain, it has been under the mastership of the host country's royal house, in this case the Royal House of Stewart, and I am the order's twelfth grand master.

Writing was a passion for King James VI and his early, rather restrained education under George Buchanan (an overrated scholar by far) came to an end when good old Buchanan died in 1582. From then on, James would insist on spending time with more erudite and liberal scholars. These included the masons of Scone, Scotland's ancient capital, where earlier kings of Scots had been enthroned over many centuries. From then on, having been invested as a nonoperative within the craft, and not forgetting that he was the craft's grand master in Scotland, James decided, following his succession to the English throne in 1603, to put the message of the craft to good use. While England became an obvious prime target for conversion, Sweden, where James had sent Scottish troops to help Gustavus II Adolphus in the Thirty Years War, became a depositary of Scottish Freemasonry as well. Following the end of this religious war, which Gustavus II won, thus making sure that Protestantism would survive in the Nordic kingdoms of Scandinavia and northern Germany, most of the Scots soldiers remained in Sweden, where they married. In fact, they took over the town of Goethenburg for themselves, and it is here that the first overseas nonoperative lodge, known as the Secret Lodge of St. Magnus, was funded. Scottish masonry had made its first intrusion into foreign soil.

By the time James VI had succeeded as king of England, Europe had gone through a vast religious upheaval that left many institutions, least of all the Catholic Church, in disarray. A new understanding of the divine, or perhaps one should call it a rediscovered understanding, rose and became established by those liberal scholars who promoted it, sometimes to the cost of their life. Within the Christian church, this would be referred to as the era of the reformers. Catholic protestors, hence the Protestant church, were debating the validity of the authority of the pope and suddenly decided to make a bid for recognition. Europe would be torn apart for almost ninety years with religious internecine quarrels, squirmishes and wars. The outcome of this religious upheaval would have far-reaching consequences in every European institution, not least Scottish Freemasonry.

In Scotland, most people tend to think the reformation party started with John Knox (born in 1512), who won the day over that "regiment of skirts," that is to say, Mary, Queen of Scots and her various female cousins ruling England, France and Spain. But this is a very narrow-minded view of the facts. People throughout Europe had been protesting against the might of Rome for years before that. Indeed, the "heresy" against Rome dated back to the latter days of the fourteenth century and what most English historians refer to as the Peasants' Revolt of 1381. Led by Tyler Watt, this revolt began, according to the history books, because the state wanted to levy a poll tax of one shilling per head and keep the workforce under fixed wage. The workforce, following the Black Death and the end of the war with France, was depleted and because of the lack of laborers, was overworked and underpaid.

More than 100,000 laborers from Kent and Essex marched to London where Watt met Richard II. I doubt many modern thinkers understand how difficult it would have been for 100,000 people to march to London from England's countryside. Let me put it another way. Never, at any given time in medieval history, has an English king managed to raise an army counting 100,000 men! Richard, then only a boy of fourteen years of age, faced the mob and said to Watt, "Tell me of your grievances and I shall resolve them." The mob, a while later, dispersed. Watt was later apprehended by the lord mayor of London and executed. This is the simple, propagandist way of explaining an event of history, seen by many as merely a historical blip in the life of fourteenth-century England. There was much more to it than that. Watt did not bring a mob but an army. To Watt, his king's word would have been enough to disperse his forces. He should have known better, even if kingship was, then, sacrosanct.

There is another man in the equation of this revolt, who has almost been eradicated from England's history. The annals of the period refer to him as an "agitator," and he too died, by execution, together with Watt and another 150 people, following the Peasants' Revolt in 1381. John Ball was a priest who fell out with the Roman Catholic Church because he started to think for himself and questioned the Bible. As far as he was concerned, there were, by far, too many anomalies in both the Old and New Testaments, and he started to preach about them, openly, in church. He is remembered for introducing his first sermon on the subject with a riddle: "When Adam delved and Eve span, who was then the gentleman?" This is the statement that truly sparked the reformation. John Ball, for some odd reason, was not excommunicated (but then his following in England was enormous), but was kicked out of the church and became what was then known, and probably not for the first time in the history of the Pauline church, as an unbeneficed priest.

Both Watt and Ball became martyrs to the cause of better wages and the right to think for oneself, something the English aristocracy, the Church and the king all clearly viewed as treason. The fifteenth century saw the rise of similar events, and priests preached a concept of self-thinking, for which many of them were burned to death throughout Europe. The church's rejection of any thinking that fell outside of strict doctrine would continue into the sixteenth century, when it rejected new astronomical data, such as Nicolas Coperincus's assertion that the world was round and not flat. The Church of Rome rejected any wisdom that did not favor its teachings, even if that wisdom had been promoted by scholars of the ancient world long before the birth of the Christian church.

By the first quarter of the sixteenth century, many opponents preached that the church was not just tyrannical, but that it also condoned poverty and illiteracy, and these opponents had shaken religious thinking to its very foundation. Their names have survived history and they would remodel the thinking of many institutions, royal and otherwise, to understand the universe in a way totally alien to that of the Church of Rome.

Desidarius Erasmus (1466–1536) defied the church and wrote a book into which he defined Christian "humanism." He was the tutor of Alexander Stewart, archbishop of St. Andrews, Duke of Ross and natural son of James IV of the Scots. Niccolo Machiavelli (1469–1527) published a book in which he explained his "thoughts on the sense of power." Sir Thomas More (1478–1535) is remembered for his views on "ideal society." Martin Luther (1483–1546) rose against the illogical concept of selling indulgences whereby, for a price, all your sins, past and future, would be forgiven and the piece of paper conferred passage to heaven without any problems. In 1520, Luther openly rejected the pope's authority, and Pope Leo X excommunicated Luther a year later. Francois Rabelais (1495?–1553) in a publication exhalted the pleasures and philosophy of life. John Calvin (1509–1564) joined and fired the church reforms movement. In 1529, Calvin, then in exile to Geneva, published his "Institution of Christian Religion." Michel Eyquem de Montaigne (1533–1592) published his "meditations on wisdom," and Giordano Bruno (1548–1600) promoted the ideal of religious toleration through the concept of astral magic and a solar cult behind which are hidden secret divine mysteries. "But surely," I can hear you thinking, "this has nothing to do with Freemasonry." Actually, it had a lot to do with it.

The common denominator that all of these people had was a belief in the lost wisdom of ancient civilizations, which, if it could be found, would give the world a new understanding of the divine, the universe, and of mankind. Remember, like today, the world between the fourteenth and seventeenth centuries was getting smaller. The Americas had been discovered by Europeans; though permanent colonies were not established in Northern America before 1607, its eastern seaboard had already been explored as early as the fourteenth century. Catholic priests, sent there by Rome, were doing their utter best to burn the historical records of those various conquered civilizations. Jesuits had traveled to Japan. Europeans were rediscovering the trade routes to China, which had been visited long ago by Marco Polo. Explorers, missionaries, traders, and other travellers radically changed people's perception of the known world, just as the television and telephone changed . . . and the computer and Internet are changing our perception of the world today.

This radical shift in religious belief and understanding made sure that, within the world of masonry, particularly within its nonoperative hierarchy, a change in philosophy took place. What must have taken place as well was astronomical confirmation of the historical aspects of operative masonry, as some masons saw for the first time the foreign temple structures built in faraway countries. Since masons were skilled at mathematics and trigonometry, their understanding of those structures would have been different than both historians' and archaeologists' understanding. The masons would have seen these buildings for what they were, structures pointing to astronomical data ("as above, so below"). The problem is that, today, no nonoperative Freemasons are aware of this. The rituals of today's Freemasons are about a few "made-up" historical events, not about mathematics, astronomy, trigonometry or sacred gemetria. To compare Freemasons of today with the operative masons of yesteryear is not acceptable.

CHAPTER 15

Operative Masonry in Scotland

It is true that the masonic tradition is old in Scotland, but ancient masons were used in order to set astronomical data in stone. There is something that all ancient civilizations on planet earth have in common, and that something is threefold. firstly, the fact that sound and vibration could help an individual reach an altered state of mind. Secondly, an incredible knowledge of the stars, showing us exact relations of constellations dating back to at least 10,500 BC, and thirdly, a measure common to all in order to set the data into stones. This secret and sacred measure was known by a special word, a word which would become known, centuries later, as "the Mason's Word," though not the one used by Freemasons today.

Premedieval masons of the Middle East, for example, built burial and ritual chambers as sophisticated acoustic sites designed to produce particular spiritual sensations among Stone-Age mourners and worshipers. New archeological research reveals that these ancient chambers were built in order to create sonic effects that convinced the worshipers that they were in touch with life beyond the grave. This, of course, is the kind of sophistication that most people do not equate with people living within that era of history.

However, it is now accepted within the Scottish archeological academia that the prehistoric society, who built these chambers across Scotland, managed to create effects such as "Helmholtz resonance" (the sound such as the one created when one blows across the top of a bottle), as well as subsonic vibrations that altered the mental state of the people attending the burial ritual. Early priests chanted and drummed, and the volume and intensity of the sounds was enhanced by the acoustics of the chamber. While the sound filled the cairn completely, it was difficult to determine the source of it, and those within the chamber would have had the disquieting impression that it was emerging from inside their heads and body. It actually produced dizziness, a sensation of ascent akin to an out-of-body experience, and helped those participating to the ritual to achieve a different state of consciousness with profound and of multisensual impressions. These cairns, numbering to about 120 in Scotland and dating as far back as 2800 BC, were the original awe-inspiring cathedrals, built by primitive masons so that their fellow men could feel to have been touched by the gods.

Then we have stone circles made of megaliths. These stones were cut at a certain angle and hewn with various distinct protrusions so that astronomical data could be obtained from them both by day and by night. Each of these stone-circle sites actually stands on a very particular longitude and latitude so that this data would be correct, not just for the era the circle was built in, but for thousands of years to come. Most, if not all, megalithic sites were built on a common measure of 2.72 feet (83 cm), a measure known as the megalithic yard.

Callanish, one of the oldest stone sites in Scotland, was built not in a circular manner as most people think, but rather in an oval or elliptical one, indicating a knowledge of the right-angled triangle, some 2,500 years before Pythagoras wrote about it in the 600 BC. Looking at Callanish from the air, we then also find that the whole structure looks like a Celtic cross. Callanish was one of the most important astronomical centers in Europe. Even though its ancient name was "the Holy Temple of the Sun," in fact, Callanish was one of the few centers in Europe collecting data related to a lunar calendar. (Stonehenge is/collects data related to a solar calendar.) We know that the great stone avenue of Callanish was accurately aligned to the rising star Capella. Meanwhile, the stones on the other side of the circle are aligned to the true north.

While Callanish related to astronomy, it also related to keeping a correct yearly geometric calendar of "time." Time was measured and divided in circle time and square time. Thus, when early masons referred to the "squaring of the circle," they were referring to their "time calendar" and its sacred geometry defined in secret numerology. There were quite a lot of those astronomical temples throughout Europe, all built on crossing ley lines.

The might of the Roman Empire and the early Pauline Christian church were terrified by the knowledge and power of the Druids (who did not build these sites in any case) and their belief in the immortality of the soul. Pre-Druidic peoples built and the Druids adotped these sites for sacred rites. Julius Ceasar, head of the Roman Empire, decided to eradicate the ancient Druidic priesthood in full. We are talking genocide here. Those who survived had to go underground, and hopefully, even somehow, passed on the knowledge to succeeding generations.

The empire of Rome was succeeded by that of the Christian church of Rome, a church run by "fathers" who understood even less of the people who lived under their domain than the Roman emperors. The church fathers, in turn, imposed an alien dogma on other civilizations, including the Jewish one from which the Christian church supposedly derives its roots. In the name of Christ, unbelievers were persecuted, libraries were burnt, and wars were engineered. Both Scotland and Ireland never were a part of the Holy Roman Empire and were persuaded rather late in their medieval history to accept and follow the Christian religion and to the Roman Catholic dogma. Both countries were lucky in the sense that they managed to amalgamate their ancient iconography with a Christian one, and create iconography that suited both the traditional understanding of past druidic spiritual life and the psyche of the people.

Early Celtic Church settlements were usually built upon ancient sacred sites and in a circular manner. This is what St. Columba, for example, did when he settled his community in Iona in AD 563. Later, when the Cistercian Order took over the Celtic Church, its bigger buildings were built upon a particular geometry—a sacred geometry that the masons building religious houses made sure would survive any onslaught. No historians have ever taken measurements of the major religious Cistercian houses throughout Europe.

Cistercian churches and abbeys are built on a different measure than normal ecclesiastical Catholic buildings. Catholic churches were built on a rectangular design: the length should be three squares of equal measure and the width two squares of equal measures. Cistercian cathedrals, churches and abbeys, however, were built on measures based on twelve squares equal in length and eight in width, thus of a proportion of two-thirds, which equals more or less the Golden Ratio of Pythagoras. A Cistercian building reflects its divine and initiated origins through its architecture and so to the "royal" art. The royal art of "architect" was even referred to by the saying "Let no one enter here unless he be a Geometrician." Today, a geometrician is known under its more modern name of "surveyor." Theophrates, in the third century AD, recalls that "sculptors and masons traveled the length and breadth of the known world with the necessary utensils to work marble, ivory, wood, gold and all sorts of metals, all of which were provided for them to build Temples on a divine model."

Few historians are aware of the exact latitude and longitude these Cistercian churches and abbeys were built on. None of them have ever wonder why some of the buildings do not face the "proper" Christian way, and few of them have ever excavated underneath these religious houses to find out if there was something there before the "Christian" era. Most historians would be extremely surprised to find out that all Cistercian abbeys were built and aligned to face the rising of the sun. While there was little building work taking place during the dark years between the Roman invasions and the policy of Pauline Christian conversion in Europe, the fact is that ancient data, historical and astronomical, was nevertheless saved through the art of iconography and the art of memory. It would later be displayed in the stone arrangement of the religious houses built by Scottish masons from the twelfth century onwards. Few people in Scotland are aware that, between the years 1113 and 1505, some eighty-four priories and abbeys were built. This is a staggering amount of building being achieved for a small country and the then population of Scotland, which is guessed to be just a few thousand by scholars who continue to argue over the numbers.

The method of quarrying stones in Scotland, and one must remember that geologically speaking Scotland is one of the oldest landmass on planet earth, had remained the same for centuries till the introduction of the steam engine in the nineteenth century. Stratified stone, being the most resistant to compressive forces, was used for buildings such as priories, abbeys, churches, cathedrals and castles. The tools used to work sandstones have changed little over the centuries and consist of mattocks, hoes, shovels, rakes and spades used for uncovering the stone, removing the overburden, or tirr as it was then called. Weights and hammers of various shapes were then used to shape the stone or drive in the drills. Picks and crowbars were, in the main, employed to lever the stone off the bed so that it could be lifted with a crane. Quarrying was all done by muscle power, either human alone or with human the help of horses or even cattle.

There was little distinction between the different types of stone workers in Scotland compared to anywhere else in Europe, particularly from the early fourteenth century. Both quarriers and workmen worked together, though the quarriers were the skilled individuals with whom the masters of works made the contracts to quarry specified amounts of stone. While the workmen did the laboring, the shaping of the stone was often done by the quarriers. They, in turn, would move up the social ladder to become masons and thus members of a trade. Most of the work was done during the summer months, and the shorter winter days were reflected in a reduced wage for quarriers and workmen as well as for masons. All worked the same amount of hours: 5 AM to 7 PM during summer time with a two-hour midday break, a half-hour break for breakfast, which they called by the medieval French word of "disjune" (hence "dejeuner"), and, except in the depths of winter, another half-hour afternoon break referred to as "nunshankis." In winter, they worked from dawn till 11:30 AM and then from 1 PM till dusk. Payday was Saturday. Incidentally, life for stone workers was never a healthy one, as proven by the comments on respiratory problems that have survived in the archives of the masters of works. Masons, who worked in groups dressing stones in sheds or lodges where much dust was created, suffered the most problems. Quarriers and workmen were luckier, as they worked in the open air.

Most historians will tell you that there was absolutely no links between operative masons and Templars and Cistercians, but that is blatantly going against the overwhelming evidences showing that the link was clearly there. Again, this link is shown in Templar iconography. Although few Templar buildings survive in Scotland, Europe has many buildings that have been saved and are now even open to the public. Many show a typical design of an early Templar cross on top of a stylized rosace and flanked on either side by a mason's plumb line. This design was used from the early years of the order in Europe (from 1128 onwards).

The Templar masons were trained in a rather special way. Their schools of architecture were religious in the sense that the masons had to go through a ritual of purification and observe the rules and secrets of St. John the Evangelist. Their apprenticeship was done by stages of initiation, whereby they learned eastern techniques of carving, such as those used by those Muslim masons—not Byzantine ones as claimed by some. When they finally gained the ultimate accolade as fully fledged masons, which took years to achieve, they would then go through the final ritual whereby their personal secret mark would be added to the book. a record book for a group of masons Early European masons' marks could be traced back to Middle Eastern masons.

The final ritual was kept secret, except to the master of the knights Templars and the ruling abbot of Clairveaux. It was held in a square chamber into which the master to be was led by a "rouleur," who had to knock three times upon the door. After being invited to enter, the apprentice was faced by three masters standing behind a square table covered with a white cloth. The square table was supposedly a reference to the tomb of Christ and the white cloth in reference to Christ's shroud but, in truth, referred to they symbolized the temple of Makkah and the shroud that covers it (although, today, the shroud is black in color). Upon the cloth could be seen a plain cross of squarish dimension, and in the middle of the cross was a rolled napkin, the representation of the crown of thorns. This shape is also, of course, the typical design of a Celtic cross. Upon each of the branches of the cross, the apprentice then would see a white plate with a candle in its middle, symbolizing the sun and the moon, and three knives, symbolizing the three nails of Christ. To this was added a piece of wood, a reference to the spear that pierced Christ's side; three pieces of rope, symbolizing the whipping that Christ had to endure; and a napkin pleated in a certain way, symbolizing the pliers with which the nails were retrieved. A cup represented the chalice of the Sang Real of Joseph of Arimathea. The wooden carving of a cockerel served as a reference to St. Peter's three denials of Christ, and a pair of dice obviously refers to the game the soldiers beneath the cross played for Christ's robe. A chest painted with symbols referred to the ark of Noah and the tabernacle of David.

On becoming a master mason, the apprentice was also given colored ribbons upon which were embroidered symbolic emblems. One emblem was the representation of a labyrinth and another was that of Hermes Trismegistus, famed for the emerald tables. The latter symbol depicted a man, standing arms and legs apart, with one hand holding a compass and the other holding a square. The whole thing was actually set within a pentagram that was itself set within a circle. (This symbol also commemorates the Cathars.)

One Scottish ecclesiastical building that demonstrates a close link to the Templars is the Cistercian Abbey of Melrose. It now stands as an extensive ruin looked after by Historic Scotland, but it has features that, by Templar standards, are unique within the iconography of the Cistercian Order. Moreover, these features are only to be found in Melrose and nowhere else in Europe. Most of the abbey today dates back to the twelfth and thirteenth centuries, except for the church and the commendator's house, which date back to 1385. It is with the church itself that we must concerned ourselves. Actually, most of the roof is missing, except for that part standing above the presbytery. Looking up, we are faced with a puzzle, which, though the guidebook shows as being of Christian design, is in fact totally Islamic in concept. The ceiling is vaulted and shows an intricate pattern of ribs and bosses, the central boss being directly positioned over the high altar.

We are faced with, outwardly, an octagon. With the inward bosses, if one is familiar enough with the number symbolism in Islamic mysticism, we can trace the various geometrical correspondence, both static and dynamic, between numbers one and twelve, relating them all to their macrocosmic and microcosmic equivalent. It is the Islamic zodiac, and within the design, one can trace the star of Isis, the sigil of the Beast and the crown of Lucifer, even in its reversed form. Interestingly, the latter three designs actually link Melrose to Rennes le Chateau and the religious mysteries of the Cathars. The design of the Judaic Tree of Life, with the sefiroth system and its twenty-two "true" ways and thirty-two paths of wisdom, as related in Cabala, can also be traced. A much older version of this same church celing can be found in the mosque of Spanish Cordoba today. This mosque was built by Abd al-Rahman I, who died in AD 788, and it was embellished over years and generations of Umayyad emirs and caliphs. It is strange to find a perfectly reproduced Islamic ceiling design in a Scottish Cistercian abbey. Melrose, by Cistercian standards, makes no sense, because unlike other Cistercian monasteries, it has Templar allegorical designs carved in the stone up to its roof. Had the vaulted ceiling over the presbytery fallen like the rest of it all, this link would have been missed. But the ceiling hasn't, and it does show that the Cistercians were privy to Templar secrets, which were Islamic rather than Christian in concept.

Interestingly, the only other Cistercian abbey with a vague Templar design, that of the cross pate, is to be found in Spain, in the abbey of Vallbona de les Monjes. There the cross pate shows in the tiburium at the base of the crossing tower. Another Spanish Cistercian abbey, that of La Huelgas, also shows some stylized geometric patterns, among which can also be found the cross pate. Altenburg, in Germany, has a restored north transept window whose main design is based on the pentagram. However, as a rule, Cistercian abbeys were plain, simple, almost austere, compared to other orders.

There is an inscription in Melrose Abbey pertaining its master mason, John Morow: "John Morow sometimes called was I and born in Paris certainly and had in keeping all the mason work of St. Andrews, the high Kirk of Glasgow, Melrose and Paisley, of Nithsdale and Galloway. I pray to God and Mary both and sweet St. John to keep this holy church from harm." It then ends by saying: "As the compass goes evenly about, so truth and loyalty shall do without doubt. Look to the end quoth John Morow." It is a strange message to say the least. Except for this inscription, nothing is known about John Morow. It isn't even sure that this was his name, but the clue is in the words "compass, truth and loyalty." It is a trinity that was once upon a time applied to the Templars. "Faith," notice, is not mentioned, so that the inscription can hardly relate to religion and the Catholic doctrine. Nor is it traditional, in the fourteenth century, to refer to the Virgin simply as Mary. However, if one remembers that the Templars revered another Mary, Mary Magdalene, and indeed St. John (though not the Baptist, but St. John the Divine), then all falls into place, and Melrose, particularly the iconography that was found in the abbey church, would have given the initiates the various clues telling them that the Templars, their secret eastern mysticism, had indeed survived in Scotland.

Most people also don't realize that the Cistercian and Templar orders can be related to one another by looking at the design on any Cistercian abbots gravestones and the several hundreds gravestones found at Kilmartin in Argyllshire. They happen to be identical, showing "atop a fourth step one single stylized cross in the form of a compass and flanked by a sword." The single difference is that while the abbots' gravestones show the four steps, those gravestones found at Kilmartin do not. But what is more surprising is that this stylized cross atop the fourth step was first found on an Islamic gold dinar of Abd al Malik and issued between AD 696 and 697. In fact, this stylized cross is a design that Sufism produced and is one that relates to "the mysteries of the Kingdom of Heaven." It is known within Christian iconography as "the sigil of the Beast" and connected to the number 666. Why is this symbol used on all Cistercian abbots' and Templars' gravestones? The answer can only be that the templars were so imbued within the revelation, doctrines and sacred art of Islamic Sufism that they adopted and followed many concepts that Catholic doctrines deemed heretical in the first place. While we have many Cistercian monasteries surviving the ravages of time, albeit now in the form of extensive ruins, the *raison d'etre* of the Cistercian Order remains a mystery today, because its lifestyle is so unknown to the world. It is a lifestyle of contemplation, austerity, oneness with the divine, and praying for a gradual awakening towards the realization of consciousness. With all due respect, this is exactly what Sufism is all about, and this lifestyle was practiced centuries before being introduced within the Cistercian Order by Bernard de Clairveaux and his successors.

Building works in Scotland grew as the Royal House of Bruce succeeded that of Dunkeld, and the works certainly became more sophisticated with the accession of the Royal House of Stewart, reaching a French style during the reign of James V. The question one has to ask is: who took care of all these working forces of thousands of people throughout the kingdom? The answer is quite simple. By the fourteenth century, these various working sites were looked after by masters of works, which came under the aegis of the king's chamberlain till the year 1424, when a subdivision of responsibility took place and a comptroller was put in charge of the architectural expenses of the king. In fact, open involvement of the royal house of Scotland dates back to 1362, when David II paid "Nicholas Mason, both mason and customar" money to pay himself, other masons and carpenters working on repairs of Stirling Castle. In 1375, we then come to the first recorded master of work (Magister Operis) employed at David's Tower in Edinburgh Castle. Sadly, his name was omitted, and only the style of his office was entered. The treasurer's account, first compiled in 1473, then deals with operative masons' accounts. Two hundred years after their appearances in Scotland, the job of these various Templar architects was fully recognized in 1507 as "master of works" by King James IV in a charter of the crown. In 1532, James V recognized the office of master mason.

What is interesting about the records pertaining to the Magister Operis is that they show almost all of these masters to be either aristocracy and gentry or abbots and burgesses. Their pay was £100 Scots per year. By 1539, it had increased to £200, and by the year 1641, the amount mentioned is £1,200 Scots. It is interesting to note that "no ordinary craftsmen" could be admitted without the approval of the masters of works. More than one "overseer" would answer to them regarding the activities of working masons anywhere within the kingdom, while their other two administrative officers, and paymasters and accountants, would direct and relate to their boss the details of management and expenditure. The fact that Scotland also employed Frenchmen as Magister Operis has to be taken into account as well. One has to remember that from 1424 onwards many Scots went to France, where they settled for a while, only to come back two generations later to Scotland, where they were able to buy lands and were granted titles.

Some people might just say that this is just pure speculation on my part. Nothing can be proved, and there are no records available justifying this particular belief. That may be the case, but isn't it strange that records show that the operative masons were, in matter of fact, already well organized—with courts where they could settle their disputes, and with the right to meet in a closed meetings once a year—survived the ravages of constant invasions?

The masons' court was referred to as "the Court of the Set Square and the Right Angle," the earlier name of which can be traced back to "the Place of Truth," the Egyptian cchool of architectural-magical art that built the houses of eternity for the pharaohs of the Eighteenth Dynasty Egypt. Funded by Pharaoh Amenhotep I, it trained masons to build royal tombs and temples based on a spiritual mathematical equation and use a magical square stone to imbue their architectural creation with a spiritual life that would help pharaoh function both in life and death.

Let us look at a few other Templar inheritances within the social life of Scotland. The knights Templar gave Scotland the word and station of "bailie," for example. The Templars had 11,000 commaderies and preceptories, and each of these was administered by a bailie. Moreover, the office of bailie first appears in Scotland in the twelfth century, following an 1128 visit by Hugues de Payens, first master of the order. On being gifted lands in Scotland by King David I, Hugues de Payens at once elected a bailie to run and make the land profitable. Years later, a bailie would be introduced within the infrastructure of Scottish burghs and then within the infrastructure of the Scottish councils.

While the Templars ruled the roost, so to speak, the three masonic schools working and building for them belonged to the Templar confraternity of Francs Metiers. By 1326, the latter had been excommunicated at the Council of Avignon by Pope John XXII and had to go underground. But the group reappeared as the "Companions of the Son of the Widow." The confraternity followed a threefold code, a trinity, of "honouring God, of preserving the wealth of the master, of sustaining the companions." This, needless to say, is the Templar rule, albeit disguised, of "Believe in God, Obey the Master, work for the Order."

The original Templar schools of architecture and the Companions of the Son of the Widow were synonymous with one another and actually can be found in the Old Testament. However, they do not have to do with the original widow within Grail history, Ruth, the Moabite and great-grandmother of David, the king of Israel. Most Masonic historians incorrectly claim that it was her son, Hyram Abiff, who designed Solomon's temple (which was actually started by Solomon's father, David and finished by his son Solomon). Nor is he referred to as the "son of the widow," which would denote him to be a descendant of Ruth and Boaz. One has to understand that the whole of Jewish society had a particular place within the secular world as well. In the family of the tribe of Levi, divided into clans, rested the tradition of providing the Temple with, not just Priests (though not the High ones, whose office was reserved for the Aaronite Priesthood), but with the choirs as well.

There is also the belief that the "Temple of the Lord" could not be built by unclean hands. Only Priestly hands could touch the stones that would be used to erect the Holy structure. It is interesting to note that, till then, the Lord our God was worshipped under a tent. In fact, the entire Hebrew Nation had lived under tents for sometime, even after settling in what would later be consolidated as the Kingdom of Israel in Western Arabia. While the Hebrew had indeed invaded and taken over cities, the original populace was not displaced. Only the new religion was imposed upon them. And since the law forbade women to marry non-Jews or to marry outside the tribes, they did not intermarry within local native society either unless their non-Jewish prospective husband agreed to circumcision. With the building of the Temple came the concept of the Hebrew population moving under a proper roof but these houses had to be built and nothing within the tradition of Israel, till then, mentioned the need of the tribes providing the state with house and Temple builders. Actually, Israelites were required by Solomon to work one month out of every three in forced labour to build the Temple. This requirement was expected of them because there weren't enough Canaanites to get on with the job. No one was paid to build the Temple. Menial forced labour was the key to have anything built.

The truth is that Solomon, states the Old Testament, wrote to the king of Tyre and asked him for an artificer versed in the art of bronze craftsmanship. The king of Tyre provided Solomon with Huram, a master bronze craftsman whose mother was a widow from the Hebrew tribe of Naphtali. Huram made in bronze the main artifacts for the temple: two columns, two bowl-shaped capitals on top of the columns, the design of interwoven chains on each capital, the ten carts, the ten basins, a tank and the twelve bulls supporting the tank. Huram might also have made the gold furnishings to be used in the temple, as well as pots, shovels and bowls. (Notice bronze, not stone. first Kings 7, verses 13 to 51, quite categorically state that is what Huram had to provide for the temple. There is nothing in the Old Testament stating that Huram was anything else than a master craftsman in bronze. As for the stones quarried for the temple foundation, eighty thousand hill-country people had cut them down. The stones were carved to size, and all the 3,300 foremen and workers had to do was put them together at the designated place in Jerusalem. It was the assemblers who put the stones, silently, together.)

Huram, artificer, is no longer mentioned in the Old Testament following the dedication of the temple. However, the name of Huram is interesting, for it was symbolic of C-Hiram or Khurum, the universal agent of the "fire spirit" required for the alchemical consummation of the Magnus Opus. The early alchemical mysteries taught initiates how to prepare a miraculous white powder of projection (monatomic gold) by which it is possible to transmute the base human ignorance into an ingot of spiritual and philosophical enlightenment, while the alchemical equation can turn lead into gold.

In other words, we are talking philosophers' stone. The exact science of human regeneration is the lost key of Masonry, for when the spirit fire is lifted up through the thirty-three segments (or degrees) of the spinal column, it finally passes to the pituitary body (Isis) where it invokes the pineal gland (Ra). This means that the Hiramic chronicles, the source of Masonic history, may be considered to embody the vicissitudes of philosophy itself, and that the pagan mystery adepts were the architects of civilization, personified by the C-Hiram (Khurum) of the sacred fire. The Masonic reference of Hiram Abiff being buried in the acacia tree is also reminiscent of the Egyptian mystery ritual of the murder and raising of the god Osiris, whose body was washed ashore near Byblos and lodged in the roots of an acacia tree. Within the Egyptian and Arabic tradition, the acacia was the symbol of the vernal equinox, the annual resurrection of the solar deity.

The Magnus Opus, or Great Work, consists of apparently four worlds or phases and is symbolized by the Hebrew stem QBL, from which derives the word "Qabala." The tradition is, contrary to popular belief, more Persian than Jewish. The first world, or phase, is Prima Causa, which is followed by the three matters of Materia Prima, Secunda and Tertia. According to alchemists' tradition, it is the fourth world, or phase (Materia Tertia), by which the Magnus Opus is achieved. According to tradition, the Magnus Opus is wholly reliant upon the perfected state of the third world/phase Materia Secunda, the production of the philosophers' stone, which is said to be the "Unfinished Workpiece" of Freemasonry. To the initiates, this process is fully portrayed within the rising degrees of perfection to be found in the Qabalistic Tree of Life and its representation of the ultimate kingship of the kingdom (both material and spiritual), which is symbolized by the sword, scepter, orb and crown. (It is interesting to note that one of those kingly and alchemical items is missing for Scotland. The country of Scotland, today, has no orb in its royal representation, only a crown, a sword and a scepter, known collectively as the Honours of Scotland. But our country did have, once upon a time, an orb, which can be seen represented upon the seal of King William I the Lion.)

You may well ask what an orb has to do with Templars and masons. The answer is nothing and everything. Nothing in the sense that pseudo-Templars and today's Freemasons would know little of the alchemical meaning attributed to the orb by the ancient artificers and everything in the sense that many Templars and medieval masons were particularly versed in the secret art of alchemy. To them, the orb represented Antimony (Stibium), referred to in the

Book of Enoch as a key element in the pursuit of enlightenment. To the medieval Templars and masons, the upturned orb (Venus symbol) is the sign of philosophical mercury, which in practical terms is the essence of the menstruum. This entire tradition was embedded within the C-Hiram/Chiram/Huram name and might relate to the secret knowledge held by Huram the artificer when he came to Jerusalem to provide the temple with holy vessels.

But as far as the Bible is concerned, Huram goes back to Tyre, and there is no mention of his being murdered. Interestingly, the name of Abiff is not mentioned in the Bible.

One theory could be that the entire concept of the alchemical aspects in Masonry had been thought out following the exile of the Royal House of Stewart and the introduction of the Electors' House of Hanover when the speculative Grand Lodge of England was set up in London in 1717.

Chapter 16

The Auld Alliance and Secret Services

Charles I is usually remembered as the "martyr" king of Great Britain who lost his head to the Cromwellian axe in 1649. In Scotland, his concept of the Christian church was defied by the Presbyterian party. Most people will have read something about a stool thrown to the minister of St. Giles by a Jenny Geddes when the poor old chap tried to read the king's proclamation on the royal wish that the Church of Scotland should adopt a new prayer book. Charles' idea was to unify British Christianity with a common basis in order to overcome the various religious tendencies that engendered division. Geddes throwing her chair is an invented event. It never took place, but to this day, people believe it actually happened. Propaganda is not and was never the monopoly of the state. In fact, the church was particularly adept in the use of it.

Charles I was, among many other things, one of the most cultivated monarchs of Europe and had an unsurpassed taste and understanding of all the arts. His reign was one of architectural, musical, theatrical, visual, written and oral liberation. He also had an interest in the esoteric and mathematics. His eleven years of reign without a parliament, in England, saw the books balanced and in the black for the first time in centuries. His knowledge of what many students refer to as "dead" languages was also equal to none. His court admitted representatives from the Church of Rome with whom he delighted in debating theological aspects of the faith in Latin as well as Greek. He never, however, aspired to become a Catholic. Astronomy, very much frowned upon by the Roman Catholic Church, was able to thrive under Charles' patronage. Also, from the beginning of his rule, Scots were able to join in the workings of England's parliament, and they introduced to "liberal" Englishmen and women some of the Scottish understanding of traditional esoterism. So much so that an "invisible" college was founded in order to promote this newly found information within English society. Prince Rupert, Count Palatine of the Rhine and Charles' nephew, would become one of the college's most prominent supporters and made sure that it was granted a royal charter of recognition during the reign of Charles II.

The invisible college was one of the various ways to promote Scottish Freemasonry, of the nonoperative trend that is, in England.

After the judicial murder of Charles I, his exiled family brought Scottish Freemasonry to France. However, the Stewarts had been in France for quite a few centuries before that, something that most people in Britain, as well as France, have forgotten. The common equation between France and Scotland is Aubignie, a French lordship that a Stewart of Lennox, royal by blood, was offered by King Charles VII of France and which the Stewart family held for generations. Most of the Stewarts were also prominent commanders in the *Garde Ecossaise*, looking after the safety of the kings of France from Charles VII to Louis XVIII.

The Scots Guard is usually perceived as just that, a military body, in France. However, there was more to it. It was extremely political, very loyal to the kings of the Scots and the body ideally suited to keep alive the Auld Alliance between Scotland and France. That it had Masonic links, there are no doubts whatsoever. In fact, each commander of the Scots Guard would be the "master" of that early Scottish trend of nonoperative masonry in France. They also initiated Francis I into their esoteric secret. When Francis I succeeded his father-in-law, Louis XII, his personal Scots Guard of twenty-four archers was commanded by none other than Lord Robert Stuart d'Aubignie.

The day of Francis' coronation, Aubignie wore a white cloth doublet adorned in front and behind with a crowned salamander. What has to be remembered is that we have now reached the Renaissance period with all its esoteric aspects and meaning. At that time, it was believed that the salamander was an elementary spirit that could live in fire unharmed and was thus a symbol of flames *in toto*. Further, it was regarded as the spiritual symbol of the righteous person who could maintain peace of mind despite psychic attacks. Its biblical link rested with the statement to be found in Daniel chapter 3: "like the three men in the furnace, the righteous man sustains no harm." (Actually, the Guard's heraldic symbol changed from time to time in relation to the various deals they made with certain political individuals or factions. Interestingly, the Islamic crescent moon became one of its heraldic symbols for a while, alluding to the French-Turkish alliance that took place in the sixteenth century.)

A few days after Francis' coronation, Robert Stuart d'Aubignie was made one of the four marshals of France with the right to be referred to as the king's cousins. Few people are aware that the people closest to the French king were either Scots or of Scottish descent. His royal almoner was Robert Cockburn. Peter Cuningham and his brother, James, Lord of Cange, together with James Stewart (later Earl of

Moray, and Mary Queen of Scots' half brother), were Francis' pages of honor. Other prominent members of the French royal household were Matthew, Earl of Lennox; Alexander Stewart, Duke of Albany; Armand Claude Gordon; Adrian and Philip Vernor; Bernard and Francis Stuart d'Aubignie; John Stuart, Seigneur de la Mothe; and James Montgomery, Seigneur de Lorges.

That they were the inner core to a greater ideal, which was liberally spiritual, there is no doubt. Some members of the Guards, such as James Stewart of Moray, would even later be of the "reformed" faith. On August 15, 1515, the French army, the king and his Scots Guard, all marched to Italy against the troops of Charles V of Spain, then under the command of Prosper Colonna. Though the first steps of the campaign were favorable to the French, it would all end in a disaster at the battle of Pavia, where Francis was taken prisoner. This event of history gave rise to an allegory showing King Francis I going hunting and, riding ahead of his party, finding himself hopelessly confused when faced with the falling darkness. Wandering aimlessly, he suddenly found himself amid a band of mystics in Scotland, who put him through a ritual of "illumination." Francis, in other words, had been initiated into the secrets of Scottish esoterism, thus becoming one of the true "brethren."

When Charles V asked Francis I to lend him a large sum of money and his men-at-arms to fight the Turks, Francis's reply is, to say the least, illuminating: "With regard to the first point, I am not a banker; as for the second, as my company of men-at-arms is the arm that bears my sceptre, I never expose it to danger when it does not accompany me to glory." Turkey, of course, was an unofficial ally of Francis I, but the Scots Guard is emphasized as being more than just a guard. To refer to it as "the arm that bears my sceptre" is tantamount to stating that it is the Scots Guard who gave him his crown and that it acted as "king maker" in France. The Scots Guard certainly acted on behalf of Francis I with Charles V of Spain and gained freedom for the French king.

Following the arrival of the infant Mary, Queen of Scots, in France in 1548, the Guard became even more important, as its duty was expanded to ensure that the lives of both the future Francis II of France and his prospective Scottish royal wife were in safe hands. From that moment up to 1559, when Mary was widowed, France and Scotland became one single entity in all but name, a reservoir filled to the brim with a philosophy particular to itself and where, certainly in Scotland, the new spiritual reform was able to function. Had Mary's first husband, Francis II, lived longer into adult life, it can be even presumed that the Bartholomew massacre, which occurred in 1572 and was a brutal attempt to supress Protestantism, would not have taken place. Catherine of Medicis would have been relegated to a minor position, while that of the pro-Catholic de Guise party would have been told in no uncertain terms that Mary allowed the Huguenots in France and the Presbyterians in Scotland to worship according to their conscience.

Both countries had exchanged, on a regular basis, masons (such as Jean Morow, who was the master of works for the masons working on the Cathedral of St. Andrews, Glasgow and the abbeys of Melrose, Paisley, Nithsdale and Galloway). From Aubignie and St. Germain, a tradition would evolve amid the French court and really come into its own when Charles, Prince of Wales and Duke of Rothesay, together with his mother, Henrietta Maria of France, landed in France prior to the death of Charles I. They would later be followed by Charles I's second-born son, James, Duke of York and Albany.

Henrietta Maria of France was the daughter of Henri III of Navarre, IV of France (born a Protestant, he thought that Paris was worth a mass and converted to Catholicism in order to succeed to the French crown) and sister of Louis XIII. On coming to France into exile, she took residence in the Chateau de St. Germain en Laye (where Mary, Queen of Scots, had previously lived as dauphine and then queen of France). Henrietta Maria arrived and set up court with quite a retinue of English and Scots people from all walks of life. In 1649, St. Germain en Laye saw the introduction of the first nonoperative Scottish lodge in France. It was simply known as Lodge St. Germain, which was, interestingly, the same name used by the kings of Scots as "secret" grand masters of the masons.

From this time onwards, nonoperative Freemasonry became the secret service of the Stewart family in exile and acted on behalf of Charles II, gathering information relating to Cromwellian policies while using the invisible college as the pro-Stewart propaganda machine with a policy to a quick royal restoration. Interestingly, Cromwell was an English nonoperative mason, and his mother was a Stewart descended from Alexander Stewart, fourth high steward of Scotland. An old family tree, produced by the Lord Lyon Court in Edinburgh in 1792, mentions the Stewart-Cromwell connection. This tree also shows that John Knox, who so intensely disliked Mary, Queen of Scots, was not against the idea of marrying into the blood royal of Scotland. Lady Margaret Stewart of Ochiltree, a descendant of the dukes of Albany, was his second wife. The reasons these two men got anywhere in life is not so much because of their own particular beliefs, but because of their connection within the world of aristocracy. Cromwell was born into the aristocracy (albeit in the lower echelons) and used it to get his way, while Knox married into it in order to gain his. And it worked. However, neither kept power for that long. Cromwell met his maker in 1658 (thus having held power for nine years), while Knox, left unchecked by the crown, departed for better pastures in 1572. Mary, Queen of Scots, left Scotland in 1567 and crossed into England, living in one prison castle after another till Elizabeth I signed her death warrant in 1587.

The Lodge St. Germain was a closed one, and no French people were invited to join. Following the restoration of Charles II in 1660, the lodge would remain secret and worked closely with Charles II in his endeavor to retain the financial help of the French king. It also made sure that Dowager Queen Henrietta Maria, who had opted to remain in France, would be able to act on behalf of her son and her daughter's marriage to the king's brother, Philippe, Duc d'Orleans. Henrietta Maria died in 1669, while her daughter Henrietta Anne (fondly nicknamed Minette by her brothers) died in 1670. The Duchess d'Orleans was inspirational in convincing both her brother, Charles II of England, and her brother-in-law, Louis XIV of France, to sign a treaty of peace between the two countries. Minette was also in charge of Scottish Freemasonry in France from 1660 till her death and was thus the official first woman to preside within a very male-orientated organization.

It would be another forty years before another Stewart princess would step into her shoes and carry on the tradition of female-led Freemasonry in France. The main protagonist of the Stewart family to succeed Minette was her niece, Louise Marie Therese, daughter of James VII and Mary of Modena. She was born in Paris, at the Chateau de St. Germain en Laye in 1692. Louis XIV and Madame de Maintenon, the king's secret wife, stood as Louise's godparents. Before her death in 1712 at age twenty, Louise acquired a definite role within French Masonic politics.

Her role can only have been symbolic. However, in those days, some members, usually the offspring of worthy brethren, could be inducted into the craft when they were as young as twelve years old. If this was the case for Louise, and there is nothing to disprove it, she would have taken her place within her aunt's old lodge of St. Germain in 1704. By 1710, Louise was firmly in charge of it.

Louise was precocious. She was also ambitious. From the time she could walk and think, she had her eyes set upon the kingdom of France. By then, the succession to the crown of France seemed pretty well assured. The Grand Dauphin Louis, son of Louis XIV, had given birth to three sons. All were called Louis. The Duc de Bretagne was born in 1705 but died within a year. While Louise, then thirteen years of age, had firmly set her eyes upon marriage to the infant, she quickly adjusted her ambition upon the second Duc de Bretagne born in 1707. But this Louis, too, would die young, at the age of five on March 8, 1712. This did not bother Louise, since another Louis, Duc de Bourgogne, was born in 1710. But her dream was short lived. Louise died on April 18, 1712, of smallpox, the very disease that had struck down her prospective royal husbands. (The Duke of Bourgogne would later marry Maria Leszczinska of Poland, his senior by seven years.)

Until her death, Louise was militant in promoting the cause of her older brother, James Francis Edward, Prince of Wales, then recognized by Louis XIV as James VIII of Scotland and James III of England. Louise was also politically astute. Taught within a highly volatile Jacobite court set up in France, Louise quickly understood that the family needed to create a movement bent on persuading the French ministry to give military help for a quick Stewart restoration. Moreover, St. Germain had been the home of her ancestress, Mary, Queen of Scots, and was a constant reminder of the achievement of her aunt Minette.

Under Louise, the first women *Loges d'Etude* (study lodges) made their appearance in Paris. Invited to join these were the wives and daughters of, mainly, cabinet ministers running France. It had become obvious to the Jacobite hierarchy in France that in order to persuade the men in charge of France's destiny to favor a Stewart restoration, they had to get the women on their side.

Louise's study lodges, while delving in many esoteric aspects of alchemical tradition, were imbued with a strong concept of virtue and loyalty. Their entire tradition, even within their hermetic concept, proved that James, her brother, was not merely the true king of Britain, but also the culmination of the biblical belief that the world would one day be ruled by one king descended from the line of Judah. The various Stewart genealogical marriages to the various European dynasties were explained within an alchemical context, and James was portrayed as the philosopher stone that the world had awaited for so long.

It was, of course, quite a dangerous course of action. All foreign monarchs could have seen red and could have objected to this idea. Some smiled, and some took it seriously. The papacy was not too sure about it, but while James lived in France, whose king was merely tolerant of the papacy in any case, there was little the pope could do. The Messianic Jacobite concept, however, appealed to many in Europe, and it made the cause of James VIII one that was expedient to being promoted within many foreign ministerial cabinets.

Though Louise died in 1712, her Masonic role was commemorated in a painting, and her successor made sure that the Masonic promotion of her brother went on. One strong supporter was George Keith, Earl Marshall of Scotland, later to become provincial grand master of the Masons in Russia. It was he and John Erskine, Earl of Mar, who organized the Raising of 1715 on behalf of James VIII, which culminated at the battle of Sheriffmuir on November 13, 1715. Scone had been readied for James' coronation, but when he landed in Scotland after the battle, he had to flee, because Scone was suddenly was threatened by a Campbell invasion. He was back in France within weeks, only to find himself required to vacate the confines of that kingdom following the triple alliance treaty between England, France and Holland. James ended up in, of all places, Rome, the only safe heaven left to him. It was a city ruled by a pope who looked upon this Stewart prince as something quite unique in Christendom.

CHAPTER 17

Excommunicate them!

In the year 1717, four lodges in London decided to amalgamate together and claim for themselves the grand title of Grand Lodge of England. This is two years following the failed Jacobite attempt of 1715 to restore the Stewarts upon their rightful throne. The leaders of those four lodges had realized that three years of Hanoverian rule had split the Whig Party in two, and the lodge members, disappointed by the events of 1715, decided to join the pro-Stuart Toriesand form the party of "the Pretender." (The Pretender was the name the Hanoverian faction used for James Stewart.) Another attempt to restore the Stewarts was thus engineered by both the Duke of Wharton and Lord Burlington. The latter was a disaffected Whig and had voted against the repeal of the Triennial Parliaments the year before. Lord Burlington traveled to France to meet with the Jacobite leaders in Paris working on behalf of Prince James Stuart. Burlington carried letters to them from the Earl of Mar and Lady Oglethorpe. By then, the titular King James VIII of the Scots, James III of England, had been required to leave French soil and was living in the small palace of Urbino, a papal estate, in the middle of nowhere. From a Hanoverian perspective, a Stewart restoration was an unlikely event. Burlington, Wharton and Oglethorpe wanted to change all that. What Burlington had in mind was to use their new Grand Lodge of England as the catalyst to the Stuart restoration, just as the invisible college had been used during the days of Charles II's restoration. They needed the agreement from their king in exile to act on his behalf.

Coming back to England, Burlington built Chiswick House as the seat of English Jacobite Freemasonry, also known as Red Freemasonry. The Masonic element is emphasized as soon as you enter the property, itself very much built in a Temple architecture. The rooms are filled with Stuart portraits and would be the scene of the Masonic Jacobite ritual, taking individuals through the usual three degrees. This ritual was followed by a progression to a higher order, later acknowledged as the Royal Arch (with its emphasis on the themes of resurrection and restoration), which took place in a red velvet room. Initiates would then be taken further to a degree based on the ancient knight-crusaders of St. John and the Templars. The complicated rituals and symbols provided a hermetically sealed network through which it was safe to carry money, arms and messages to Jacobite agents all over Europe. (Today Burlington House is open to the public and is managed by English Heritage. It is well worth a visit.)

The biggest problem that the hierarchy of those four lodges had to face was the fact that their legality was in question. Their right to exist was given to them by previous rulers of England, coming down from James VI of the Scots when he succeeded Elizabeth I in 1603. (Had not Scotland's James VI come to England as its new king (James II) in 1603, Freemasonry would not have been introduced into England.) Few English have ever wondered when these four independent lodges in London were founded in the first place. These lodges merely amalgamated in 1717, in the same manner that two businesses might merge today, but they were alive and well and active long before 1717. Their right to exist would have been given to them through the assent of previous rulers of England coming down from James VI of the Scots when he succeeded Elizabeth I in 1603. Remember that England was still a feudal society, even in 1717, with only Anglicans having rights to do anything. Catholics, Quakers or Jews did not have the right to function officially within English society. With the rightful king having been disposed of and replaced by interlopers, the lodges needed to ask for and gained patronage from the very king they supported.

The other main problem that the newly set up Grand Lodge of England faced was that there were hundreds of independent lodges throughout England, and they were quite happy with their autonomy. Most current English Freemasons tend to believe that the Grand Lodge of England was able to lord its authority over all the kingdom overnight. This assumption is quite wrong. The Grand Lodge's authority took years to achieve and, from 1723 onwards, the way the London lodge achieved it was through infiltration. Think of it, the north of England was mainly Catholic and pro-Stewarts. Wales was, in the main, pro-Stewart, as was the vast majority of the population in Ireland, save Ulster, which had been peopled with extreme English Anglicans since the days of Elizabeth I and fanatical Scots Presbyterians from the reign of James VI. Scotland, since 1707, irrespective of religious denominations and regardless to what conventional historians would like you to believe, was also in favor of the return of the Stewarts on the throne. Freemasonry lodges existed independent from one another in each of the three kingdoms, and all had previously worked towards the restoration of Charles II. The Stewarts over the water decided to put the power of all these lodges throughout Great Britain and Ireland to good use in helping them achieve a second restoration. Clearly, the one institution in England that was likely to lose its power over the people was the Church of England, since it was the church that had plotted the Stewart downfall and brought the interlopers over. Interestingly, the protagonists of all four London lodges were closely linked to the Church of England.

The other thing we have to remember is that Catholics, in those days, could be Freemasons. In fact, it was the only organization in England that afforded them equality within society since the day King James VII of the Scots (James II of England) had been deposed. (He had wanted everyone within the boundaries of his kingdoms to worship according to their own conscience.) With the Stewarts out of the political picture in Britain, "liberty of conscience" and the concept of equality were firmly ousted. This meant that politics reverted back to the status quo, and no one but Anglicans had any rights at all. In order to retain this status quo, all lodges in England, or as many as possible, were to be taken over, subverted, even eradicated if necessary. Although 1717 saw a new, London-based Masonic impetus, working to restore the Stewarts to their rightful inheritance, the plan was foiled after the failure of the Atterbury plot to overthrow George I in 1722. In 1723, at the end of the Duke of Wharton's grand mastership, the Grand Lodge of England was taken over by Hanoverian infiltrators. I have no doubt that this facet of the history of English Freemasonry irritates the present-day hierarchy of Grand Lodge of England. (It is interesting to note, in passing, that the lodge's archival records, from its inception in 1717 to June 24, 1723, have totally vanished.)

When it comes to Jacobite attempts to restore the Stewarts, people tend to think of three dates: 1690 (the date of the battle of the Boyne, Ireland), 1715 (the battle of Sheriffmuir, Scotland), and 1745 (the battle of Culloden, Scotland). The Scottish restoration attempt of 1718 tends to be forgotten in the annals of history. It involved the Spaniards and the Duke of Liria (James VIII's half-brother and a Freemason), and the Irish and the Scots, particularly the Earl Marshall of Scotland, who stood high within the hierarchy of the Scottish Masons. The scheme was foiled from its beginning, as the Hanoverian government gained inside information of the approaching Spanish armada from infiltrated lodges both in England and Ireland. Even if the prevailing wind had not put the Spanish fleet to flight, England was ready to deal with the Spanish invasion. Clearly, from the Stewarts point of view, this was a disaster.

By 1725, the Earl of Derwentwater, who was also an illegitimate cousin of James VIII, a grandson of Charles II and a Jacobite Freemason to boot, opened the second Jacobite lodge in France. This was done in order to strengthen the power of Lodge St. Germain. From that date onwards, Freemasonry spread like wildfire throughout France, and charters were granted by Derwentwater *au nom du Roy* ("in the king's name"), in this instance King James VIII, III, who was also the theoretical king of France. The same was also done by the Duke of Berwick, then a citizen of the crown of Spain. (Today, the former Berwick family holds the titles of Duke of Liria and Alba.)

In Italy, the first lodge to be founded was the Lodge Lord George Seton in Rome. Established in 1715 (thus two years prior the birth of the Grand Lodge of England in London), it influenced the papacy, in this instance Pope Clemens XI, to support the Stewart king in exile. Pope Clemens XI supported the Stewarts, even though the previous pope had cost them the crowns of Great Britain in the first place. Indeed, it was Innocent XI who gave William III of Orange (a Dutch Protestant) permission to employ a majority of Catholic mercenaries in his army, with which William effectively invaded England. (For those doubting Thomases, the original letters written by the pope to William III of Orange regarding the invasion of England were found in 2001 by Italian historians.) The second Italian lodge was instituted in 1735, again in Rome, with King James VIII's approval. Against all records, tradition claims Prince Charles Edward Stewart as one of its members. All members were Jacobites, mostly Scottish and a few French.

The interesting point within this equation was that Freemasonry, following the Stewarts' loss of their crowns, spread first within countries, such as France and Sweden, which had no links with the Holy Roman Empire. The Hanoverians, on the other hand, were electors within the Holy Roman Empire and one of the many families who elected a Holy Roman emperor, the temporal head of the empire. Seemingly, the Netherlands stood within the same equation. It, too, was part of that Holy Roman Empire. So was the Roman Catholic Church, since the popes were the spiritual heads of that empire. What transpires is that Jacobite Freemasonry itself had to infiltrate the politics of the Papacy and managed to do so without too much trouble.

However, if the Stewarts were doing well within Europe, in Britain, things were going from bad to worse. James VIII/III decided that action was needed and asked his cousin, Pope Clemens XII (born Lorenzo Corsini), if he could help in the matter and possibly publish a bull advising British Catholics not to join Masonic lodges at home. This, in James' estimation, would help to find those rotten apples working for and informing the government of the usurper, George II of Hanover.

Unfortunately, Clemens XII was one of those individuals who saw Freemasonry as a thorn in the side of the church. He saw Freemasonry as far too liberal, far too pagan and rejecting the authority of the papacy. Further, he failed to understand that Freemasonry was the secret service of the very exiled king he supported. On April 28, 1738, the pope promulgated his antimason's bull "In Eminenti." All Catholics wanting to join Freemasonry were thus threatened with papal wrath and excommunication. James VIII/III was appalled on seeing the people supporting his cause and enjoying the membership of all Christian religious denominations taken to task by the papacy, instead of just at home as he has asked. James was fully recognized, as had been his father before him, as the secret grand master of Lodges all over Europe. His eldest son, Charles Edward, was a Freemason, and Charles was constantly grumbling against the papacy, particularly since the death of his too-pious mother, Maria Clementina of Poland, who had died in 1735. The papal bull, to him, looked like another betrayal akin to that of Pope Innocent XI in 1688.

To be truthful, the papal bull was not that much effective. Dominicans and Jesuits ignored it and joined lodges everywhere regardless of the bull. In fact, these were the factions within the Roman Catholic Church who supported fully the return of the Stewarts to Britain and worked tirelessly towards a restoration. Not only that, they jumped into bed, regardless of religious inclination, with anyone supporting a Stewart restoration. In their eyes, elected popes came and went, as did papal policies. Hereditary kingship, on the other hand, was the stability upon which nations and Christianity truly depended. The Hanoverian electors came upon the throne by the wish of parliament, thus being merely elected into office, James VIII /III was king by the right of being his father's son and belonged to the oldest royal house in Christendom.

The second lodge in Rome was founded in 1735, and its members were rather all impressive. That it was ecumenical in concept is proven by the membership. It included Protestants as well as Catholics and Episcopelians. John Cotton of Cambridgeshire was, for example, a nonjuror and thus an English Protestant. Charles Slezer was a Jacobite whose father, John, had been a friend of Charles II. Dr. James Irvin was James VIII's personal physician and became a member of the Royal Company of Archers in 1715. He died in 1759. His son, James, was also a member of the lodge. Thomas Twisden was the son of Sir William Twisden, fifth Bart of Twisendem, in Kent. William Hay, son of the sixth Earl of Kinnoul, had been created Earl of Inverness by James VIII. John Stewart of Grantully had been an officer of the cavalry during the rising of 1715. George Seton, fifth Earl of Wintoun (who had opened the first lodge in Rome in 1715) was master of the second lodge from August 1736. John Murray of Broughten, who would become secretary to Prince Charles Edward Stewart during the Jacobite uprising of 1745, became a member of the lodge in August, 1737. Other members were Mark Carse, of Cockpen; Count Soudavini; and Henry fitzMaurice. The people who were received into the lodge are no less impressive. Captain Thomas Archdeacon was received on

January 4, 1736. Dr. Alexander Cunningham, son of Sir William Cunningham of Caprington by his wife Janet Dick (the only child of Sir James Dick, Bart of Prestonfield and a cousin to Andrew Lumsden, secretary to King James VIII), was received on January 2, 1737. Two other notables were the Scottish painter Allan Ramsay and the French Marquis de Vasse.

On May 9, 1737, an Edinburgh merchant by the name of Halliburton joined the lodge. The name Halliburton is interesting for it was one of the aliases that Charles Edward Stuart used when crossing back to Glasgow and Edinburgh under the guise of a wine merchant. It may very well be that Charles Edward Stewart, for the sake of both secrecy and safety, was the same as person as Edinburgh merchant Halliburton.

There are no more records available following that last meeting and the lodge went underground, though it did not dissolve, following the publication of Pope Clemens' bull in 1738.

Three years prior to the publication of the papal bull, Prince Charles Edward Stewart was to have his first military experience when he took part of the siege of Gaeta and the war between the houses of Bourbon and Austria over succession to the kingdom of Naples. Although he was related to both houses—to the Bourbon on his father side and to the Hapsburgs on his mother side—the Bourbons' argument won the Stewarts to their cause. France had claimed both Sicily and Naples since the days of King Francis I, who died in 1547. By the eighteenth century, whoever was king of Naples was also king of Sicily, and whoever held Sicily could be said to hold a naval enclave within the Mediterranean. Since a Bourbon, Philippe, Duc d'Anjou, had become king of Spain, it was felt by the Bourbons of France and Spain that both Naples and Sicily should be ruled by Carlos, fifth son of Philippe d'Anjou, then Philippe V of Spain. It is this war of succession that saw the rise of the political branch of the Sicilian M.A.F.I.A., "*Morte Alla Francia, Italia Anela,*" meaning "Death to all the French, Italy cries." The population of Sicily, however, was keen to decide for itself who should rule them and, admittedly, the Spanish prince was not their first choice.

Charles Edward Stewart, as most people know, came to Scotland in 1745 to liberate the whole of Britain from the suppressive yoke of the House of Hanover, but was defeated by the Duke of Cumberland in April 1746 at the Battle of Culloden. What is not commonly known is that Charles Edward had held a Templar meeting within the walls of the Palace of Holyroodhouse in September 1745 and had been recognized by those attending it as their new master.

Many people, particularly those in the Masonic craft, have asked me if Charles Edward was a Freemason. The answer is a resounding yes. Those who were in charge of his education were Freemasons, and their aim was to create the embodiment of a Masonic king, a king who would be liberal, who would believe in justice and who would stand for an enlightened monarchical democracy. We are now entering the age concept of the "crowned democrat." Actually, they wanted to create the concept of a monarch leading with a republican spirit. With Charles Edward, Freemasonry would suddenly reach a revival that would span across oceans, nations, and religions and that would spark revolutions. It would also create the United States of America.

The revival started with Freemason from both Scotland and Sweden, with Michael Andrew Ramsay (1686–1743) and Emanuel Swedenborg (1688–1772), with the support of the Tessin family in Sweden and Jonathan Swift, with the Parisian Masonic Jacobite bankers Tourton and Baur, and with the Irish colonel Daniel O'Brian. Those who know something of Jacobite history will be aware that Michael Andrew Ramsay was Charles Edward's tutor. Ramsay became something of a hero for Charles, and he thought Charles to be quite precocious. Indeed, from the earliest days of his life, Charles Edward was aware that he had a mission and a destiny to fulfill. Ramsay imbued Charles' mind with Masonic liberalism, with a distrust of the Roman Catholic Church and with a Celtic literacy that would come to help Charles Edward understand the land of his ancestors during the days he had to roam the Highlands following the 1746 defeat at Culloden.

When not teaching his prince, Ramsay wrote orations on behalf of Freemasonry, and these papers, sent under strict secrecy to various pro-Stewart sympathizers working for the various governments in Europe, were read avidly and disseminated throughout the land. Working with Ramsay was the Earl Marshall of Scotland, Keith by name. It is he who initiated Charles Edward into the educating Roman lodge of the "Order of Tobosco" in 1731. The study lodge of Tobosco was a training school for teenage Masons and schooled them in the rituals of grand masters, Templar idealism and chivalric knighthood. The secrecy, the politics, the analysis, the royal embassies visiting the lodge, such as that sent by the king of Sweden and headed by Axel Wrede-Sparre, all appealed to Charles Edward's sense of destiny. Following the siege of Gaeta of 1734, there was no stopping the true heir of Britain from revitalizing the Masonic networks working on behalf of the restoration of his father. The boy of fifteen had become a man of action, a man of ideas, the idealistic Masonic king in waiting.

The Swedes, certainly in those days, were a force to be reckoned with, particularly within the frame of Freemasonry. Moreover, the Swedish masons were overtly pro-Stewart. Their representative in Rome was Count Nils Bielke, brother-in-law of both the Masonic Swedish leaders, Wrede-Sparre and Tessin. Furthermore, Bielke also served as secret agent for King Louis XV of France and was an intimate of the Jacobite court at Rome. It was, in fact, Bielke who arranged for Swedenborg to meet James VIII and his sons in the Mutti Palazzo in Rome. Swedenborg, in his diary, mentioned his "reverential awe" at meeting the royal Stewarts. Charles Edward Stewart, seemingly, based his military training on that of Sweden's late warrior-king, Charles XII.

While James VIII took a passive political stand, Charles Edward decided that action was best. Aggressiveness was the key, Charles thought, and aggressive recruiting was the policy Charles advocated. Enter Baron von Hund onto the Jacobite scene of 1743. Von Hund was initiated in Paris by proxy by the Earl of Kilmarnock, Lord Clifford, and by Alexander Seton, tenth Earl of Eglinton and Knight of the Red Feather. (Although von Hund believed he was initiated by Charles, but Charles was in Rome at the time.) Von Hund soon became a Masonic liaison officer between the Jacobites in the French court and those in the court of Frederick the Great of Prussia. The latter had been initiated into Freemasonry in an *Ecossais* lodge prior to 1743.

By late 1743, Swedenborg was in Holland, waiting, in total secrecy, for his orders to cross to London. While at The Hague, he was initiated into a mystical Jacobite society. Blindfolded, wrapped in a death shroud, led through darkened rooms, Swedenborg was given a new order name and hailed as an "honest" Jacobite. Reaching London in May 1744, he recorded political observations in code and referred in his letters to "the Jacobites who would settle in the sanctuary of the North and rebuild the Temple of Wisdom." He further became involved in the shadowy Royal Order of Scotland, which had suddenly made an appearance in London in 1741 and practiced the high degrees developed by Andrew Michael Ramsay. (It was, in fact, a French military officer by the name of Pierre Lambert de Lintot, living as a clandestine in London and working under the guise of an engraver, who developed the rite of seven degrees by tying them to the Royal Order of Scotland.)

General James Keith, then in Sweden, was preparing a large contingent of both Swedish and Russian troops to cross to Scotland and join Charles Edward. By then, Charles Edward had made his way to Paris. February 1744 was when the Masonic enterprise went into full-scale alert. Backed by Jewish and Irish cash; backed by Masonic Jacobite lodges; backed by Prussia, Russia and Sweden, the Jacobite raising of 1745, had it succeeded, would have probably changed the shape of European politics. America might not have become an independent republic, France might be ruled today by a Stewart king in succession to an extinct house of Bourbon, the imperial House of Romanov might still be in charge of Russia and two world wars might have been averted.

Coming back from Scotland in 1746, Charles Edward created, in 1747, the Jacobite Masonic lodge of Arras, and it is to that one particular lodge that many others in France and Belgium trace their ancestry. Many Hanoverian Masonic historians take the view that this claim is unfounded and that the Arras lodge was not created before 1765. Their claim, however, can be easily refuted on the grounds that the 1765 Masonic chart is nothing more than a solicitor transcript, made in 1765, of the original 1747 charter signed by Charles Edward. Further, while they claim that he signed the charter "Charles R" (thus claiming, so they say, to be king), the truth of the matter is that the original, as mentioned on the solicitor's 1765 transcript, quite simply states that Charles Edward merely signed "*Pour le Roy*, Charles PR" ("For the King, Charles P[ro] R[ex]"). Charles held his charter of regency from his father since 1744, so he was quite entitled to sign as prince regent. Moreover, there is a print, extant, showing Charles Edward, accompanied by the Comte de St. Germain, giving the Masonic chart to the brothers of Lodge Arras.

Charles Edward's influence on the world of western Freemasonry of the eighteenth century was, to say the least, immense. In fact, the records of the French, Spanish and Swedish Masonic hierarchies state quite categorically that Charles Edward was their sovereign grand master. In the introduction to his biography of Prince Charles Edward Stewart, J. Cuthbert Hadden mentions the fact that Charles Edward, through many of his travels and dealings with foreign courts, "left traces of occult enterprises outlined in cabinets of foreign governments, in the Senate of Great Britain, in the British Navy itself—busy, mysterious phantoms of tradition, more nearly applied to the romaunt of the Middle Ages than to the history of modern times; and leaving such evidence of his spirit and conception, that there is no event connected with his name of which it may be said: 'it is credible, because it is improbable.'"

Long before the event of Culloden when he was twenty-six years of age, Charles Edward was a European political power to be reckoned with. Unlike his father, who used passive policies, Charles believed that God helped those who helped themselves. By the age of fifteen, following the Siege of Gaeta, the Stewart heir had truly come of age. His uncle, the Duke of Berwick, James fitzjames Stewart, took him under his wing and groomed him to take over, within a year, the reins of the Masonic entities in Europe. In those days, the age of entry into Freemasonry was sixteen, or twelve if your father was a Mason. (This business of having to be twenty-one is very much a modern thing.) Charles Edward was, one has to remember, a cousin to the Holy Roman Emperor, to the kings of France and Spain, and to the Comte de St. Germain, and he could count numerous popes as ancestors. His was a pedigree spanning some three thousand years, and he was heir to the oldest kingdom in Europe. That the Masonic world in Europe should set its eyes upon this one individual could only be expected. It was, after all, nothing less than a family tradition. Charles decided to shape this underground establishment by emphasizing its antiquity. Esoteric coats of arms were introduced, new Masonic titles were created, an active Templar tradition was forcefully introduced within this new trend of Freemasonry, together with the concept of the liberal arts so detested by the Roman Catholic Church.

To the House of Hanover, this pro-Stewart Masonic threat could only be dealt with in one particular way. Everything about Scottish Freemasonry had to be debunked, had to be derailed, had to be, in short, anglicized. Three men rose to the challenge: Edward, Duke of Kent, and his brother Frederick, Duke of Sussex, both sons to King George III, and Thomas Dunkerley, an illegitimate son of King George II. The Hanoverian York rite was about to raise its ugly head.

CHAPTER 18

Divide and Conquer
The End of an Auld Lang Sine

I mentioned in my first book, *The Forgotten Monarchy of Scotland* that Charles Edward Stewart was offered the crown of America by a delegation sent by Colonel George Washington following the defeat of the British army at Yorktown. Washington was, of course, a Freemason himself. Further, the very people who were involved in his endeavor to free America from the yoke of Westminster came from Jacobite stock. Their fathers and grandfathers had fought for King James VIII and for Prince Charles Edward both in the 1715 and 1745 Jacobite raisings. Most of them had been Scots Masons as well. In fact, one of Charles' natural sons was a personal friend of Washington himself and had kept his father informed on the American nationalistic developments on a regular basis through private letters and American newspaper reports.

When it came to decide as to what kind of democratic representation the Americans should opt for, many people were divided on the matter. There had been no a precedent for electing an individual to be the legal, presidential representative of any nations. The concept was decidedly new. Washington, who could trace his ancestry back to early Scottish kings, was offered the crown by a common vote of those involved in the proceedings of the "what do we do now?" committee. He rejected it on the grounds that while his ancestry may have been royal, albeit tenuously, it was not good enough to grant him the recognition over other more legitimate kings from Europe. Many people in America today would probably say, "Why should he have cared about Europe?" Bear in mind that, at that time, except for the descendants of those early settlers who came, and survived, in the seventeenth century, the majority of the white population in America in 1784 came from Europe. Most of them were born from parents who had migrated to America from Europe. American's link with Europe was much stronger in those days than it is today.

The Jacobite faction in America opted for the next best thing to naming their liberator as king. It decided to give America to the man who had a better claim to rule it than England's George III. George Washington, a Freemason, sent a delegation to King Charles III, first Count of Albany, at the Guadigni Palazzo in Florence, in Italy. Charles Edward declined the invitation, and America became a republic.

Charles Edward, by then, had become once again a focus point for many people and pro-Stewart European governments. During the 1760s, the Duke of Clermont, with the blessing of both King Louis XV of France and Charles Edward, issued all French lodges certificates in the name of Charles Edward, Grand Master. This lasted till the death of Clermont in 1771. By then, Sweden was very keen to relaunch the mystical aura of the Stewarts in exile. Throughout the 1770s and 1780s, the king of Sweden resolved to strengthen the Swedish-Jacobite Masonic links and networks. It was with the support of the then king of Sweden, Gustavus III, that Charles Edward was able to divorce and repudiate Louise de Stolberg Guedern (technically his second wife). Now Gustavus III of Sweden asked Charles to make him the legal heir to the grand magistry of both the Templars and Masons in Europe, and certainly those in Sweden. Charles' imprimatur was thought to be of such importance that without it, a Masonic entity, anywhere in Europe, had no value.

While the Swedes were reaching a deal with Charles Edward, Prussia and Denmark were making overture to Charles as well. Denmark and Prussia were, by then, pro-Hanoverian. Charles decided to send them on a wild goose chase by claiming that he had nothing to do with either Freemasonry or Templarism. Charles' statement of denial has been quoted by many Masonic historians as sacrosanct. They are, of course, mistaken. Even the Stewart papers at Windsor do contain a Masonic-Swedish passport issued to Charles Edward under the style of "Knight of the Golden Sun." Contemporary letters from both the French duc de Clermont and the king of Sweden and his brothers refer to Charles Edward as their "Supreme Authority" and "Secret Grand Master." None would have made these statements without being aware of all the facts.

Britain, of course, was a different kettle of fish. Charles' supreme authority over Freemasonry in England came to an end in 1774. Lambert de Lintot, the French secret agent working in London, sent a memo to Paris stating that in June of that year, in a meeting held in London, no less than seventy brothers voted to remove Charles Edward from his position as "Grand Master, Grand Commander, Conservator, Guardian of the Pact and Sacred Vow of the Christian Princes." They also affirmed this resolve "by denying any recognition to any constitution in the name of the said Charles Edward, in the three kingdoms of Great Britain." However, their resolve could only apply to England, since no brethren from Scotland and Ireland were present at that meeting. But this statement alone proves that Charles Edward Stewart had had the recognized right to create lodges in Great Britain (the three kingdoms) for some forty years.

There was a reason for England doing this, albeit not a good enough one to reject the man that had done so much for Freemasonry as a whole. Many English lodges had been declared "irregular" by the Hanoverian usurper and government surveillance was suddenly on the increase. Survival was of the essence. They had to abandon Charles and seek another champion, one that lived in Britain and was, preferably, a member of the ruling royal family. Their choice fell upon the Duke of Cumberland. This was not the infamous Butcher of Culloden (he died without issue), but rather a brother of George III. Henriech Friedriech, Prinz von Hannover, Duke of Cumberland and Strathern, did not get on well with his brother. In fact, they loathed each other, so much so that Cumberland expressed his contempt for George III by constantly working with the opposition party and the French-affiliated Masonic lodges abroad. Choosing the duke to lead the lodges in England was a clever move because though the duke was linked to the Royal House of Hanover, his disaffection made sure that the rite of seven degrees would continue to attract political dissidents and "irregular" Masons. Charles Edward must have had a good chuckle at all the decision, as it really meant that nothing had changed and it was business as usual.

Another propagandist of Charles Edward Stewart was, of course, Robert Burns, Freemason, poet and Scotland's national bard.

He was, of course, a contemporary of Prince Charles Edward Stewart and was, in effect, related to him, though very distantly. Less known of Burns' background is that, though born within humble financial circumstances, he was kin to the best blood of Scotland through his Keith ancestry and had Scottish earls, dukes and marquises as cousins. Most of them, including Burns' paternal great-grandmother's family, fought on behalf of the Stewarts. There is no doubt that Rabbie was well aware of this, and confirmation can be found in a letter of his written to Lady Winifred Maxwell Constable, a woman of staunch Jacobite tendency. He saluted her "as a common sufferer in a cause where even to be unfortunate is glorious. The cause of heroic loyalty." He then goes on to say that "though my fathers had not illustrious honours and vast properties to hand down, though they left their humble cottages only to add so many units more to the unnoted crowd that followed their leaders, yet, what they could, they did and what they had, they lost. With unshaken firmness and unconcealed political adventure, they shook hands with ruin for what they esteemed the cause of their King and Country."

Though born a decade after "the 45," Burns' Jacobitism was rampant and made all the more obvious when he took part to the birthday celebration of Charles Edward Stewart held in Edinburgh on December 31, 1787. This, in itself, was still a treasonable act for which he could have been arrested and lost his life without trial. Fortunately, George III would have had to arrest most of Scotland's leading aristocracy, something he could hardly afford to do. Also participating to the true king's birthday bash were the following people: Lady Nairn, author of "Will Ye No Come Back Again" (whose father had been Prince Charles' aide de camp); James Murray of Abercairney; the Earl and Countess of Seaforth; the Duke of Perth; Oliphant of Gask (whose father had organized Prince Charlie's coronation in the abbey of Holyrood House in September 1745); and Thriepland of fingask and Stewart, Lord Provost of Edinburgh. Burns and they, it must be noted, shared the same table on that glorious evening, when all stood and drank "to the King over the water."

That Burns was a patriot can be seen by many of his physical actions. Visiting the grave of his ancestor Robert Bruce at Dunfermline Abbey, he knelt and kissed the stone. The winter of 1788/89 marked the centenary of the so-called glorious English revolution. Sick with disgust, he wrote to the *Edinburgh Evening Courant* a defense of the Stewarts, in which he states "the Stewarts have been condemned and laughed at for their folly and impracticability of their attempts in 1715 and 1745. I cannot join in the ridicule against them . . . Let every man, who has a tear for the many miseries incident to humanity, feel for a family, illustrious as any in Europe, and unfortunate beyond historic precedent."

Burns wrote such Jacobite works such as *Lament for James, There'll Never Be Peace Till Jamie Comes Hame, Scots Wha Hae, Caledonia: A Ballad, Charlie, He's My Darling, Lament for Mary, Queen of Scots, On the Approach of Spring, Address to Edinburgh* and *The Bonnie Lass of Albany*. All these works show a fervent wish for the return of his lawful royal house and Scottish sovereignty and made Burns a growing threat to the British establishment. The bigger the following Burns was able to create, the bigger the threat of a Stewart restoration.

The Freemason tradition came down to Burns through his Keith ancestry, and the brotherhood of man had a place of prime importance in his life. The outcome of his belonging to Freemasonry was a song that probably has been sung all over the world. *A Man's a Man for A' That* was the opening hymn of the Scottish Parliament in 1998.

Liberty and equality were things that Robert Burns treasured as well. But somehow, his *Ode for General Washington's Birthday* is one of the lesser known of his works, even in the United States of America. On the eve of the French Revolution, Burns wrote *The Rights of Woman* and even bought a canon that he was going to donate to the people of France. The canons, however, were confiscated before they could make their way from Edinburgh to France. The fact that Burns' financial circumstances obliged him to work as an excise-man in Dumfries on behalf of a government he neither believed in nor supported shows him to be a practical man, what is referred today as "a canny Scot." His work entailed traveling the countryside, where his newly found fame as a successful writer involved him in an excess of conviviality and private parties. However, he was never the addicted drinker as so many historians claimed.

Dying so young, in the prime of his years, we are reminded of our own mortality. We are also reminded that, no matter how short a life, anything is possible if we believe in the concepts of ideals and principles. Reading Burns' poetry, we become quickly aware that there is an answer for all situations. His *Address to a Toothache* just proves the point. For those short of cash, and this will, no doubt, apply to us all (except the Windsors of course), simply read Rabbie's *Lines Written on a Bank-note*. For those who fought in either of the world wars, a quick look at Burns' *Soldiers Return* will show that nothing much had changed between Burns' days and theirs. If he was a man of vision, he was also a man of wisdom, a bard for all nations, and he is revered and celebrated the world over.

Following his death in 1796, his children by Jean Armour became, against their mother's wishes, wards of the State and were forcibly taken to London and brought up in a pro-Hanoverian environment. None of his descendants would bother the State ever again.

When Charles Edward died in Rome in 1788, the Hanoverian government saw it as an opportunity to erase the Stewart tradition for once and for all. The next three years would see the propaganda machine working overtime. Three things stood in favor of the British government in this Machiavellian scheme. firstly, Charles' brother, Henry, was a acrdinal of the Roman Catholic Church, and though he now claimed to be king "by the will of God but not the will of men," the man would be a pushover to deal with. Henry has been referred by many of his contemporaries as both "amiable" and "boring." He was no Charles Edward Stewart. Secondly, Charles' own lawful progeny was merely two years old when his father died. Prince Edward James Stewart, second Count of Albany and first Duke of Kendal and Kintyre, would not become a contention to deal with for some years. He might, it was hoped, even die before he reached his dynastic majority. Certainly, the death of Charles' legitimated daughter, Charlotte, in 1789 was a godsend to the British government. Thirdly, the man in charge of the Stewart Masonic tradition was now the king of Sweden, Gustavus III, and, obviously, to most people in Britain, that might as well be the other side of the world.

By 1791, one of George II's illegitimate sons, Thomas Dunkerley, viewed amicably by George III, was forcibly imposed as provincial grand master on numerous provinces in England and formed the Supreme Grand and Royal Conclave of England. Under Dunkerley's advice, Prince Edward, Duke of Kent, was elected overall patron to English Masonry. Dunkerley died in 1795, and Kent took over the reign of Masonic England. By then, Gustavus III had been shot dead in 1792, and his son (in fact, the natural son of Gustavus III's wife, Sophia of Denmark), Gustaf IV Adolph, had taken over as king. Gustaf IV, unlike his stepfather, was anti-French and thus could be thought of as an ally of the Hanoverian government of Britain. In 1809, he was forcibly deposed and replaced by his uncle, Charles XIII, a pro-Stewart in politics. Seemingly, Gustaf IV was never made aware of the Masonic inheritance, and it thus reverted back to the Stewarts in Rome.

Then, in 1793, Rome was invaded by the French under the leadership of General Joseph Bonaparte, brother of the man who became Emperor Napoleon I of France. Seemingly, both brothers, in fact all Bonaparte brothers, were Freemasons. Joseph met with Henry Benedict Stewart and his nephew Edward James in Rome a few days before Rome was invaded by the French. The life of Edward James Stewart, even though he was only seven years of age, was too important to leave to the vagaries of war. Joseph Bonaparte advised the Stewarts to leave Rome and to make their way to Sardinia. While Henry, a cardinal of the Roman Catholic Church, remained in Rome, Edward James and his mother made their way to the court of King Charles Emmanuel IV of Sardinia.

The sudden disappearance from the political scene of the Stewart heir was a blessing in disguise to the Hanoverian government, but it would be short-lived. Edward James and his mother came back to Rome in 1802, accompanied by none other than Charles Emmanuel IV, ex-king of Sardinia. By 1807, the Masonic political scene in Britain came, once more, to the fore. That year, Henry Benedict Stewart, Duke of York and Cardinal of Frascati, died. Since 1799, he had been a financial pensioner of the Hanoverian crown to the tune of £5000 per year. His death, compounded by a rather confusing second will leaving his right to the three crowns "to that Prince to whom it descends by virtue of blood relationship," allowed the Hanoverians to make their final and last move that would hammer the knell blow to Jacobite Freemasonry. British propaganda claimed the Royal House of Stewart had died out and was extinct. Henry Benedict Stewart's first will, known to all in Europe, from kings to the pope, was totally ignored, and Edward James, certainly in Britain, was sent into the historical annals of nothingness.

The leadership of Jacobite Freemasonry on mainland Britain would, suddenly, be contested by two Hanoverian princes. The Duke of Kent (who later became the supposed father of Queen Victoria) and the Duke of Sussex, Prince Augustus Frederick, fifth in line to the throne, made a bid to take over what had been a thorn in the side of the family since 1714. Kent was rejected, but Sussex was successful in succeeding as grand master. There was a reason behind the English Jacobites' acceptance of Sussex. His wife, Lady Augusta Murray, daughter of John, fourth Earl of Dunmore, came from a strong and staunch Jacobite family. They were married in Rome, against the wishes of George III, in 1793 and had two children, Sir Augustus Frederick d'Este and Lady Emma Augusta d'Este. By royal decree, their children were deprived of the style of "Royal Highness" and the title of prince and princess. It was also known that they had met, on numerous occasions, with Henry Benedict Stewart and his nephew, then styled Count Stuarton. The d'Este surname was borrowed by Sussex and his wife for their children to commemorate the last true queen consort of Great Britain, Queen Maria Beatrix d'Este, Princess of Modena, the wife of King James VII of the Scots, James II of England.

During Sussex's rule as grand master, Alexander Deuchar, a Scots engraver, suddenly decided that the whole of Scottish Freemasonry should follow an English ritual known as the York Rite. This meant that, even though Scotland had its own grand lodge based in Edinburgh, any remnant of the original ritual from pre-Hanoverian era simply went into oblivion. Scots lodges all over the country were ransacked, and old rituals were confiscated and, one must assume, destroyed.

Deuchar's history is worth mentioning here because, as a whole, the man did more to destroy the original rites of Freemasonry in Scotland than the Hanoverians ever where able to do over a period of some one hundred years. In my views, Deuchar was nothing less than a traitor, one of those many individuals who, for reasons of pure profit and power, saw fit to create the abominations that all Scots Masons have to put up with today, including the alleged requirement that the national anthem should be sung at the opening or closing of a lodge. Deuchar's brother, a captain in the British army, actually stole a cross from the former Templar church of Tomar in Portugal and brought it back to Scotland. The family boasts a genealogy stretching back to Scottish kings (though a few generations are missing to make it a fact and a history claiming that they fought at Bannockburn in the army of Robert Bruce. The latter, to grant them their due, may be correct, and the family could produce the sword that had fought on behalf of Scotland's independence up to the end of the nineteenth century. What is interesting to note is that, although Deuchar was a major mover of Scottish Freemasonry towards the York Rite, there are, to date, no biographies about him. Even the world of Scots Freemasonry is totally silent about the man, as if it is ashamed of having to acknowledge him at all).

Another fact that helped the Hanoverians to truly take over Scottish Freemasonry was that the original line of the Sinclairs of Roslyn becoming dormant in the 1780s. Sarah Sinclair, daughter of William Sinclair, ninth

Baron of Roslyn, died without issue. Her cousins, James and Francis, were then living in Italy and were officers in the Neapolitan army. Whether or not they have descendants is not known today, but research is presently taking place to find the heir of line of the ancient barons of Roslyn. What is clear, however, is that a new title of Earl of Roslyn was created for Alexander Wedderburn on April 21, 1801, by George III. Dying without issue, Wedderburn's sister, Janet, then married to Sir Henry Erskine, fifth Baronet, who succeeded to the title, and the family adopted the double-barreled name of Erskine-Sinclair. It is from that unconnected line to the original Masonic lairds of Roslyn that the present earl is descended. While this family had no connections with Freemasonry before, it is now capitalizing on the Masonic link with Roslyin Chapel charging an entrance fee to view a religious building that is otherwise open to most people for public worship. Interestingly, a Masonic portrait of a Templar knight at Roslin Chapel has the face of Prince Charles Edward Stewart, alluding to his being the secret grand master of the Masonic Templars. One must, however, look at the portrait upside down. There is no denying, from that portrait alone, that Charles Edward was of immense importance to the Masonic painter and Scots Masonic Templars themselves, even up to the nineteenth century. It proves of a Stuart involvement within Scottish masonic Templarism.

The final nail in the coffin of Scottish freemasonry was hammered by the earls of Elgin. Together with the Erskine-Sinclairs of Roslyn, the Bruces of Elgin made sure that Scottish Freemasonry would be subverted to become part of the British establishment by promoting the idea that the Grand Lodge of Scotland should answer to Grand Lodge of England. The Scots, needless to say, refused to go that far. Becoming hereditary provincial grand masters, the Bruces of Elgin then decided to make a play as the heirs of Robert Bruce, who acknowledged the Royal House of Hanover Saxe Coburg Windsor as being the rightful heirs to the three crowns of Britain. It is, of course, quite untrue that the earls of Elgin are descended from Robert Bruce. If they were, they would have succeeded David II, Bruce's son, and would probably be ruling Scotland today.

The truth of the matter is that, though the family name is indeed Bruce, they cannot trace their descent to the original lords of Annandale; two missing generations in their genealogy to prove the case. Indeed, the younger son from whom they claim to be their Annandale descent cannot be found in the Scottish records but only in the English ones. Nor can they claim to be descended from Robert Bruce from the wrong side of the blanket. Peerages of Scotland state that this simply cannot be the case. In fact, the real heir of line of that branch of the Bruce family is not the Earl of Elgin, but the would be heir of the dormant branch of the "Bruces of Rait." Extensive research is presently taking place to find the individual that should take over as head of Clan Bruce.

The reason I mention this is to show that the wrong people are in charge of an institution that was actually created to take Scotland forward in a more liberal way, not to bring it to a standstill within the British political status quo. There are, today, no Scottish Freemasonry rituals dating back to the seventeenth century to be found in Scotland. What our ancestors performed within the four walls of their respective lodges cannot be described. Or can it?

Interestingly, the answer is to be found in the Russian archives in Moscow and will soon be revealed to the Masonic world at large. As most of us know, Adolf Hitler was a man who was heavily involved with the occult, particularly the black side of it, and had gathered a tremendous amount of Masonic archives from the various countries Germany invaded during the Nazi era. The records were all taken to be stored in Berlin. In 1945, when Germany fell to the Allied forces, these archives were taken away by the Russians and deposited in Moscow in various heavy cardboard boxes. There, they would be left, untouched, on dusty shelves. Until, that is, Perestroyka exploded in a liberating way, and Russian communism faded in the background.

It was then that an American researcher accidentally fell upon the Masonic find in Moscow. Looking for something totally different, the researcher fell upon these old closed boxes, some of them looking rather despondent, from which protruded some single sheets of paper. His nose got the better of him and he pulled one sheet out, then realizing that what he held was part of an original eighteenth-century Masonic ritual. He said nothing, pulled out some more sheets, and brought them back to the United States for further analysis. Once his team realized what they had found, there was no stopping them. Although it took years to get permission from the Russian state to finally view the archives, the data is presently being collated so that the information can be passed on for posterity. What is special about these archives is the fact that most of them refer to Scottish Freemasonry, all date back to the seventeenth and eighteenth centuries, and they contain original rituals from the period, rituals that have not been performed for over two hundred years. This is what is going to redress the balance and break the so-called status quo that has brought Scottish Freemasonry to a standstill for so long. Moreover, they will prove the unequivocal involvement of the Stewart kings as hereditary grand masters.

What the archives will also prove is the influence that Freemasonry had upon the European world and, subsequently, Europe's worldwide colonies. With British Freemasonry subverted to support the unwanted Hanoverian succession, the ideals of Scottish sovereignty, liberty and equality would be shelved away and replaced by the concept of English feudalism and the British status quo. It cannot last much longer in its present form, and there are many murmurs now, asking questions, seeking answers, wanting to make changes that would be more than welcomed by most brethren of the Masonic craft, particularly in Scotland.

Times are changing, and we have learnt, over the past two hundred years, that nothing we have been told should be taken for granted. In fact, let us remember that Freemasonry was intended as a progressive science and not a stagnating one. Let us, today's Freemasons, prove ourselves equal to the task of finding our true roots, those of truth and justice, of fraternity and philanthropy, of enlightenment and liberty, whether these be civil, religious or intellectual. Let us reject the restricted platform that has been imposed upon us against our will for so long. Time to put the ancient principle of ancestral conviction into action. It is time to see the light and be the corner stone of the Sacred Universal Law. It is time to remember.

The Mohammedan descent of Hugues de Payens and Teresa, ruling Countess of Portugal

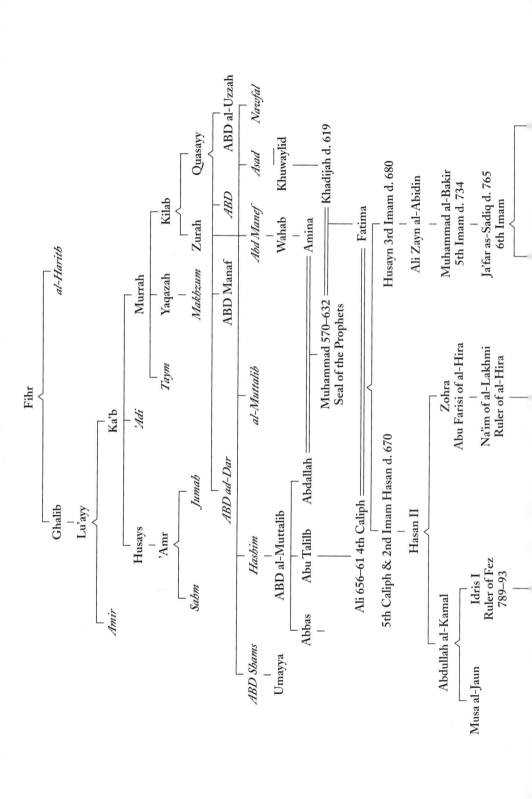

		Ismail
		|
		V
		Ismailite Orders of Assassins & Nusayri
	Musa al-Qadhim 7th Imam d. 799	
	|	
	Ali Ridha d. 818 8th Imam	
	|	
	later Imams	
	Itaf	
	|	
	Amr (took residence in Seville)	
	|	
	Aslan	
	|	
	Abbad	
	|	
	Qara'is	
	|	
	Isma'il, Iman of Seville	
	|	
	Muhammad I Kadi abu'l-Kasim Emir of Seville d. 1042	
	|	
	Muhammad II al-Mu'tadib Emir of Seville 1042–1069	
	|	
	Muhammad III al-Mu'tamid Emir of Seville 1069–1091	
	|	
	Zaida (Ximena) d. 1107 Alfonso VI of Castille & Leon	
	|	
	Teresa, Countess of Portugall Henri of Burgundy d. 112	
	|	
	Alfonso I Enriques King of Portugal	
	|	
	Kings of Portugal	
	From whom all the ancient dynasties of Europe	
Idris II 793–828		
|		
Umar		
|		
Abdullah		
|		
Ali		
|		
Ahmad		
|		
Mamun		
|		
Abu Ahmad		
|		
Muhammad d. 1008 al-Mansur, Emir of Cordoba Abba of Pamplona		
|		
Abd ar-Rahman an'Nasir (Prince Sanchuelo) Jimena of Cordoba		
|		
Theobaldo, Lord of Gardile Angelica Doukas		
|		
Thibault de Payens Lord of the Castle of Martigny Helie de Montbard		
|		
Hugue de Payens 1st Master of the Order of the Knights Templar Elizabeth		
|		
Thibault, Abbot of Abbey of St. Colombe		

Acknowledgments

I wish to thank the late Sir Jack Robertson. Without his constant input, I doubt that this book would have ever started. A special mention should go to the late Dom Lorenzo Abruneddo, Metropolitan Archbishop of the Orthodox Catholic Church, Jurisdiction of New York, formerly the Sovereign Grand Master of the Sovereign Order of the Order of St. John of Jerusalem, the Knights of Malta. He opened his invaluable knowledge and the archives of the Order in New York for me to peruse. Brother James Munro, who explained Roslyn Chapel like no other can do. Sir Laurence Gardner, for his impeccable research on the subject of Freemasonry. His book *The Shadow of Solomon* was an inspiration. Tim Wallace-Murphy, for nagging at me, constantly, to finish the work. Dr. Margaret Tottle-Smith, who kept sending information on a regular basis. Brother Bob Cooper, the librarian of Grand Lodge of Scotland, who gave me the opportunity to view and search the Charles Morrisson Collection all those years ago. The Vatican and Corsini libraries. Monica van der Hoff, the Grand Master of the mixed Grand Lodge of the Netherlands, Grand Orient, Amsterdam, for her incredible support. Sir Abel de Lacerda Botelho, for taking me to Sintra and that magical Masonic castle. The Trustees of the said castle, for a visit that I shall never forget. To my Masonic friends in the Middle East. They were so prompt and so keen that the truth should be told. Their intellect and Masonic knowledge have been unique in helping us write this book. To my Mother, for telling us "to get on with it." Last but certainly not least, Caroline Pincus, Brenda Knight, Jan Johnson, and the entire team at Red Wheel/Weiser.

—HRH Prince Michael of Albany

Bibliographies

Islam (Arabian Conquest to Spain, including Genealogies)

Al-Makkari, Almed ibn Muhammad. *History of the Mohammedan Dynasties in Spain.* Translated by Pascual de Cyangos. London: Oriental Translation Fund of Great Britain and Ireland, 1840.

Barber, Forrest E. "Arab Blood Royal." *The Augustan* 18, no. 4 (1977).

Bearman, P., T. Bianquis, C. E. Bosworth, E. van Donzel, and W. P. Heinrichs, eds. *Encyclopaedia of Islam.* Leiden, the Netherlands: Brill Academic Publishers, 1999.

Becker, Udo, ed. *The Element Encyclopedia of Symbols.* Translated by Lance W. Garmer. Dorset, U.K.: Element, 1994.

Bosworth, Clifford E. *The Islamic Dynasties: A Chronological and Genealogical Handbook.* Edinburgh: Edinburgh University Press, 1967.

Daftary, Farhad. *The Assassin Legends: Myths of the Isma'ilis.* London: I. B. Tauris, 1994.

———. *The Isma'ilis: Their History and Doctrines.* Cambridge, U.K.: Cambridge University Press, 1990.

Douka, Jean. "Ceasar & Moine: son jeu politique a Byzance de 1060 a 1081." Translated by B. Leib. *Analecta Ballandina* 68 (1950).

Duckworth, John. *Muhammad and the Arab Empire.* St. Paul, Minn.: Greenhaven Press, 1980.

"East Meets West." *Burke's Royal Families of the World.*

Evans, Charles. "The Princess Zaida." *The American Genealogist* 39 (1963): 157–160.

Fletcher, Richard. *Moorish Spain*. Berkeley: University of California Press, 2006.

Frederick, T. *A Closer Look at the Ancestry of Hugues de Lusignan*. London,1879.

Glick, Thomas F. *From Muslim Fortress to Christian Castle: Social and Cultural Change in Medieval Spain*. Manchester, U.K.: Manchester University Press, 1995.

Hammer, *Les Assassins*.

Hitti, Philip Khuri. *History of the Arabs*. 10th ed. New York: St. Martin's Press, 1970.

Hourani, Albert. *A History of the Arab Peoples*. New York: Warner Books, 1991.

Jackson, Peter, trans. *The Mission of Friar William Rubruck: His Journey to the Court of the Great Khan Möngke, 1253–1255*. London: The Hakluyt Society, 1990.

Jacob, Charles. "A Suggested Moslem Descent for Eleonor of Provence and Eleonor of Castile." *The Augustan* (1969).

Jambet, Christian. *La Grande Resurrection d'Alamut*. Paris: Éditions Verdier, 1990.

Jayyusi, Salma Khadra, ed. *Legacy of Muslim Spain*. 2nd ed. Leiden, the Netherlands: Brill, 1992.

Johar, Ibn, Abu-Al Alkar, and Abou-firas. *Chronicles of the Crusades*. N.p., n.d.

Jordanian embassy in London. Unpublished information on the Ashemite dynasty (genealogies).

Lane-Poole, Stanley. *Saladin and the Fall of the Kingdom of Jerusalem*. Beirut: Khayats, 1964.

Landay, Jerry M. *The Dome of the Rock*. New York: Newsweek Book Division, 1972.

"Le veritable Hasan Sabbak-Faik Bulut." Translated from the Turkish.

Lourie, Elena. *Crusade and Colonisation: Moslems, Christians and Jews in Medieval Aragon*. Aldershot: Variorum, 1990.

Kaegi, Walter E. *Byzantium and the Early Islamic Conquests*. New York: Cambridge University Press, 1992.

Krey, August. C. *The first Crusade: The Account of Eyewitnesses and Participants*. Princeton, N.J.: Princeton University Press, 1921.

Pickthall, Mohammed Marmaduke. *The Meaning of the Glorious Qur'an*. New York: A. A. Knopf, 1930.

Pidal, Ramón Menéndez. "La Mora Zaida." In *La España del Cid*. Madrid: Espasa-Calpe, 1947.

Ponsoye, Pierre. *L'Islam et le graal: etude sure l'ésoteérisme du Parzival de Wolfram von Eschenbach*. Milan: Arche, 1976

Provencal, E. Levi. *Hispano-Aribica, La Mora Zaida, femme d'Alfonse VI de Castile*. N.p.: Hesparis archives Berberes et bulletins des Hautes-Etudes Marocaines, 1934.

Rahman, H. U. *A Chronology of Islamic History*. London: Ta-Ha Publishers, 1995.

Saifullah, M. S. M. "Ka'bah as a Place of Worship in the History." *Islamic Awareness*, http://www.islamic-awareness.org/History/kaaba.html.

Salibi, Kamal. *The Bible Came from Arabia*. London: Jonathan Cape, 1985.

Settipani, Christian. *Our Ancestors From Antiquity*. Daggett, Calif.: The Augustan Society, 1997.

Watt, W. Montgomery. *The Influence of Islam on Medieval Europe*. Edinburgh: Edinburgh University Press 1972.

Willoughby, Rupert. "The Golden Line: Byzantine, Arab and Armenian Ancestry of the Russian Ruricks." Part I, *Genealogists' Magazine* 23 (March 1991), 321–326; Part II *Genealogists' Magazine* 23 (June 1991), 369–372.

Ye'or, Bat. *The Decline of Eastern Christianity Under Islam: From Jihad to Dhimmitude: 7th – 20th Century*. London: Associated University Presses, 1996.

Yohaf, Yasef. "Les Assassins, qui sont ils?" From a French Masonic lodge.

France

Agiles, Raimundus de (Raymond D'Aguilers). *Historia Francorum qui Ceperunt Iherusalem*. Translated by John Hugh Hill and Laurita L. Hill. Philadelphia: American Philosophical Society, 1968.

Anselme, Pere Augustin Dechausee. *Histoire genealogique et chronologique de la Maison Royale de France*. . . . Paris, 1890.

D'Arbois de Jubainville, H. *Histoires des Ducs et des Comtes de Champagne*. Paris, 1869.

Aubert de la Chenaye-Desbois, Francois Alexandre. *Dictionnaire de la Noblesse, genealogies, l'histoire et la chronologie des famille nobles de France*. . . . Paris: Schlesinger frères, 1863–1877.

Auzias, Leonce. *L'origine Caroloringienne des Ducs Feodaux d'Aquitaine et des Rois Capetiens.Revue Historique* 173, no. 59 (1934).

Barrau, Hippolyte de. *Documents de Rouergue*. 1860.

Barrau, Hippolyte de. *Documents historiques et genealogiques sur les familles de Rouergue*. N.p.: Rodez, 1853.

Bernard of Clairvaux. *The Letters of St. Bernard of Clairvaux.* Translated by Bruno Scott James. Chicago: H. Regnery, 1953.

Bladé, Jean-Francois. *Comtes Caroloringiens de Bigorre et les premiers Rois de Navarre. Revue de l'Agenais* (1878).

Bresc-Bautier, Genevieve. *Le Cartulaire du Chapitre du Saint Sepulchre de Jerusalem.* Paris: l'Academie des Inscriptions et des Belles Lettres, 1984.

Briollet, Maurice. *Une descendance des seconds Rois d'Austrasie les Vicomtes de Limoges.* N.p., 1965.

Calmette, Joseph. *Les Grands Ducs de Bourgogne.* Paris: Albin Michel, 1949. (Or Calmette, Joseph. *The Golden Age of Burgundy.* Translated by Doreen Weightman. London: Weidenfeld and Nicolson, 1962.)

"Cartulary of St. Michael." Original monastery records at the Bibliotheque de Tonnerre.

Chalandon, Ferdinand. *Histoire de la domination Normande en Italie et Sicille.* Paris: Librairie A. Picard et fils, 1907.

Chaume, Maurice. *Comtes de Bar-sur-Seine et de Tonnerre.* Dijon, 1947.

———. "Les Anciens Sires de Bourbon." *Annales de Bourgogne* (1930).

———. *Les origins du Duche de Bourgogne.* 4 vols. Dijon: Imprimerie Jobard, 1925–1937.

Grierson, Philip. "Maison d'Everard de Frioul et les origins des Comtes de Flandres." *Revue du Moyen-Age* (1938).

Latrie, M. *Tresor de Chronologie, d'Histoire et Geographie.* Paris: Palme, 1889.

Mantayer, George de. "Manasses, Comte de Chaunois, et Garnier, Comte de Troies." *Bulletin des Etudes Historiques des Hautes Alpes* (1925).

Morenas, Henri Jongla de. *Grand Armorial de France.* 6 vols. Paris: Les Éditions Héraldiques, 1934–1939.

Moriarty, George Andrews. *The Origin of the Carolingiens.* Boston, 1944.

Moriarty, George Andrews. "The Origins of the Capets." *New England Historical & Genealogical Register* 99 (April 1945): 130–131.

Paz, August du. *Histoire generalogique de plusieurs Maisons illustrees de Bretagne.* Buon, 1619.

Waquet, Jean Claude. *Receuil des Chartes de l'Abbaye de Clairvaux: XIIe Siécle.* Troyes, France: Archives départementales de l'Aube, 1950.

Judaism (relating to family trees)

Baer, Yitzhak. *A History of the Jews in Christian Spain.* Translated by Louis Schoffman. 2 vols. Philadelphia: Jewish Publication Society of America, 1993.

Benjamin of Tudela. *The Itinerary of Rabbi Benjamin of Tudela.* Translated by Marcus Nathan Adler. N.p., 1907.

Bevan, Edwyn. *Jerusalem Under the High-Priests: five Lectures on the Period Between Nehemiah and the New Testament.* London: E. Arnold, 1904.

Cumont, Franz. *Les religions orientales dans le paganism romain: conferences faites au college de France 1905.* Paris: Librairie Orientaliste Paul Geuthner, 1963.

Danby, Herbert, trans. *The Mishnah.* London: Oxford University Press, 1964.

Driver, G. R. *Caananite Myths & Legends.* Edinburgh: T & C Clark, 1956.

Goodblatt, David M. *The Monarchic Principle: Studies in Jewish Self-Government in Antiquity.* Tübingen, Germany: J. C. B. Mohr (P. Siebeck), 1994.

Goode, Alexander. "The Exilarchate in the Eastern Caliphate 637–1258." *Jewish Quarterly Review* 31 (1941), 149–169.

Ibn Daud, Abraham ben David, Halevi. *Sefer Ha Qabbalah: The Book of Tradition.* Oxford; Portland, Ore.: Littman Library of Jewish Civilization, 2005.

Johnson, Marshall D. *The Purpose of the Biblical Genealogies: With Special Reference to the Setting of the Genealogies of Jesus.* London: Cambridge University Press, 1969.

Jones, A. H. M. *Cities in the Eastern Roman Provinces.* Oxford: Clarendon Press, 1971.

———. *Herods of the Judaea.* Oxford: Clarendon Press, 1967.

Klausner, Joseph. *Jesus of Nazareth: His Life, Times, and Teaching.* Translated by Herbert Danby. New York: Macmillan, 1953.

Klausner, Joseph. *From Jesus to Paul.* Translated by William F. Stinespring. Boston: Beacon Press, 1961.

Milman, Henry. *The History of the Jews.* London: Darf, 1986.

Neusner, Jacob. *A History of the Jews in Babylonia III: From Shapur I to Shappur II.* Atlanta: Scholars Press, 1999.

Schurer, Emil, Geza Vermes, Fergus Miller, Martin Goodman. *A History of the Jewish People in the Age of Jesus Christ (175 BC–AD 135).* 3 vols. Edinburgh: T & C Clark, 1973.

Thiele, Edwin R. "A Comparison of the Chronological Data on Israel and Judah." *Vetus Testamentum* 4, no. 2 (April 1954), 185–195.

Vincent, Louis-Hugues. *Jerusalem de l'Ancien Testament: Rechersches d'Archaeologie et d'Histoire.* Paris: Gabalda Editeur, 1956.

Wilson. Great Survey of Jerusalem. Palestine Exploration Fund, 1864.

Zacuto, Abraham ben Samuel. *Yuhasin ha-Shalem* [*A Book of Lineage*]. Frankfurt am Main: M. A. Vohrmann, 1924.

Zuckerman, Arthur. *A Jewish Princedom in Feudal France, 768–900.* New York: Columbia University Press, 1972.

Byzantium

Allen, Jelisaveta Stanojevich. *Author Index of Byzantine Studies*. Zug, Switzerland: IDC, 1985.

Bierbrier, Morris L. "Modern Descendants of Byzantine families." *The Genealogists' Magazine* 20, no. 3 (Sept. 1980), 85–96.

Brosset, Marie Felicite, ed. and trans. *Collection d'historiens Armeniens*. St. Petersburg: Impr. de l'Académie impériale des sciences, 1874–1876.

Chalandon, Ferdinand. *Les Comnenes, Jean et Alexius*. Paris, 1913.

Fletcher, Richard. *The Conversion of Europe: from Paganism to Christianity 371–1386*. London: Fontana Press, 1998.

Fletcher, Stella. *The Longman Companion to Renaissance Europe 1390–1530*. Harlow, England; New York: Longman, 2000.

Haldon, John F. *Byzantium in the Seventh Century: A Transformation of Culture*. Cambridge, U.K.: Cambridge University Press, 1990.

Herrin, Judith. *The Formation of Christendom*. London: Fontana Press, 1989.

Lewis, Lionel S. *Joseph of Arimathea at Gladstonebury: Or the Apostolic Church of Britain*. London: James Clarke & Co., 1955.

Mamikonian, Jean. *Histoire du Taron*. Paris, 1896.

Norwich, John Julius. *Byzantium: The Decline and Fall*. London: Viking, 1995.

Psellus, Michael. *Fourteen Byzantine Rulers: the Chronographia of Michael Psellus*. Translated by E. R. A. Sewter. Harmondsworth: Penguin, 1966.

Sturdza, Mihail-Dimitri. *Dictionnaire Historique et Genealogique des grandes familles de Grace, d'Albanie et de Constantinople*. Paris: M-D Sturdza,1983.

Toumanoff, Cyril. "Armenia and Georgia." *The Cambridge Medieval History*. Edited by J. M. Hussey. Vol. 4.1. Cambridge, U.K.: Cambridge University Press, 1966.

Vajay, Szalbolcs de. "Eudecie Comnene, l' Imperatrice des Troubadours." *Genealogica & Heraldica. Report of the 14th International Congress of Genealogical and Heraldic Studies in Copenhagen* (August 1980).

The Crusades

Eisenman, Robert. *The Dead Sea Scrolls and the first Christians*. Shaftsbury, U.K.: Element, 1996.

Foucher of Chartres. *The Chronicle of the first Crusade*. Translated by Martha Evelyn McGinty. Philadelphia: University of Pennsylvania Press, 1941.

Krey, August C. *The first Crusades: The Accounts of Eye-Witnesses and Participants*. Gloucester, Mass., Peter Smith, 1958.

Lamonte, John L. "The Significance of the Crusaders' States in Medieval History." *Byzantion* 18 (1940–1941).

Mayer, Hans Eberhard. "Etudes sur l'histoire de Baudouin Ier, Roi de Jerusalem." *Melanges sur l'histoire du Royaume Latin de Jerusalem*. Paris: Institut de France, Memoires de l'Acad. des inscription et Belles-Lettres, 1984.

———. *Kings and Lords in the Latin Kingdom of Jerusalem*. Aldershot, Hampshire, U.K.; Brookfield, Vt.: Variorum, 1994.

Munro, Dana C. *The Kingdom of the Crusaders*. New York, London: D. Appleton-Century, 1935.

Prawer, Joshua. *The Crusaders' Kingdoms: European Colonialism in the Middle Ages*. New York: Praeger, 1972.

———. *Histoire du Royaume de Jerusalem*. Paris: Éditions du Centre National de la Recherche Scientifique, 1969–1970.

———. "The Settlements of the Latins in Jerusalem." *Speculum* 27 (1952).

Riley-Smith, Jonathan. *The Crusades: A Short History*. London: Athlone Press, 1990.

The Register of the Great Seal of Scotland, Volume II, AD 1424–1513. Edinburgh: Scottish Record Society in conjunction with Clark Constable, 1984.

The Templars

Addis William A. and Thomas Arnold. *A Catholic Dictionary: containing some account of the doctrine, discipline, rites, ceremonies, councils, and religious orders of the Catholic church*. 8th ed. London: Kegan Paul, Trench, Trubner & Co., 1909.

Albon, Guigues Alexis Marie Joseph André. *Cartulaire General de l'Ordre du Temple, 1119?–1150: Fascicule Complémentaire Contenant la table des Sommaires des Actes et L'Identification des Noms de Lieux*. Paris: H. Champion, 1922.

Amargier, Paul. "La Defense du Temple devant le Concile de Lyons en 1274." In *1274, année charnière: mutations et continuité* [Actes du Colleque Intetrnational, 30 Septembre–5 Octobre 1974]. Paris: Centre national de la recherche scientifique, 1977, 495–501.

Bartolini, Charles. Hugues de Pagan, le fondateur Provencal de l'Ordre du Temple. *Revue Arcadia* (1999).

Benassai, Alessandro. "The Mystery of the Templars." *Archeosofica* (1987).

Bonneville, Nicolas de. *Maçonnerie écossoise comparée avec les trois professions et le secret des Templiers du 14e siècle*. N.p.: Orient de Londres, 1788.

Bordonove, Georges. *La tragedie des Templiers*. Paris: Pygmalion/Watelet, 1993.

Burman, Edward, *The Templars: Knights of God*. Wellingborough, Northamptonshire, U.K.: Crucible, 1986.

Caroff, Fanny. *L'iconographie des croisades*. Thesis.

Cerrini, Simonetta. "Il faut une nouvelle regle pour concilier priere et combat." *Historia special* 53 (May–June 1998), 16–25.

———. "Un Ordre tres hierarchies." *Historia* (1998).

Clement, Claude. *Saint Bernard ou la puissance d'un grand initie: de la Kaballe a la mystique*. Paris; Editions Fernand Lanore, 1996.

Demurger, Alain. "Templiers, Attention aux myths." *Historia* (1998).

———. *Vie et mort de l'Ordre du Temple, 1184–1314*. Paris: Editions du Seuil, 1989.

"Deposition du Frere Jean de Chalon." Secret Archives of the Vatican.

Falque de Bezaure, Bernard. *Sur les traces des Templiers des Alpes-des-Haute-Provence*. Mallemoisson: Editions de Provence, 1996.

Favier, Jean. *Philippe le bel*. Paris: Fayard, 1998.

Feather, Robert. *The Copper Scroll Decoded: One Man's Search for the Fabulous Treasures of Ancient Egypt*. London: Thorsons, 1999.

Galimard de Flavigny, Bertrand. *Les Chevaliers de Malte: des hommes de fer et de foi*. Paris; Gallimard, 1998.

Graffin, Robert. *L'Art Templiers des Cathedrales*. Paris: Editions Jean Michel Garnier, 1993.

Gylmour-Brisson, Anne. "Le Procés des Templiers dans les Etats du Pape." From the Vatican Library.

"La Maison du Temple a Paris." Found in the Archives Nationales, Paris.

Lavocat, Louis-Leon-Lucien. *Proces des Freres et de l'Ordre du Temple: d'apres des pieces inedites publiees*. Paris: Plon, 1888.

The Lost Books of the Bible and the Forgotten Books of Eden. Cleveland: Collins/World Publishing, 1926.

Maillard de Chambure, C. H. *Regle et statuts secrets des Templiers*. Paris: Brockhaus et Avenarius, 1840

Martin, Georges A. D. *Le Provence et le graal: mission secrete en Occident*. Le Coudray-Macouard: Cheminements, 1999.

Michelet, Jules. *Le Procés des Templiers*. Paris, 1851.

Partner, Peter. *Templiers, Francs-macons et societes secretes*. Paris: Pygmalion, 1992.

Pennick, Nigel. *Sacred Geometry: Symbolism and Purpose in Religious Structures*. Wellingborough, Northamptonshire, U.K.: Turnstone Press, 1980.

Rolland, Jacques. *L'Assassinat programme des Templiers*. Saint-Leu-la-Forêt, France: Table D'Emeraude, 2000
———. *L'Ordre noir des Templiers*. Paris: Editions Traditionelles, 1997.
Saint Hilaire, Paul de. *Les sceaux Templiers et leurs symboles*. Puiseaux, France: Pardes, 1996.
Sans, Joan Fuguet. *L'architecture des Templiers en Catalogne*. [French translation of *L'arquitectura Dels Templers a Catalunya*. Barcelona: Rafael Dalmau, 1995.]
Schonfield, Hugh J. *The Essene Odyssey: The Mystery of the True Teacher and the Essene Impact on the Shaping of Human Destiny*. Shaftesbury: Element, 1984.

Christianity and the Papacy

Addis William A. and Thomas Arnold. *A Catholic Dictionary: containing some account of the doctrine, discipline, rites, ceremonies, councils, and religious orders of the Catholic church*. 8th ed. London: Kegan Paul, Trench, Trubner & Co., 1909.
Aquinas, Thomas. *Summa Theologiae: A Concise Translation*. Timothy McDermott, ed. London: Eyre and Spottiswoode, 1989.
Augustine. *Confessions*. Translated by Henry Chadwick. Oxford, New York: Oxford University Press, 1991.
Banck, Laurentius. *Roma triumphans seu actus inaugurationis & coronationis Innocentii decimi pont. max. brevis descriptio, cum omnibus triumphis & cermoniis ediem actui additis*. Frankfurt: Johannes Dhuiringh, 1645.
Baigent, Michael and Richard Leigh. *The Dead Sea Scrolls Deception*. London: Jonathan Cape, 1991.
Baigent, Michael, Richard Leigh and Henry Lincoln. *The Messianic Legacy*. London: Jonathan Cape, 1986.
Carpenter, Clive. *The Guinness Book of Kings, Rulers & Statesmen*. Middlesex, U.K.: Guinness Superlatives Ltd., 1978.
Chrysostom, John. "To the Fallen Monk."
Eisenman, Robert. *The Dead Sea Scrolls and the first Christians*. Shaftsbury, U.K.: Element, 1996.
Eusebius. *The History of the Church from Christ to Constantine*. Translated by G. A. Williamson. Revised and edited by Andrew Louth. London, New York: Penguin Books, 1989.
Fletcher, Richard. *The Conversion of Europe: from Paganism to Christianity 371–1386*. London: Fontana Press, 1998.
Gardner, Laurence. *Bloodline of the Holy Grail: The Hidden Lineage of Jesus Revealed*. Shaftesbury, U.K.: Element, 1996.

———. *The Magdalene Legacy: The Jesus and Mary Bloodline Conspiracy Revelation Beyond the Da Vinci Code*. London: Element, 2005.
Herrin, Judith. *The Formation of Christendom*. London: Fontana Press, 1989.
Hislop, Alexander. *The Two Babylons*. London: S. W. Partridge & Co., 1929.
Lewis, Lionel S. *Joseph of Arimathea at Gladstonebury: Or the Apostolic Church of Britain*. London: James Clarke & Co., 1955.
Pliny the Elder. *Natural History*. Edited by T. E. Page. Translated by H. Rackham. London: Heinemann, 1938.
Pryce, John. *The Ancient British Church: A Historical Essay*. London: Longman, Green, 1878.
Stanford, Peter. *The She-Pope: A Quest for the Truth Behind the Mystery of Pope Joan*. London: Arrow Books, 1999.
Torjesen, Karen Jo. *When Women Were Priests: Women's Leadership in the Early Chruch and the Scandal of Their Subordination in the Rise of Christianity*. San Francisco: Harper San Francisco, 1993.
Warren, F. E. *The Liturgy and Ritual of the Celtic Church*. 2nd ed. Wolfsboro, N.H.: Boydell Press, 1987.

OTHER SOURCES

Carr, Harry, ed. *The Minutes of the Lodge of Edinburgh, Mary's Chapel No. 1 (1598–1738)*. London: Quatuor Coronati Lodge, 1962.
Gardner, Laurence. *The Shadow of Solomon: Lost Secrets of the Freemasons Revealed*. London: Harper Element, 2005.
Hay, Richard A. *Genealogie of the Saintclaires of Rosslyn, including the Chartulary of Rosslyn*. Edited by J. Maidment. Edinburgh: T. G. Stevenson, 1835.
Knoop, Douglas. and G. P. Jones. *The Genesis of Freemasonry: An Account of the Rise and Development of Freemasonry in Its Operative, Accepted, and Early Speculative Phases*. Manchester, U.K.: Manchester Univeristy Press, 1947.
———. *Handlist of Masonic Documents*. Manchester, U.K.: Manchester University Press, 1942.
Macgibbon, David D. and Thomas Ross. *The Castellated and Domestic Architecture of Scotland from the Twelfth to the Eighteenth Century*. Edinburgh: D. Douglas, 1887–1892.
Mackenzie, Kenneth R. H. *The Royal Masonic Cyclopaedia*. Wellingborough, Northamptonshire, U.K.: Aquarian Press 1987.
Montgomerie, Alexander. *The Poems of Alexander Montgomerie*. Edinburgh, London: Scottish Text Societies, W. Blackwood and Sons, 1887.

Mylne, Robert Scott. *The Master Masons to the Crown of Scotland and Their Works*. Edinburgh: Scott & Ferguson, 1893.
The Philalethes 42, no. 4 (August 1998).
Stevenson, David. *The first Freemasons: Scotland's Early Lodges and Their Members*. Aberdeen, Scotland, U.K.: Aberdeen University Press, 1988.
———. *The Origins of Freemasonry: Scotland's Century, 1590–1710*. Cambridge, U.K., New York: Cambridge University Press, 1993.

FREEMASONRY

From the library of Grand Lodge of Scotland, works from the Charles Morrison collections.
Auld, William. (*152.) Published 1761.
Binning, Thomas. (*429.7.)
Bonneville, Nicolas de. (*65.) Published 1778.
Bordas. "Chambres des grades sur le chapitre d'Arras" (*559.1). Published 1802.
Burness, James. "Knights Templar" (*432). Published 1837.

FAMILY TREES

The Egyptian descent of the Royal House of Judah and Zadokite High Priests
The High Priests of Jerusalem (post second Temple building)
The Hasmonean Kings and the House of David (their relationship)
The Ptolemic descent of St. Bartholomew
The Barka descent of St. Bartholomew
The Seleucid Kings to Ardashir of Persia
From Ardashir of Persia to Raymond of Toulouse, Crusader Count of Tripoli
The Byzantine descent of Raymond of Toulouse
The biblical descent of Muhammad, the Seal of the Prophet
The Mohamedan descent of Hugues de Payens
Kings of al Hira and Khosites (Christian Arab Royal Houses)
The Neapolitan and Byzantine descent of Hugues de Payens
The Pamplonese descent of Hugues de Payens
Sinclairs relationship with Hugues de Payens
The royal descent of St. Bernard de Clairvaux (Merovingien), showing the genealogical relationship between the original Templar leaders.
A second royal descent of St. Bernard of Clairvaux (Caroloringien)
The House of Champagne

The House of Bruce of Elgin
The Barons of Roslyn
The Royal House of Stewart
The Royal Esoteric Scottish Succession (from ancient to modern days). (By painter Peter Robson)

To Our Readers

Weiser Books, an imprint of Red Wheel/Weiser, publishes books across the entire spectrum of occult and esoteric subjects. Our mission is to publish quality books that will make a difference in people's lives without advocating any one particular path or field of study. We value the integrity, originality, and depth of knowledge of our authors.

Our readers are our most important resource, and we appreciate your input, suggestions, and ideas about what you would like to see published. Please feel free to contact us, to request our latest book catalog, or to be added to our mailing list.

Red Wheel/Weiser, LLC
500 Third Street, Suite 230
San Francisco, CA 94107
www.redwheelweiser.com